NIETZSCHE IN CONTEXT

Nietzsche in Context presents a comprehensive reinterpretation of Nietzsche's thought, placing Nietzsche in the context of the philosophers of his own time. Offering a survey of important philosophical themes, Robin Small identifies the writer or writers with whom Nietzsche most felt himself to be engaging in dialogue. This historical dimension is complemented by original analysis and interpretation of the ideas under discussion.

Nietzsche in Context takes Nietzsche scholarship into new and fruitful directions. By locating his ideas within a broader context, this book provides a comprehensive reinterpretation of Nietzsche's thought adding to the continuing interest of his contributions to philosophy.

For Anna

Nietzsche in Context

ROBIN SMALL

LONDON AND NEW YORK

First published 2001 by Ashgate Publishing

2 Park Square, Milton Park, Abingdon, Oxon OX14 4RN
605 Third Avenue, New York, NY 10017

Routledge is an imprint of the Taylor & Francis Group, an informa business

First issued in paperback 2021

Copyright © Robin Small 2001

Robin Small has asserted his moral right under the Copyright, Designs and Patents Act, 1988, to be identified as the author of this work.

All rights reserved. No part of this book may be reprinted or reproduced or utilised in any form or by any electronic, mechanical, or other means, now known or hereafter invented, including photocopying and recording, or in any information storage or retrieval system, without permission in writing from the publishers.

Notice:
Product or corporate names may be trademarks or registered trademarks, and are used only for identification and explanation without intent to infringe.

Publisher's Note
The publisher has gone to great lengths to ensure the quality of this reprint but points out that some imperfections in the original copies may be apparent.

Disclaimer
The publisher has made every effort to trace copyright holders and welcomes correspondence from those they have been unable to contact.

A Library of Congress record exists under LC control number: 2001022190

Typeset by Manton Typesetters, Louth, Lincolnshire, UK.

ISBN 13: 978-1-138-73009-0 (hbk)
ISBN 13: 978-0-367-24931-1 (pbk)

Contents

Acknowledgements vii
A Note on Sources and Translations ix
Introduction xi

1 Spir and Time   1
2 Dühring and Time   21
3 Teichmüller and Perspective   41
4 Zöllner and Space   59
5 Mechanism and Beyond   81
6 Possibility, Probability and Finality   99
7 The Mathematics of Eternal Recurrence   117
8 The Physics of Eternal Recurrence   135
9 Sensualism and Knowledge   153
10 *Ressentiment*, Revenge and Punishment   171

Bibliography 189
Index 199

The Pictures and their Sources used on the Paperback Cover

Nietzsche (centre)
Source: Ernst Pfeiffer, *Friedrich Nietzsche Paul Rée Lou von Salomé. Die Dokumente ihrer Begegnung.* Frankfurt am Main: Insel Verlag, 1970, facing p. 48. Attribution: "aus dem Nachlass von Lou Andreas-Salome".

Clockwise from top

Paul Rée (1849–1901) Chap. 10
Source: Joachim Köhler, *Nietzsche and Wagner: A Lesson in Subjugation*, trans. Ronald Taylor. New Haven: Yale University Press, 1988, illustration 11, p. 132. Attribution: Rowohlt Verlag Archives, Reinbeck bei Hamburg.

Johann Carl Friedrich Zöllner (1834–1882) Chap. 4
Source: Fanny Moser, *Der Okkultismus: Täuschungen und Tatsachen.* München: Verlag von Ernst Reinhardt, 1935, Tafel 4. Attribution: "Nach einer Photographie im Deutschen Museum in München".

Elisabeth d'Espérance (1849–?) Chap. 4
Source: Elizabeth D'Espérance, *Shadow Land of Light from the Other Side.* London: George Redway, 1897, frontispiece.

Julius Robert Mayer (1814–1878) Chap. 8
Source: Eugen Dühring, *Robert Mayer der Galilei des neunzehnten Jahrhjunderts und die Gelehrtenuntaten gegen bahnbrechende Wissenschaftsgrössen.* Reprint of 2nd edn. Darmstadt: Wissenschaftliche Buchgesellschaft, 1972, frontispiece.

Roger Joseph Boscovich (1711–1787) Chap. 1 and Chap. 5
Source: L.L. Whyte (ed.), *Roger Joseph Boscovich.* London: Allen and Unwin, 1961, frontispiece.

African Spir (1837–1890) Chap. 1
Source: African Spir, *Right and Wrong*, trans. A.F. Falconer. Edinburgh: Oliver and Boyd, 1954, frontispiece.

Friedrich Albert Lange (1828–1875) Chap. 3
Source: F.A. Lange, *Geschichte des Materialismus und Kritik seiner Bedeutung in der Gegenwart.* 7th edn. Leipizig: J. Beidecker, 1902, Band I, frontispiece.

Eduard von Hartmann (1842–1906) Chap. 2
Source: Eduard von Hartmann, *Philosophy of the Unconscious*, trans. C.K. Ogden. New York: Harcourt, Brace and Company, 1931, frontispiece.

Acknowledgements

This research was supported by Monash University and other institutions which at various times offered hospitality and assistance: the Australian National University, the University of Edinburgh, the University of Toronto and the University of East Anglia. The resources of the British Library and the Cambridge University Library were invaluable in locating source materials.

Individuals who have given their encouragement, advice and support include Babette Babich, Colin Evers, Reg Hollingdale, Klaus Spiekermann and Lynne Broughton. In particular, Gabriele Lakomski has been a loyal friend and colleague over many years. I am happy to have this opportunity to express my sincere gratitude towards these people for all they have contributed to the completion of this work.

Some material included in this book has appeared previously in the following forms:

'Nietzsche, Spir, and Time', *Journal of the History of Philosophy*, 32 (1994): 85–102.

'Nietzsche, Zöllner, and the Fourth Dimension', *Archiv für Geschichte der Philosophie*, 76 (1994): 278–301.

'Nietzsche, Dühring, and Time', *Journal of the History of Philosophy*, 28 (1990): 229–50.

'Possibility, Probability and Recurrence', *International Studies in Philosophy*, 18 (1986): 29–46.

'Incommensurability and Recurrence: From Oresme to Simmel', *Journal of the History of Ideas*, 52 (1991): 121–37.

'Boscovich Contra Nietzsche', *Philosophy and Phenomenological Research*, 46 (1986): 419–35.

'We Sensualists', in Babette E. Babich and Robert S. Cohen (eds), *Nietzsche, Epistemology, and Philosophy of Science: Nietzsche and the Sciences II* (Dordrecht: Kluwer Academic Publishers, 1999), 73–89.

'Ressentiment, Revenge and Punishment: Origins of the Nietzschean Critique', *Utilitas*, 9 (1997): 39–58.

A Note on Sources and Translations

In quoting from the published works of Nietzsche, and from the notes included in *The Will to Power*, I have used the English translations of Walter Kaufmann and R.J. Hollingdale, with occasional modifications. All other translations are my own, unless otherwise stated.

The following abbreviations are used in citing the writings of Nietzsche:

KGB: Nietzsche, *Kritische Gesamtausgabe: Briefwechsel*, ed. Giorgio Colli and Mazzino Montinari (Berlin: de Gruyter, 1975 –).

KGW: Nietzsche, *Kritische Gesamtausgabe: Werke*, ed. Giorgio Colli and Mazzino Montinari (Berlin: de Gruyter, 1973 –).

Introduction

I

Friedrich Nietzsche has always been recognized as an original thinker, one who stands apart from and outside the philosophical schools and tendencies of his time. This is the way he continually presented himself, from his early writings onwards: as a writer sharing none of the assumptions and conventions of contemporary authors, as an 'untimely' thinker, one belonging to the future rather than the present day. Many readers have accepted this self-interpretation at face value. Yet there is another side to Nietzsche's thinking which shows not only an awareness of contemporary writers, but an engagement with their ideas which is often both intense and sustained. My intention is to explore this side in detail, by surveying various themes in his philosophical thinking with such links in mind. It is important to avoid one misunderstanding, though. This book is not designed to show that Nietzsche derived his ideas from various other thinkers. In that sense, it is not necessarily about 'sources', or even about 'influences'. Rather, it shows that his independence and originality developed in dialogue with other thinkers. Those qualities are no less real for that reason: in fact, I believe that they can be appreciated all the more by being placed in the context of his relations to other philosophers.

Which philosophers, though? In keeping with his claims for untimeliness, Nietzsche preferred to disguise or conceal many links. Often they are signalled by uncredited quotations, or by verbal allusions which are left for his readers to identify – if they can. Today's readers are not well placed to do this. The trail has in many cases been lost, and what remains is a relatively narrow range of references. Hence, commentators have argued for connections between Nietzsche and Schopenhauer, or other important philosophers such as Kant or Hegel, as well as with writers such as Emerson, who may or may not be labelled as a philosopher but is in any case acknowledged as a major literary figure. The drawbacks of this approach can be indicated by an illustration. More has been written about Nietzsche's relation to Leibniz than about his relation to Johann Gustav Vogt. We can guess the reason: Leibniz is an important thinker, known to every philosophical scholar, while Vogt was, and will no doubt remain, a very obscure writer indeed. Yet it is quite possible that Nietzsche never read a word of Leibniz. On the other hand, there is good evidence that he managed to work his way through Vogt's enormous treatise on cosmology: in fact, he not only annotated his own copy but made notes on several passages, and drew upon Vogt's ideas in works such as *The Gay Science*.

This example can usefully be broadened. What Nietzsche did read was not Leibniz himself as much as various contemporary authors who might reasonably be described as vulgar Leibnizians. Here I am thinking of writers such as Otto Caspari, Maximilian Drossbach, Johann Gustav Vogt and others. Despite differences, they share a common tendency, marked by a hostility towards the materialism associated with British empiricism, and an emphasis on 'inner' forces within the elements of matter. Although practising scientists such as Hermann von Helmholtz were not in sympathy with this approach, it was prominent in German popular writing. Often these writers introduced a political dimension, attributing differences in philosophy to contrasts between the English and German national characters. They argued that the success of the English in devising mechanical machinery such as the steam engine was behind their preference for a mechanistic model of physical reality; and the old dispute between supporters of Newton and Leibniz was continued by some writers with barely diminished enthusiasm. Similarly, it was suggested that Darwin's idea of the struggle for existence was an expression of the English ideology of market forces (a claim still popular today in the sociology of science). Nietzsche was far from being a German chauvinist, but from time to time echoes of this context within which his impressions of scientific ideas were gained do occur in his thinking.

The tendency just described was not an isolated phenomenon. The later nineteenth century was something of a golden age of philosophical vulgarization. Looking at the German literature of the period, we also find not only vulgar Leibnizians but vulgar materialists (Büchner, Vogt and Moleschott), vulgar positivists (Dühring), vulgar Darwinists (Haeckel), and vulgar Schopenhauerians (Hartmann and Mainländer).[1] Nietzsche kept up with these and other developments in philosophy, as well as in physical science, and took the trouble to study some relevant books, making notes on his reading and sketching out arguments or conclusions useful for his own purposes. His correspondence contains frequent requests to his publisher or to friends to be supplied with recent publications. His friend Heinrich Köselitz shared many of these interests, and raised topical issues in his letters to Nietzsche. Hence, it is not surprising that many of the philosophers read by Nietzsche were well-known in their day. Eugen Dühring is perhaps the best example here: a versatile and prolific author, whose books sold well. Nietzsche knew how well, because his own books were brought out by the same publisher, Ernst Schmeitzner, who kept Nietzsche informed of Dühring's high sales, as well as regaling him with stories about Dühring's eccentric behaviour.[2]

For all that anyone knew then, Dühring was to remain a highly influential thinker into the following century. We know now, of course, that this did not turn out to be the case. Dühring was generally forgotten by the time of his death in 1921, and since then has enjoyed only the doubtful privilege of being identified as the systematic target of Friedrich Engels' elaboration of the philosophy of dialectical materialism in a series of articles published in book form as *Herr Eugen Dühring's Revolution in Science* – more commonly known as *Anti-Dühring*. It must be remembered that Nietzsche did not know this, just as others of his time cannot reasonably be criticized for failing to foresee how Nietzsche would come to be regarded in the following century.

Introduction

We need to be aware of the dangers of hindsight in our assessment of these points of philosophical reference, especially where they are contemporary ones.

What is surprising in all this is how good and discriminating Nietzsche's tastes were. His judgements on F.A. Lange and Eduard von Hartmann – favourable and unfavourable, respectively – show a sound capacity for comparative assessment. His exploration of contemporary literature was wide-ranging. To some extent, he simply read what everyone else was reading – for example, the popular lectures of well-known scientists such as Hermann von Helmholtz, Emil du Bois-Reymond and Karl Ernst von Baer. He had no prejudice against philosophers working outside an academic environment, such as African Spir and Léon Dumont. In these cases, his choices were rather variable in standard. Spir, although an amateur, was a competent thinker and writer, and had a broader view of the literature than many of his professional counterparts, as his references to British empiricist philosophy indicate. Dumont was another amateur of rather less expertise, but still not a waste of time. In other instances, Nietzsche's choices were curious. Why, for example, would anyone, even then, use a good deal of time studying the elaborate construction of an entire physics and cosmology on the basis of highly arbitrary *a priori* assumptions – the case of Vogt? And why would someone prefer such eccentric ideas to the scientific account of force offered by a genuine researcher, Robert Mayer? This is a puzzle which we may not be able to solve, although I will make some suggestions in due course.

Nietzsche's writing career took place when philosophers and scientists were preoccupied with two recent scientific theories of extraordinary importance. One was the theory of evolution through natural selection, as set out in Darwin's 1859 work *The Origin of Species*. By eliminating the separation between humanity and other species, Darwin had given strong encouragement to naturalistic accounts of human nature and to corresponding theories of culture and morality. The other important debate of the time concerned the second law of thermodynamics, with its startling consequence for the future of the physical world. For the educated general public, this issue was raised by Hermann von Helmholtz's 1854 lecture 'On the Interaction of Natural Forces'. There Helmholtz spelled out what William Thomson had left unsaid: that the progressive elimination of all thermal differences would eventually lead to 'the end of the history of the universe'.[3] Both of these scientific controversies exercised German writers during the second half of the nineteenth century, and both figure prominently in Nietzsche's own reading in natural philosophy. However, Nietzsche's understanding of modern science was obstructed by his ignorance of mathematics. This alone would have made his passing idea of undertaking further study at the University of Vienna very hard to achieve.[4] Hence his bias towards writers like Friedrich Zöllner, who used very little mathematics and indeed deplored its status as the central part of scientific theorizing.[5]

II

If this is one part of the context in which Nietzsche's thinking is located, the situation of philosophy is the other. An indication of the direction in which we should be looking here is given by Nietzsche's own understanding of his position. He saw himself as a successor of certain recent writers who, he thought, had brought a certain kind of metaphysical thought to its ultimate conclusion. In *Twilight of the Idols* he described this development as the final stages in 'the history of an error'.[6] The earlier stages are presented in these terms:

1. The true world – attainable for the sage, the pious, the virtuous man; he lives in it, *he is it.*
   (The oldest form of the idea, relatively sensible, simple, and persuasive. A circumlocution for the sentence, 'I, Plato, am the truth'.
2. The true world – unattainable for now, but promised for the sage, the pious, the virtuous man ('for the sinner who repents').
   (Progress of the idea; it becomes more subtle, insidious, incomprehensible – *it becomes female*, it becomes Christian.)
3. The true world – unattainable, indemonstrable, unpromisable; but the very thought of it is a consolation, an obligation, an imperative.
   (At bottom, the old sun, but seen through mist and scepticism. The idea has become elusive, pale, Nordic, *Königsbergian*.)

Up to this point, Nietzsche has provided clear indications of the particular doctrines which correspond to these general positions concerning the relation between the apparent and real worlds. In effect, he has given a summary history of Western thought from its beginnings up to the early nineteenth century, mentioning Plato, Christianity and Kant as primary points of reference. What follows is another three sections, designed not only to continue the account to his own time, but to point towards what is to come. The metaphor of a setting sun is now taken further: another day comes with a new dawn, morning and hour of noon. Here, however, Nietzsche is less specific in his references.

4. The true world – unattainable? At any rate, unattained. And being unattained, also *unknown*. Consequently, not consoling, redeeming or obligating: how could something unknown obligate us?
   (Grey morning. The first yawn of reason. The cockcrow of positivism.)
5. The 'true' world – an idea which is no longer good for anything, not even obligating – an idea which has become useless and superfluous – *consequently* a refuted idea: let us abolish it!
   (Bright day; breakfast; return of *bon sens* and cheerfulness; Plato's embarrassed blush; pandemonium of all free spirits.)
6. The true world – we have abolished. What world has remained? The apparent one perhaps? But no! *With the true world we have also abolished the apparent one*.
   (Noon: moment of the briefest shadow; end of the longest error; high point of humanity; INCIPIT ZARATHUSTRA.)

Who are the representatives of those later phases which culminate in the appearance of Nietzsche's own spokesman, Zarathustra? The closer he comes to himself, the more Nietzsche covers his tracks. In *Beyond Good and Evil*, he provides some clues in a discussion which is closely parallel to this passage.[7] He credits several contemporary thinkers with making the idea of a true world 'good for nothing', incapable of serving even as an ideal which, although unattainable, might guide us in either our claims to knowledge or our moral lives. It would be wrong to assume that the philosophers Nietzsche has in mind were motivated by a hostility towards any idea of a reality beyond the world of the senses. On the contrary, they were concerned to vindicate that concept by eliminating from it any elements which are derived from, and therefore apply only to, the objects of experience. In their view, previous metaphysical doctrines had failed to fulfil this demand in a rigorous way. Hence, these philosophers deny the validity of appearance, but allow themselves no right to make assertions about the nature of a genuine reality.

The first contemporary Nietzsche refers to in section 10 of *Beyond Good and Evil* is the Russian-born philosopher African Spir (1837–1890). Spir's metaphysical standpoint is uncompromisingly Parmenidean; starting from the absolute status of logical truth, he argues that reality can contain neither plurality nor change. Nietzsche praises Spir (albeit without naming him) for his courageous will to truth, which leads him to 'prefer even a handful of "certainty" to a whole carload of beautiful possibilities'. On the other hand, it is clear to him that this is a 'hopeless position', and he concludes that preferring 'a certain nothing to an uncertain something' is a form of nihilism – the expression of a weak and despairing spirit. I will look at the case of Spir in greater detail in Chapter 1. Although Nietzsche certainly rejects Spir's metaphysics, my discussion will show that he can often be seen to follow Spir's analyses closely, especially in approaching the infinite divisibility of time and the concept of absolute becoming.

After these remarks, Nietzsche turns to what he describes as 'stronger and livelier thinkers', apparently on account of their vigorous attacks on the claims of empirical knowledge. One of these is a well-known writer, Friedrich Albert Lange (1828–1875), whose *History of Materialism* is still recognized as a valuable contribution to philosophy. Nietzsche encountered this work at an early stage and found it very useful as a source of both instruction and stimulation.[8] Lange provides not only a chronicle of materialism from its ancient origins to his own time, but also a survey of current natural science as this enters into philosophical debates. Yet Lange's own philosophical position is very different from materialism. He follows the tradition of Kantian idealism, regarding the objects of experience as mere appearances constructed by the organization of our own sensibility and understanding. This includes even our own bodies: hence Nietzsche's admiring comment that such thinkers are willing to 'let their securest possession go'.

Mixed in with this allusion to Lange's idealism is a reference to another contemporary whose role as a precursor is particularly valued by Nietzsche. This is his former Basel colleague Gustav Teichmüller (1832–1888) who certainly does 'speak of "perspective" with a new arrogance'. Like Spir's, his philosophy is a metaphysical doctrine which deprives the intelligible world of any interest and relevance to experience. This is metaphysics taken to its ultimate conclusion. But for Nietzsche, such a *reductio ad absurdum* is a prelude to his own philosophy, which takes the world of appearance as the only one. Again, one might imagine that he would find nothing of positive use in Teichmüller's system but, on the contrary, Nietzsche takes up its key elements for his own purpose. These are signalled by a frequent use of such key words as 'projection', 'sign language' or 'semiotic' and, above all, 'perspective'. The theme of perspective is the clearest and most frequent debt of Nietzsche's thinking to Teichmüller. We will see in Chapter 3 how his use of this metaphor changes and develops as a consequence of his encounter with Teichmüller's system.

Any dialogue between Nietzsche and his contemporaries should be seen as including a third group of participants as well – the early Greek thinkers. His lectures on the pre-Platonic philosophers, and his unfinished essay 'Philosophy in the Tragic Age of the Greeks', are very relevant here. So are his notebook sketches on Democritus, for the light they throw not only on his approach to early Greek thought, but also on his attitude to the materialism of his own time, in links that he tends to make by relying mainly on Lange's account. It must be acknowledged that Nietzsche's approach to the ancient thinkers often imports the ideas of the nineteenth century in an arbitrary and anachronistic fashion. In his lectures on pre-Platonic philosophy, for instance, he illustrates Heraclitus by a summary of Karl Ernst von Baer's 1860 lecture proposing a naturalistic account of the differences in awareness of time amongst different living species.[9] The revised version, given the title *Philosophy in the Tragic Age of the Greeks*, includes similar assimilations. For instance, Heraclitus's conception of time is explained by a long quotation from Schopenhauer, rationalized by an assurance that 'As Heraclitus thinks of time, so does Schopenhauer'.[10] African Spir stands in for Parmenides, but is also used against him. This work was never finished: it goes only as far as Anaxagoras, and would presumably have included Empedocles, Democritus and Socrates as well. Presumably it would have followed earlier drafts in associating Friedrich Albert Lange with ancient scepticism, modern materialism with Democritus, and Darwin's theory of natural selection with Empedocles. Here, we must remember Nietzsche's claim that all the possible philosophical standpoints had already been presented in their purest forms by early Greek thought.[11] Given that proposition, what could remain but to identify modern accounts of the world as versions of these original standpoints?

III

This book is designed to work through the range of themes in Nietzsche's philosophical thinking about space, time and matter, about the nature of science and knowledge. In each case I have focused on the dialogue, or dialogues, which seemed most relevant to that subject. The early chapters deal with the broadest concepts such as space and time, and later ones with the physical theories which draw on these ideas. The concept of force is important here, for Nietzsche saw it as basic to a comprehensive model of reality which would be, if not derived from, then at least consistent with natural science. Much of this second half will be devoted to the controversial doctrine of eternal recurrence, within which many of these themes come together. Finally, I will turn to some themes surrounding the role of sensation and feeling in our knowledge of the world and our ethical concepts.

My starting-point is one of Nietzsche's characterizations of his own thinking. In several places, he classifies himself as a follower of Heraclitus: that is, he proclaims his support for the Heraclitean doctrine of becoming, according to which reality as a whole is to be characterized by a constant change which rules out any stable being. Absolute becoming is an elusive concept, however. One of the few philosophers of Nietzsche's time prepared to say much about it was African Spir, who took his lead from J.F. Herbart's earlier treatment. Herbart had claimed that three characteristics can be attributed to absolute becoming. First, change is continual, never pausing and having no beginning or end. Second, change proceeds at a constant rate, with the same amount of alteration occurring in the same time. Third, change always goes in the same direction, never returning upon itself – that is, never repeating an earlier state.[12] My discussion will look into the first and third of these propositions in detail, since the questions they raise are crucial to Nietzsche's thinking. Herbart's first 'law' of absolute becoming raises the two questions of the infinite divisibility and the infinitude of time. His third thesis is a direct challenge to the notion of recurrence. In each case, Nietzsche has ideas of his own to offer to such philosophical debates.

His Heracliteanism inclines him to the view that 'Nature is just as infinite inwardly as outwardly'.[13] Hence, he is inclined to support both aspects of Herbart's first proposition. Yet he supports them in his own way, and for his own purposes. The infinite divisibility of time is important for Nietzsche, primarily in his critique of epistemology. It implies that what we perceive can never be more than a minute fraction of the course of becoming. Our concepts are designed to cover up and rationalize this incapacity.[14] Thus, the notion of cause and effect assumes discontinuities which are in fact products of our own failure to apprehend the flow of becoming. Our belief in separate 'things' is just as much an illusion. At the same time, these are fortunate errors, since they serve our practical interests by enabling us to organize experience in regular patterns and thereby cope with our environment. Hence the dilemma that runs through Nietzsche's approach to epistemology: the need for illusion is one of our conditions of life, and yet the will to truth sets itself the task of uncovering and destroying all such falsehoods.

The second proposition about infinitude and time also relates to broader issues. Nietzsche was drawn to assert an infinity of past time not only by his rejection of any doctrine of divine creation, but also by his own thought of eternal recurrence. In defending the adequacy of understanding a past infinity in terms of an infinite regress from the present moment, he attempted to rebut the opposing arguments of several contemporary philosophers: Eduard von Hartmann (1842–1906), Philipp Mainländer (1841–1876) and, most importantly, Eugen Dühring (1833–1921). Yet Nietzsche did not simply reject Dühring's thoroughgoing finitism. He accepted Dühring's so-called 'law of definite number', which states that whatever can be counted – for example, the elements which constitute the physical world at a given time – must have some definite and limited magnitude. From this follows an *a priori* answer to the question about the finitude of the world. Where the finitude of space is concerned, however, Nietzsche's thinking shows the influence of another contemporary, the controversial astrophysicist Friedrich Zöllner. Here the full story is a complex and interesting one, involving remarkable changes in Nietzsche's attitude towards Zöllner over a number of years. In Chapter 3, I will correlate these with other aspects of his development and also use them to throw some light on *Thus Spake Zarathustra*.

One important feature of Nietzsche's approach to science was shared with writers such as Zöllner – an emphasis on epistemology as the determining factor in scientific theorizing. Hence, his interest is just as much in the methodology as in the content of physical theories. This comes out most strongly in his attitude towards the version of materialism he calls 'mechanism', a theory which is atomistic in its content and reductionist in its method. For Nietzsche, mechanism is not just one scientific theory among others, but the most advanced and successful kind of science. Sometimes he attacks it in strong terms, yet he often goes in the opposite direction, and even takes up what looks like a reductionist approach in his own thinking. What we need to bear in mind is that Nietzsche's concern is with the ongoing scientific programme, rather than with its current state. He attacks mechanism as he encounters it, and yet sees himself as 'completing' its programme by, on the one hand, attacking the assumptions of atomism and, on the other, addressing the question of a final state of the universe.

This completion involves the idea of an eternal recurrence, one of the most disputed areas in Nietzsche's thinking. In Chapter 7, we will look more closely at the assumptions and arguments that he uses to support this theory, and in the following chapter at the physical model which he thinks corresponds to the concept of eternal recurrence. Nietzsche's reading in natural philosophy was biased towards approaches which seemed to build upon the dynamic theory of Boscovich, rather than the mainstream tradition of atomism. The contemporary writers he found of most interest were those who made the concept of force, rather than matter, central to their view of the world. One of these has already been mentioned: Gustav Vogt (b.1843), whose 1881 book *Die Kraft* offered an elaborate and comprehensive account of the natural world based on a few simple assumptions. The other contemporary writer whose ideas about force were an influence on Nietzsche was Julius Robert Mayer (1814–1878), recognized as giving the law of conservation of energy its first definite statement. Concepts drawn from these writers led Nietzsche not only to propose a physical model for his doctrine of eternal recurrence, but also to link the theme of force with the concept of *power* which became prominent in his later thinking.

Another theme arising from Nietzsche's confrontation with scientific materialism concerns the role of the senses in knowledge. 'Materialism trusts the senses', Lange had written in his magisterial work.[15] Following his lead, Nietzsche shows the same apparent inconsistency here as he does towards materialism in general. He can write 'Today all of us are sensualists', yet elsewhere attack belief in the senses as a vulgar prejudice. The ambiguity is resolved by separating theoretical and practical versions of sensualism: Nietzsche supports its role as a methodology, but denies it any dogmatic claim to truth. In Chapter 9 I will explore three themes related to the role of the senses in knowledge: the association of sensualism with materialism; the relation between the vocabulary of sensory qualities and the categories of science; and the special cases of pleasure and pain, showing how sensualism figures as an important point of reference in Nietzsche's later thinking.

My concluding chapter considers Nietzsche's thinking on justice and punishment. In some ways, this takes us in a different direction from the previous discussions, and yet here, too, his ideas arise out of a dialogue with several contemporary writers. Eugen Dühring had argued that the source of the concept of justice is a natural feeling of *ressentiment* against those who have harmed us. He concluded that punishment, even in its impersonal legal form, is always an expression of revenge. It is society's strategy for controlling this dangerous passion, by giving it a legitimate but carefully limited outlet. In a powerful critique of moral concepts, Nietzsche turns this theory on its head. For Dühring, the fact that *ressentiment* comes 'naturally' to human beings is sufficient for it to have a moral value, identified as the sense of injustice. For Nietzsche, the real question is: what are the reactive drives that appear in *ressentiment*? He identifies them as belonging to one kind of life rather than another – namely, to a weak and unhealthy life – and so places their value in question. In this way, the theory of *ressentiment* becomes a powerful lever for negating the valuation of justice which Dühring wants to rationalize.

Nietzsche's critique of moral concepts owes much to another contemporary writer. He borrowed his 'historical' approach from Paul Rée (1849–1901), who suggested that the utilitarian origin of punishment had been forgotten and obscured by practices which appear to be directly linked with moral guilt. Nietzsche takes up the idea of a hidden prehistory of morality, but finds Rée's account too simple in its assumption of an original rationality in social practice. He responds that punishment has quite different purposes and meanings at different times, so that any single explanation or justification is inadequate. Thus Rée's uncritical acceptance of an utilitarian valuation appears to be as naïve in its own way as the retributivism that he wants to explain, or rather, to explain away.

It is in this final chapter that the main argument of my book emerges most clearly. For the area of values and morality is where Nietzsche has most often been credited with an originality which owes little or nothing to either familiarity or interaction with other philosophical thinkers. It is commonly supposed that the introduction of the concept of *ressentiment* into moral theory was his own contribution. This is simply wrong, and yet we can see that he transformed the concept and turned it into a much more powerful instrument of theorizing than it had been in the hands of its originator. Similarly, Nietzsche's genealogical approach to morality is a development of 'historical' philosophizing which is no longer concerned just to explain moral feelings and judgements, but achieves a change of perspective which in turn constitutes a radical revaluation. These examples confirm what I have maintained: that Nietzsche's originality is not placed in question when his relations with other authors are considered. Rather, it is this context which helps us to see more clearly where his starting-points were, and how they acted as the impetus for his most striking and original contributions to many subjects, from natural science and epistemology to ethics and cultural theory.

Notes

1. This does not count those philosophers who acted as their own vulgarizers – and here one may be forgiven for thinking of Nietzsche himself.
2. Dühring had accused Schmeitzner of cheating him by understating the production of his books. Nietzsche may have accepted Schmeitzner's story at the time, knowing of Dühring's well-earned reputation as a quarrelsome and litigious personality, but later he came to have his own suspicions, and severed relations with Schmeitzner in a rather Dühring-like way.
3. Hermann von Helmholtz, *Popular Scientific Lectures* (New York: Dover Publications, 1962), 90.
4. See his letters of June and July 1882: KGB III/1, 208, 223 and 226.
5. Friedrich Zöllner, *Wissenschaftliche Abhandlungen*, Band III (Leipzig: Commissionsverlag von L. Staackmann, 1878), 92.
6. Friedrich Nietzsche, *Twilight of the Idols*, 'How the "True World" Finally Became a Fable: The History of An Error'.
7. Nietzsche, *Beyond Good and Evil*, sect. 10.
8. Nietzsche's relation to Lange has been the subject of a full-length study, George J. Stack's *Lange and Nietzsche* (Berlin and New York: de Gruyter, 1983).
9. KGW II/4, 267.
10. *Philosophy in the Tragic Age of the Greeks*, sect. 5.
11. Ibid., sect. 1.
12. J.F. Herbart, *Sämtliche Werke*, ed. K. Kehrbach and O. Flügel (Aalen: Scientia Verlag, 1964), Band 4, 171; and African Spir, *Denken und Wirklichkeit. Versuch einer Erneuerung der kritischen Philosophie* (Leipzig: J.G. Findel, 1873), Band 1, 270.
13. KGW II/4, 270.
14. See Robin Small, 'Absolute Becoming and Absolute Necessity', *International Studies in Philosophy*, 21 (1989), 125–34.
15. F.A. Lange, *Geschichte des Materialismus und Kritik seiner Bedeutung in der Gegenwart* (Iserlohn: Verlag von J. Baedecker, 1866), 345.

Chapter 1

Spir and Time

Nietzsche's commitment to the doctrine of becoming is expressed in many places in his writings, from his early lecture courses to his last notebook entries. He often uses expressions such as 'eternal flow' and 'absolute flow' to signal the concept he has in mind.[1] An *eternal* flow is one that has neither a beginning nor an end but extends throughout infinite time, both in the past and the future. An *absolute* flow is one that allows no exception to the rule of constant change. It cannot contain within itself any pause of the sort that an enduring substance, however brief its duration, would imply. Nietzsche is willing to assert infinite divisibility, not just for time, but in a very general way. In his lectures on early Greek thought, he says: 'Nature is just as infinite inwardly as outwardly: we now get as far as the cell and the parts of the cell: but there is no limit at which one could say that here is the last point inwards: becoming never ceases, into the infinitely small.'[2] Ten years later, in the poetic 'prelude' to *The Gay Science*, he repeats the assertion: 'Infinite is the smallest piece of the world!'[3] The case of time is different in one respect for Nietzsche, since he is prepared to allow that it is infinitely great as well as infinitely divisible. Apart from that, he takes the world to be finite in all its features, and even asserts the finitude of space.[4] In the case of time, he also asserts on several occasions that 'time is infinitely divisible'.[5] Finally, he refers to 'the absolute momentariness of the will to power'.[6]

What influences can we detect in these statements? First and foremost, no doubt, that of Heraclitus.[7] But for any elaboration of the doctrine of becoming, we must look elsewhere. The problem here is that few later thinkers have considered the idea in its uncompromising form as worthy of serious consideration, and even fewer have been willing to adopt it as an account of reality, if only on an experimental basis. Nevertheless, Nietzsche did find in the work of one contemporary philosopher a useful treatment of absolute becoming.

Nietzsche and Spir

African Spir is a more interesting writer than his lack of continuing reputation would suggest.[8] A Russian officer who served in the Crimean War, he retired on a private income to Germany and later Switzerland, in order to pursue an interest in philosophy. Working outside the university system, Spir published a number of books in German and French.[9] The most important of these are *Forschung nach der Gewissheit*, published in 1869, and his definitive work *Denken und Wirklichkeit*, which appeared in 1873 and in a new edition in 1877.[10] Nietzsche studied and drew on this work on its first publication, and returned to it more than once in later years.[11]

Spir here presents a metaphysical system which rests on a sharp and uncompromising separation between the world of appearance and an absolute reality. What makes his position unusual is its insistence that there can be no relation between the two: what is unconditioned cannot be a condition of anything: 'For it is already clear that no intermediate element at all is possible between the unconditioned and the conditioned, since the concepts 'unconditioned' and 'conditioned' form an exhaustive disjunction.'[12] All we can know of the unconditioned is that it must accord with the logical principle of identity, and from this we can infer that it cannot contain either plurality or change, since both of these would compromise its absolute identity. It is a kind of Parmenidean One. Spir's development of his position proceeds mainly through criticism of the doctrines of Kant and Herbart. Unlike many of his German contemporaries, he also shows a good knowledge of the British philosophers of the empiricist tradition. The subtitle of the book is *Versuch einer Erneuerung der kritischen Philosophie*, but Spir is certainly not a neo-Kantian. He does not want to eliminate the thing-in-itself, as Otto Liebmann had proposed in initiating that movement a few years earlier.[13] Rather, it is Herbart's metaphysical system that comes closest to his own. One could say that if Herbart was 'a Kantian of the year 1828', then Spir is a Herbartian of the year 1873. This does not exclude important differences in doctrine, however. Spir rejects Herbart's conception of an unconditioned reality consisting of a plurality of simple and changeless 'reals', which provide an ontological basis for the phenomena of our experience. He asserts that the absolute principle of identity rules out this plurality, as it does any such relation to the conditioned.

Nietzsche's reading of Spir is evident in *Philosophy in the Tragic Age of the Greeks*, written in 1873, where Parmenides is presented as basing his system on the logical principle of identity, as the only certainty available to human knowledge.[14] The expressions that Nietzsche uses here, and the line of thought, are very similar to those of Spir. In *Human, All-Too-Human*, Nietzsche several times refers more openly to Spir, not by name, but as a 'distinguished logician'.[15] By 'logician' he seems to mean not a specialist in formal reasoning, but rather someone who *believes in* the absolute status of logical truth. It is Spir's consistent application of this standard that leads to his conception of the unconditioned. Many philosophers, Nietzsche observes, think they can infer something from experience about the nature of the thing in itself.

> As against this, more rigorous logicians, having clearly identified the concept of the metaphysical as that of the unconditioned, consequently also unconditioning, have disputed any connection between the unconditioned (the metaphysical world) and the world we know: so that what appears in appearance is precisely *not* the thing in itself, and no conclusion can be drawn from the former as to the nature of the latter.[16]

Nietzsche is open in his admiration for some metaphysical thinkers. In *Beyond Good and Evil* he praises those who have the integrity and courage to take their line of thinking to its ultimate consequence, even if this means holding a hopeless position. Such a will to truth 'may ultimately prefer even a handful of "certainty" to a carload of beautiful possibilities'.[17] The reference seems to be to Spir's *Forschung nach der Gewissheit*, in which certainty is postulated as the *sole* aim of philosophy. A single proven proposition, Spir says, is worth ten philosophical systems in which nothing is really proven: 'The only way for free thinking is thus, first and foremost, to establish what is immediately certain and then to investigate what consequences, drawn with certainty, can be derived from it.'[18]

Yet if the content of this certainty amounts to nothing, it is a form of nihilism. Here we should recall Nietzsche's view that to push an idea to its utmost limit is to bring it 'to the point of nonsense'.[19] The postulation of an unconditioned reality wholly unconnected with the world of experience turns the notion of a 'true' world into 'an idea which is no longer good for anything, not even obligating – an idea which has become useless and superfluous – *consequently*, a refuted idea'.[20] As such, it is just a prelude to Nietzsche's own view, that the world of experience is the only world. Thus, by driving metaphysical thinking to its point of destruction, Spir is preparing the way for his anti-metaphysical successors – the 'new' philosophers amongst whom Nietzsche counts himself.

Nietzsche himself is no 'logician'. Much of *Human, All-Too-Human* is a systematic attack on what he sees as the 'tyranny' of logic over philosophy.[21] Logic, he argues, presupposes that there are 'identical things', but this is an unfounded assumption, as indeed is the notion that there are 'things' at all. Moreover, the value of logic for life is doubtful. Human beings could not live without the illogical; everything that makes our lives worthwhile comes from drives and feelings to which no logical justification can ever be assigned.[22] The same themes run through Nietzsche's later writings: for example, in *The Gay Science* he suggests that the 'logical' has emerged from the 'illogical' through a process of natural selection, favouring those beings whose illusions give them an advantage in the struggle for life.[23] Many similar passages could be cited; to this extent, Nietzsche's ideas are often developed in criticism of Spir's doctrines.

In view of his rather austere view of ultimate reality, it may seem surprising that much of Spir's philosophy is concerned with the world of experience. In fact, the lack of connection between the two is an advantage, for it enables Spir, like Parmenides, to give an account of the 'way of belief' which is not predetermined by the metaphysical 'way of truth'. Here it is his treatment of time which particularly impressed Nietzsche. Arguing against both Kant and Herbart, Spir insists on the empirical reality of time, while denying its *a priori* status.[24] Kant's error, according to Spir, is to treat space and time on the same basis, a bias attributable to his love of symmetry.[25] Succession in time is *given* to us immediately, and so its reality is undeniable. Space, in contrast, is merely our construction. Since time is nothing apart from succession, we cannot imagine an empty time, whereas we can imagine an empty space, and even assign it a definite size.[26] Time is thus neither something existing in its own right, nor a necessary form of intuition on the part of the subject.[27] It is an abstraction which expresses what given successions have in common with one another.

Many of these points find a close echo in Nietzsche's thinking. On renewing his study of *Denken und Wirklichkeit* in 1885, he noted down Spir's description of time as 'a mere abstraction' and his denial of its *a priori* necessity.[28] Anything supporting an attack on dogmatic thinking was useful to Nietzsche in formulating the ideas of *Beyond Good and Evil*, and Spir's empiricist view of time was as congenial as his critique of the notion of 'immediate certainty' in psychology.[29] But to assess the influence of Spir on Nietzsche's thinking, we need to look more closely at particular aspects of the concept of time, beginning with the question of continuity, and proceeding to the more difficult question of absolute becoming.

The Infinite Divisibility of Time

In rebutting the idea of time as something in its own right, Spir draws on an argument used by Herbart.[30] It asserts that such an idea is inconsistent with the fact that different successions occur at different *rates*. If time were a common medium in the way that space is for bodies, it would have its own speed, and impose that upon every process falling within it. The force of this argument is slightly elusive, but it seems to concern the *divisibility* of time. The suggestion is that if time were something more than a mere abstraction, it would provide its own measure, without reference to real successions. There would be, so to speak, a natural unit of time. Hence, any proof of the infinite divisibility of time will assist in showing that it is not a thing in its own right. This interpretation of Spir's argument is supported by what he goes on to say:

> With the rotation of the earth, for example, a point on the equator moves with a million times greater speed than a point located close to the pole: and yet both points complete their revolution in exactly the same time, and occupy this time with the same continuity and uniformity. The slower moving point never stands still, any more than the faster moving one. How then could the same time, if it were not a mere abstraction but something distinct from real successions, be occupied by two so different quanta of succession in a uniform and, to that extent, equal way? It would obviously be impossible.[31]

Here Spir is drawing on a very traditional argument. To appreciate its significance, we need to go back at least as far as Aristotle's attempt to establish the infinite divisibility of both time and space.[32] Aristotle proceeds from the assumption that things may move with different speeds in the same time. After explaining the meaning of 'faster' and 'slower', he outlines a systematic procedure which leads to the desired conclusion. We can summarize it in the following way. Suppose that A is the faster and B the slower object. Then if B covers a given distance d_1 in a time t_1, A covers the same distance in a shorter time t_2. During this time, the slower object B covers a lesser distance d_2. But the faster object A covers this second distance in a time t_3, which is shorter than t_2. Now Aristotle says that:

> ... we can carry on this process for ever, taking the slower after the quicker and the quicker after the slower alternately, and using what has been demonstrated at each stage as a new point of departure: for the quicker will divide the time and the slower will divide the length. If, then, this alternation always holds good, and at every turn involves a division, it is evident that all time must be continuous.[33]

If Aristotle's argument is valid, the continuity of space and time must stand or fall together, for if in following the alternating procedure we arrive at some indivisible period of time, any further division of space will be precluded. Thus, if there is a natural unit of time, there must be one of space, and vice versa.

It is clear that one challenge facing this argument will be directed against its assumption that there are faster and slower processes. The reply will suggest that such differences are only apparent, and that in fact all processes occur at the same rate. If some seem to be slower than this rate, it is because they include *pauses* which are overlooked when the process is supposed to be slower. And if some seem to be faster, it is because the moving object is *jumping over* some parts of its path, and this too is being overlooked. In one case, then, there are units of space which correspond to more than one unit of time, and in the other there are units of space which correspond to no unit of time.

How can one reply to this objection? An elimination of these anomalies is achieved by showing that slower and faster processes both involve a one-to-one correspondence between moments of time and positions in space. Aristotle does not provide any such demonstration; that was left for his successors. Sextus Empiricus sets out the required argument in his treatise *Against the Physicists*, and it is this that Spir invokes in the passage cited above. We are asked to consider a rotating rigid body, such as a ruler turning about one of its ends.[34] Different points marked along the ruler complete their revolutions in the same time, but have travelled quite different distances; thus it must be allowed that some are moving faster and others slower. But what about the objection already raised? It cannot be the case that some run ahead or that others lag behind, since in that case the ruler would bend or break as it revolved. Hence, we must conclude, it is possible for moving bodies to have different speeds without discontinuities in their motion, so that Aristotle's argument for the infinite divisibility of both space and time remains a sound one.

This further argument was taken up by many later philosophers. Perhaps the best-known version is that of Moses Maimonides, whose example is a millstone, presumably as solid an object as one could imagine.

> Have you seen a millstone making a complete revolution? Has not the part that is at its circumference traversed the distance represented by the bigger circle in

the same time in which the part near the centre has traversed the distance represented by the smaller circle? Accordingly the motion of the circumference is more rapid than the motion of the inner circle. And there is no opportunity for you to assert that the motion of the latter part is interrupted by a greater number of units of rest as the whole body is one and continuous, I mean the body of the millstone.[35]

Spir refers to points located at different latitudes on the rotating earth. While one point moves more slowly than the other, he says, it clearly does not stand still at any time; so that the same time corresponds to quite different amounts of succession. Nietzsche must have noted this line of thinking, for in an 1881 notebook we find the following entry:

> Only succession produces the idea of *time*. If we were to sense not causes and effects but a continuum instead, we would not believe in time. For the process of becoming is *not* composed of points at rest or lines at rest. The outer periphery of a wheel is constantly moving, just like the inner periphery, and although slower, *not* at rest in comparison to the faster inner one. The difference between slower and faster movement is not to be determined in terms of 'time'. In absolute becoming, force can never be at rest, never be non-force: its 'slow and fast movement' is not measured in a unit which is not there.[36]

Most of the themes in this are taken up from Spir, and the example of a moving wheel is another version of the standard argument which reappears in *Denken und Wirklichkeit*.[37] Nietzsche makes an obvious error in saying that the wheel's outer edge moves slower than its inner edge, but he arrives at the intended conclusion that there is no given unit of time. How far Nietzsche's train of thought goes beyond Spir's account, however, is seen in his introduction of absolute becoming into the discussion, leading on towards a radical relativization of space and time.

The note begins with an idea taken directly from Spir – the dependence of our concept of time upon succession. Spir remarks that someone who sleeps soundly for eight hours may suppose that only a moment has elapsed, since the time between his falling asleep and waking up has not existed for him.[38] Nietzsche, referring to his doctrine of eternal recurrence, says: 'You think you have a long rest until rebirth – but do not fool yourselves! Between the last moment of consciousness and the first appearance of new life lies "no time" – it passes by like a stroke of lightning, even if living creatures measure it in terms of millions of years or could not measure it at all.'[39] Like Spir, he holds that our idea of time is bound up with our experience of a succession of different states. This is where causality enters into our thinking, to account for such a transition, in terms of a necessary connection between successive states of affairs. In *The Gay Science* Nietzsche writes:

> Cause and effect: such a duality probably never exists – in truth we are confronted with a continuum out of which we isolate a couple of pieces, just as we only ever perceive a motion as isolated points, and so infer it without actually seeing it. The suddenness with which many effects stand out misleads us; but it is a

suddenness only for us. In this second of suddenness there are an infinite number of processes that elude us. An intellect that could see cause and effect as a continuum and not, in our fashion, as an arbitrary division and dismemberment, that could see the flow of occurrence – would repudiate the concept of cause and effect and deny all conditionality.[40]

Similarly, in a notebook entry of the same period he writes:

> A continuum of force contains no succession and no coexistence (this too assumes the human intellect and gaps between things). Without succession and without coexistence, there would be no becoming, no multiplicity *for us* – we *could* only take that continuum to be one, at rest, changeless, not a becoming, without time and space. But this is just the human antithesis.[41]

If the duality of cause and effect is an illusion, how does it arise? First of all, Nietzsche asserts that we perceive very little of the process of becoming: 'Sensations and thoughts are something extremely insignificant and rare in relation to the innumerable occurrences in every moment.'[42] As a consequence of this selectivity on the part of our perceptual faculties, we form a conception of separate and discontinuous things; then we are faced with the task of re-establishing some connection between them, and draw on our notion of cause and effect for that purpose. A corollary of the point Nietzsche is making here concerns the relativeness of our grasp of *duration*. This is a theme he touches on in many passages. A process that we take to be 'sudden' only appears so because we overlook the inner continuity of its real content. Nietzsche takes this to mean that a period of time may be much longer than we take it to be. He says for instance:

> To the actual course of things must correspond an actual time, quite distinct from the feelings of longer or shorter time that knowing beings have. Actual time is probably unspeakably much slower than we human beings feel time: we perceive so little, although even for us one day appears very long against the same day in the feeling of an insect.[43]

One main source for this idea of the relativity of awareness of time is an influential lecture given in 1860 by the naturalist Karl Ernst von Baer.[44] Nietzsche draws on this text in his early lectures on the pre-Platonic philosophers, in order to illustrate the Heraclitean view of time. According to von Baer, Nietzsche says, different living beings experience the length of a given period of time in very different manners, in accordance with the rates of their own life-processes. If our lives went much more quickly, we would take plants to be as unchanging as we now take mountains to be.[45] The movements of animals would be too slow for us to perceive; instead we would have to infer them as we do now with the motions of the heavenly bodies. On the other hand, if our lives were to slow down enormously, the changing of the seasons would appear a very sudden series of alternations. Nietzsche concludes: 'If we could perceive much faster, we would have the illusion of permanence much more strongly: if we imagine the infinitely fastest, but still human, perception, then all motion would cease and everything would be eternally unchanging.'[46]

This point is closely related to the theme of space. Nietzsche claims that space is a secondary phenomenon in relation to time. Our conception of space is dependent on our sense of time. In the first place, it arises out of our need to separate and sort out things which we take to be in existence at the same time. Yet, according to Nietzsche, this coexistence is always an illusion, the result of our inability to perceive succession. He concludes that space is merely imaginary: 'Of the space that belongs to the eternal flow of things we know nothing.'[47] In the second place, our idea of the *size* of space is directly related to our sense of time. The more events we are aware of yet fail to perceive as a succession, the more we need to use space in order to imagine them as existing together. Thus to the extent that we overestimate the speed that forces have, we also overestimate the amount of space that they occupy. In abnormal states, such as those induced by narcotics or by extreme stress, this effect may become even more pronounced: 'Hashish smoking makes space much more extensive, because much more than usual is seen in the same time.'[48] But, even in our normal state, we magnify our environment and ourselves as well, and for this reason perhaps see ourselves as more important than we really are. Nietzsche concludes: 'It is possible that everything is much smaller. Thus the actual world smaller, but moving much more slowly, yet infinitely richer in movements than we notice.'[49] His critique of our sense of time is thus turned into a critique of our idea of space. In its most radical form, this critique begins with a repudiation of the idea of simultaneity: 'Let us be mistrustful of all seeming "simultaneity"!'[50] But in that case any real justification for using the notion of space disappears altogether. However, Nietzsche is usually more cautious, and restricts himself to a critique of our judgements concerning the speeds of forces.

Absolute Becoming and Eternal Recurrence

Having examined Nietzsche's treatment of our ordinary awareness of time, and its relation to Spir's approach, I turn to the difficult theme of absolute becoming. Spir's discussion of absolute becoming is closely linked to Herbart's treatment of the concept, although its conclusions are different. For this reason, I begin with Herbart who, in his *Lehrbuch zur Einleitung in die Philosophie*, approaches absolute becoming by way of a 'trilemma' arising from the concept of change.[51] Change either has a cause or has no cause; and, if it does, the cause is either an external or an internal one. Hence there are three possible accounts of change: *mechanism*, which explains change in terms of external causes, a view also shared by common sense; *self-determination*, which Herbart identifies with the Kantian concept of transcendental freedom; and *absolute becoming*, which is defined in the first instance as a complete denial of causality. Herbart considers the alternatives in this order. After finding the first two to be either incoherent or burdened with contradictions, he proceeds to consider the remaining option, absolute becoming. The problem here is to grasp the content of this unfamiliar idea. Certainly there can be no causal rules in absolute becoming, but this does not mean that things change in an irregular or unpredictable way, since that implies some degree of stability, both before and after the changes. Herbart insists that a radical but consistent conception requires setting aside our usual ideas about things and their qualities. A doctrine of absolute becoming, he says, makes three main claims about change:

1   Change is continual, never pausing and having no beginning or end.
2   Change always proceeds at the same rate, with the same amount of alteration occurring in the same time.
3   Change always proceeds in the same direction, never returning to an earlier state.[52]

Understood along these lines, Herbart goes on to argue, absolute becoming involves logical inconsistencies, since we cannot give content to such propositions except by using a vocabulary which, for example, allows different qualities to belong to the same things. And in that case we are led to paradoxical statements like those of Heraclitus. By itself, the mere concept of becoming does not contain a contradiction.[53] But as soon as we try to say anything concrete about it (*what* it is that becomes, for example) we are caught up in insoluble logical problems.[54]

In *Denken und Wirklichkeit*, Spir sets out Herbart's three 'laws' of absolute becoming, and proceeds to criticize them, or at least the last two.[55] How, he asks, can we attribute uniformity of either speed or direction to absolute becoming? These concepts involve a correlation (*Zusammenhang*) of the elements in a succession, but if they have nothing whatever in common with one another, that is plainly impossible. Herbart is right in observing that no causal laws could be present in absolute becoming, but he is wrong in characterizing the content of absolute becoming as arising from nothing and disappearing into nothing. Spir insists that 'nothing' cannot have any relation to something existing, and certainly cannot 'turn itself into' something existing. Furthermore, Herbart is wrong in suggesting that constant change *is* somehow the content of absolute becoming, and its only possible content at that: such an identification of form and content is a conceptual impossibility. Like Herbart, however, Spir does not believe in absolute becoming, or even in change as a property of the real world, as distinct from the world of appearance.

Nietzsche stands sharply opposed to these metaphysicians, and yet it is their formulation of absolute becoming that influenced his thinking. We can outline his conception by comparing it with Herbart's analysis in the following way:

1   Nietzsche clearly agrees with the first proposition; he holds that change has neither a beginning nor an end, and that the time in which it occurs is infinite, in both the past and future. (Chapter 2 will discuss this proposition in detail.) Further, he insists that not even the most momentary

pause is possible, since its occurrence would bring becoming to an end once and for all.[56]
2   Nietzsche holds that absolute becoming is not uniform, but contains variations in 'tempo'. He speaks of the 'slow and fast movement' of force, while denying that the rates can be measured in a given unit of time. Such differences in tempo, he says, are variations in degree that we turn into oppositions, like that between rest and motion.[57]
3   Nietzsche's doctrine of eternal recurrence stands in direct contradiction to Herbart's third 'law'; it means that the flow of becoming does turn back into itself, again and again.[58] As Zarathustra's animals put it, 'The path of eternity is curved'.[59]

The central problem remains: what can we say about absolute becoming, given that our usual concepts express a bias in favour of being, and even a denial of becoming? There seems to be no vocabulary for a Heraclitean view of the world. Whether we can escape from this predicament is very problematical: 'We cannot think of *becoming* other than as the transition from one persisting "dead" state of affairs into another persisting "dead" state of affairs.'[60] Nietzsche seems to be suggesting that we are forever limited to the concepts that express our human perspective, that we are 'unable to see round our corner'.[61] He writes: 'We cannot change our means of expression at will: it is possible to understand to what extent they are mere signs.'[62] Accordingly, when he comes to express his own doctrine of eternal recurrence, he uses words like 'state of affairs' (*Zustand*) or 'general state' (*Gesammtlage*) to characterize what it is that is supposed to recur eternally. No doubt we can bear in mind that these terms are 'mere signs' and that, strictly speaking, what is supposed to recur is the process of becoming which is simplified – and falsified – in being reduced to successive states. But assuming that 'Linguistic means of expression are useless for expressing becoming',[63] the fact remains that the static vocabulary is what we have at our disposal.

Or is it? Nietzsche's frequent use of the term *Geschehen* is important here. It is hard to find an English word that corresponds to this term as he uses it. Usually we find it translated as 'event' or 'events'.[64] However, something like 'occurrence' or even 'process' would very often be more accurate.[65] More radically, one could resort to a coinage such as Benjamin Lee Whorf's 'eventing'.[66] These alternatives would avoid the suggestion of discrete particularity that attaches to the English word 'event', as recent philosophers have noted and made explicit.[67] Their 'reification' of events, as W.V. Quine candidly calls it,[68] takes us in the opposite direction to Nietzsche's thinking. In the passage of *The Gay Science* quoted earlier, he characterized absolute becoming as a 'flow of occurrence'.[69] This is his label for the reality that underlies the succession of states that our knowledge of the world represents as real.[70] He seems here to use a concept while denying its availability. For example, he argues that the necessity of the connection between cause and effect is not a genuine problem; since there is really a *single* process here, rather than two discrete states, the only necessity we need to invoke is the necessity by which everything is itself rather than something else.[71] This is what he means in writing that 'Occurrence (*Geschehen*) and necessary occurrence is a *tautology*'.[72] Our usual notion of becoming is an attempt to reconstruct a concept out of its negation: understandably this runs into the sorts of logical difficulty that Zeno brought to light in his paradoxes. Despite his own warnings, Nietzsche is hopeful that an attempt to achieve an authentic concept of becoming could meet with success. His use of *Geschehen* is one step in this direction, but not the only one, as we shall see.

Nietzsche's conception of absolute becoming is open to objections of various kinds, but of particular interest are those that arise from his own arguments concerning time. The first of these arises out of Spir's argument for the reality of time, which Nietzsche borrows in *Philosophy in the Tragic Age of the Greeks* as an effective reply to the Parmenidean denial of the reality of change. He quotes Spir's own words: 'One can say: "It merely seems to me that conditions and ideas change", but this semblance itself is something objectively given. Within it, succession indubitably has objective reality; within it something actually follows upon something else.'[73] In later years, Nietzsche repeatedly made use of this argument. For instance, his reflections on the impossibility of a 'final state' led him to an argument (to be looked at more closely in Chapter 6) which appeals to the status of the present moment as crucial premise. If there had ever been a moment of 'being' in the strict sense, Nietzsche argues, 'there could be no more becoming, and so no thinking of or observing a becoming either'.[74] The fact of 'mind' shows that the present moment is one of becoming, and thus proves that the world has no final state.[75] Clearly, this is Spir's claim for the self-evident reality of becoming as guaranteed by our own thinking.

The problem is that a similar *ad hominem* argument can be brought against Nietzsche's own theory of absolute becoming, in so far as it implies that the separateness of things or events is an illusion. Even if it merely seems to us that there are separate things, one could say that the semblance is itself separate from other semblances, and if the reply is that this is merely another illusion, the same comment can be made about that further semblance, and so on indefinitely. So it appears that, if we take this line of argument seriously, a case can be made for the reality of distinct things, as much as for the reality of change. It is hard to see how Nietzsche could reply to this objection. He insists that 'in truth, all our doing and knowing is not a sequence of facts and empty intervals, but rather a continuous flow'.[76] In a later note, he argues that the mental states which seem to be separate, and to stand in causal relations to one another, have a merely epiphenomenal status: 'All succession in consciousness is completely atomistic.'[77] The question remains, however, whether this consignment of much of our experience to the realm of illusion does not invite a reply like the one that Nietzsche borrowed from Spir to defend the reality of change.

A second objection to Nietzsche's idea of absolute becoming is based on one of his own arguments, designed to support the doctrine of eternal recurrence. In various texts, he argues that, whereas only a finite number of states of affairs are possible, the time within which they occur is infinite, so that in the course of time the same states must occur again, and indeed occur infinitely many times. Now we can turn this argument in a different direction by replacing one premise. If time is infinitely divisible, then within any finite period there are an infinite number of moments at which different states of affairs can occur. But if only a finite number of such states are possible, must not they all occur within, say, the next minute? So must not the present state occur again within this time? But it seems quite certain that this is not the case. Hence, one can conclude, the infinite divisibility of time is an assumption which should be abandoned in order to avoid an absurd conclusion.

The only difference between this and Nietzsche's own argument for eternal recurrence is the replacement of infinite magnitude with infinite divisibility. Is his reasoning any less valid in this form? It seems quite evident that the present state of things does not recur within a short period of time. In fact, this is supported not just by experience but by the impossibility of any contrary experience: as many commentators have pointed out, there can be no *direct* evidence of any kind for a recurrence of the total state of things. The impossibility of recognizing a total state of the world as a recurrence of some previous state follows from the strict identity of the *total* state of affairs, of which one's own experience is just a part. For that reason, it cannot include an element of memory or recognition that was not present in its earlier occurrence. The argument makes another assumption, however, which is open to question: that a particular series of states can occur within any given time. This is not consistent with our experience, which testifies that processes occur at their own finite rates. Not only does Nietzsche recognize this fact; he identifies it as a philosophical problem, for his own standpoint and for others. In an 1881 notebook he suggests an argument for units of time based on this point: 'Everything measurable by everything: but outside things there is no measure: therefore every magnitude by itself is infinitely great and infinitely small. On the other hand, perhaps there is a unit of *time* which is fixed. Forces take definite times to become definite qualities.'[78] Understandably, Nietzsche is tentative in making this suggestion, since it is really a problem for his doctrine of becoming. He is faced with a problem in any case: how can forces 'take time' in this sense? Does this involve their acting at a distance in time?

'Time Atoms' and Action at a Distance

One answer to this question is found in a lengthy notebook entry dating from early 1873, in which Nietzsche suggests that 'time is not a continuum' but consists instead in distinct 'time-points' which act at a distance on one another.[79] In many ways this sketch is an anomaly in Nietzsche's thinking about time. It makes several assertions which are contradicted more than once by his later writings on the subject, and yet some aspects of the ideas seem to remain a continuing presence. The 'theory of time-atoms'

(*Zeitatomenlehre*) shows the influence of a recent reading of Boscovich's *Theory of Natural Philosophy* and, even more importantly, Zöllner's *Über die Natur der Cometen*. However, it also draws upon Nietzsche's own reflections on the validity of human experience of space and time. In this further development, he uses his critique of the sense of time to provide an argument for eliminating the idea of space. If our common applications of the concept of simultaneity are mistaken, then any justification for according an objective status to space disappears, at least on the assumption that this claim rests on its indispensability for the individuation of simultaneous events or objects. But if space is eliminated, or reduced to a single point, what remains? That is the question that Nietzsche tries to answer in his theory of time atoms. He presents a thoroughgoing programme of reduction which he summarizes as consisting of three stages.

It is possible:

1 to trace the world at hand back to a pointlike space-atomism,
2 to trace this again back to time atomism,
3 time-atomism finally coincides with a theory of sensation. The dynamic time-point is identical with the sensation-point. For there is no simultaneity of sensation.[80]

The source of the first stage of this theoretical programme is clearly Boscovich's theory of unextended 'points of matter' as the ultimate constituents of the physical world. But Nietzsche takes this merely as the starting-point for a line of thinking which departs entirely from anything attributable to Boscovich. His next step is to argue for the unreality of space, by claiming that the spatial law of force proposed by Boscovich is inadequate when the role of time is taken into consideration. From that he argues that the underlying pattern which constitutes the order of the world is a purely temporal one. Hence, it is unextended points of time, rather than space, that are related in lawlike ways.

Nietzsche's line of thought here is only given in note form, but its crucial first step is clear: a denial of *persisting* things. He poses a dilemma: we can have unchanging atomic elements, or we can have acting forces, but not both.[81] For nothing can act without undergoing its own alteration – without being, as he puts it, 'absolutely changeable'.[82] It follows that forces must be wholly impermanent: 'If we take what acts in *time*, then what acts is something different in each smallest moment of time.'[83] But the effect of this is to prevent forces from acting on other forces at all, since any such process would require some period of time to cover the distance between the points, and in that case the two forces would never be in existence together. Nietzsche concludes that forces cannot act on other forces in time: they can be related in a lawlike way only through a timeless law of spatial relations. In that case, he says, we think of the world as given 'at one stroke', and concepts like that of motion are simply eliminated.

Since this result is unacceptable, the alternative path is to discount the concept of space and try to grasp the relations between forces in terms of time alone. On this assumption, there is just one point in existence at a given moment of time. But since time is infinitely divisible, there is room for an infinite number of points in any interval between points. This is where Nietzsche denies the continuity of time and suggests that we should speak not of 'time' at all, but only of time-points: 'Time is not at all a continuum: rather there are only totally distinct points, not a line.'[84] This view is quite opposed to the Aristotelian approach to time, in which indivisible moments figure only as the limits of continuous periods of time. On that view, continuity is primary, whereas beginning with points of time forces us either to give up continuity or to attempt to reconstruct it out of infinite collections of points – a task that has occupied mathematicians for the last hundred years, without an accepted solution yet in sight.

At this stage, we are left with a series of points of time, separated from one another by greater or lesser intervals. How different magnitudes are to be assigned to these intervals is left unexplained and, indeed, is hard to grasp. Nietzsche's idea is that these variations allow patterns to emerge, so that an observer can recognize some such pattern and identify it with a previous one. An analogy with what Nietzsche has in mind might be a Morse code signal, where it is letters of the alphabet that we recognize as 'the same' whenever their characteristic patterns occur within the sequence of tones. The fact that many different patterns are perceived as occurring *concurrently* leads to a hypothesis of different 'things' which exist alongside one another, presumably at different locations in space. Thus a reconstruction of simultaneity and spatiality emerges from the time atom theory, and from that beginning one can proceed towards scientific theories in something like their usual form.

Ultimately, Nietzsche says, the points of time coincide with the elementary sensations upon which all knowledge is based. His notebooks of this period take up the epistemological approach of Schopenhauer and more recent writers such as Zöllner, in which the primacy of sensation is taken as a basic principle.[85] Even space and time, it is argued, are only interpretations of what is given in sensation which, taken by itself, is neither spatial nor temporal. 'It seems to me to emerge from this', wrote Zöllner, 'that the phenomenon of sensation is a much more fundamental fact of observation than the mobility of matter, which we are forced to add to it as the most general property and condition of the intelligibility of sensory alterations.'[86] Hence, the properties of space and time, as well as matter, must be explained in terms of sensation. That Nietzsche's theory of 'time-atoms' is intended to provide a framework for that process can be observed by reading it backwards – that is, proceeding from atomic sensations to points of time, and then in turn to the temporal patterns which enable the construction of persisting objects and spatial relations.

Action at a distance in time is a problematical concept, however. So is action at a distance in space, and the objection is similar in each case: how can a thing act where (or when) it is not? Zöllner strongly defends the idea of action at a distance and discusses it at some length, arguing that Newton was in fact a defender of this concept, despite what seems to be a plain denial in his correspondence with Richard Bentley.[87] He also supports the notion of action at a distance in time, quoting the physicist Carl Neumann, who had said in an 1868 address:

> If one accepts (as occurs almost universally since Newton) that objects separated in space act on each other immediately, then it is just as legitimate to accept an immediate causal interaction between objects which are separated from each other in time: assuming naturally that such an assumption leads to consequences as fortunate as those of the first one.[88]

The issue here is the relation between causality and time. A good example of argumentation on this question can be found in Hume, who denies action at a distance in space but goes on to insist that cause and effect can never be simultaneous. For if one cause could be simultaneous with its effect, he argues, then all causes could be simultaneous with their effects, so that the whole course of events could occur at once.

> The consequence of this wou'd be no less than the destruction of that succession of causes, which we observe in the world; and indeed, the utter annihilation of time. For if one cause were co-temporary with its effect, and this effect with *its* effect, and so on, 'tis plain there wou'd be no such thing as succession, and all objects must be co-existent.[89]

Hume's argument here is closely linked with his later discussion of the notion of causal power or efficacy. He denies that we really have any such idea, since we cannot point to any experience from which it could be derived.[90] Anyway, if there were such a thing, why would not it produce its effect straight away? In some ways, Nietzsche's time-atom theory is in close accord with Hume's approach. For it too appeals to the regular occurrence of patterns of events as the only available basis for a lawlike organization of the objects of experience into a general representation.

Several years later, however, Nietzsche is able to arrive at a quite different solution. '*All conflict* – every process (*Geschehen*) is a conflict – *takes time*,' he writes. 'What we call "cause" and "effect" leaves out the conflict and therefore does not correspond to the process. It is consistent to deny time in cause and effect.'[91] As he does elsewhere, Nietzsche is attacking the concept of causality here. Because it reduces any process to an ordered pair of 'dead' states of affairs, causality cannot account for the duration of the transition from one to the other. Why cannot cause and effect be simultaneous? Nietzsche says that there is no inconsistency in supposing that to be the case; in fact, this remark understates his own position. He thinks that there is an *in*consistency in affirming time in cause and effect, because this involves the notion of action at a distance in time. It is impossible to act upon something that does not yet exist, or to be acted upon by something that no longer exists: 'Two successive states: the one cause, the other effect, is false. The first state has nothing to effect, the second has been effected by nothing.'[92] This point recalls the account of absolute becoming offered by Herbart and Spir. At any rate, it indicates to Nietzsche that causality cannot provide an answer by, so to speak, doing the job of the becoming it has replaced.

His own reply is that every process has to be understood as a struggle between forces. Whereas duration would be imposed arbitrarily on becoming by a unit of time, it is here assigned to something within the process itself. Temporality is constituted by a continual conflict between the forces whose interaction gives rise to the properties and qualities we encounter in experience. It is the impossibility of a stable equilibrium that rules out any moment of rest, and so ensures that becoming will proceed endlessly in the future, just as it has in the infinite past. But conflict is also important in explaining the *variations* in becoming without which there would be no determinate durations. No struggle is a uniform process; rather, a succession of phases is implied, with the sorts of contrast which, in Nietzsche's view, are expressed in our simplistic oppositions between rest and motion. Nietzsche takes this line of thought further in his theory of the 'will to power'. In its essence, the concept is an attempt to achieve what both Herbart and Spir had judged to be impossible – a characterization of absolute becoming. Not surprisingly, language is a main problem confronting Nietzsche here. In the end he is drawn into a poetic mode of discourse, as in the text which his editors used as the final section of *The Will to Power*: there he describes the world as 'a play of forces and waves of forces, at the same time one and many, increasing here and at the same time decreasing there; a sea of forces flowing and rushing together, eternally changing, eternally flooding back, with tremendous years of recurrence ...'.[93] If this is a long way from the style of his contemporary, Spir, it is not so far from the philosopher near whom, Nietzsche said, he felt 'altogether warmer and better than anywhere else'[94] – that is, Heraclitus.

Notes

1. KGW V/2, 397–401 and 452; VII/1, 140; and VII/2, 161.
2. KGW II/4, 270.
3. Friedrich Nietzsche, *The Gay Science*, Prelude, sect. 55; KGW V/2, 37.
4. See, for example, his letter of 23 July 1885 to Heinrich Köselitz; in KGB III/3, 69.
5. KGW III/4, 178. Cf. ibid., 50 and 119.
6. KGW VII/3, 387.
7. Friedrich Nietzsche, *Ecce Homo*, 'The Birth of Tragedy', sect. 3.
8. He is the subject of a useful article by Mary-Barbara Zeldin, 'Spir, Afrikan Alexandrovich', in *The Encyclopedia of Philosophy*, ed. Paul Edwards (New York: The Macmillan Company and The Free Press, 1967), Vol. 7, 544. The 'Vie de A. Spir' of his daughter Hélène Claparède-Spir, in A. Spir, *Nouvelles esquisses de philosophie critique* (Paris: Félix Alcan, 1899), is more hagiography than biography. However, the same author's article 'Friedrich Nietzsche und Afrikan Spir', *Philosophie und Leben*, 6 (1930), 242–50, is worth reading for its account of her dealings with Elisabeth Förster-Nietzsche, head of the Nietzsche-Archiv.
9. Only one of Spir's books is available in English: *Right and Wrong*, trans. A.F. Falconer (Edinburgh: Oliver and Boyd, 1954).
10. African Spir, *Forschung nach der Gewissheit in der Erkenntnis der Wirklichkeit* (Leipzig: Förster und Findel, 1869); and *Denken und Wirklichkeit. Versuch einer Erneuerung der*

kritischen Philosophie (Leipzig: J.G. Findel, 1873). The latter work is in two volumes, although the first is not labelled 'Band I' and has the appearance of a self-contained work. At the end of his '*Vorwort*', Spir says:

> I have the intention to subject various problems and subjects, which could be touched upon only briefly in the present volume, to a more thorough treatment and discussion, which perhaps with time will also be published ...

The time came a few months later. In the 'Vorwort' to Band II Spir explains:

> The present work was planned from the beginning as two volumes. But since I did not have the intention to publish the two volumes together and did not want to commit myself at all to the publication of a second volume, I allowed the first to appear an independent work, which it in fact is.

The version of *Denken und Wirklichkeit* that constitutes the first two volumes of Spir, *Gesammelte Schriften* (Leipzig: Verlag von J.G. Findel, 1883–84), contains major alterations; although the doctrine is the same, its presentation has been brought closer to the systematic approach of *Forschung nach der Gewissheit*, the importance of the principle of identity being emphasized at the outset and repeated throughout; another difference is the disappearance of many of the references to British writers.

11   He borrowed the first volume from the Basel University library shortly after its publication in 1873, borrowed both volumes in 1874, and acquired his own copy of the second edition in 1877. Elisabeth Förster-Nietzsche, writing in 1909 to Hélène Claparède-Spir, stated that she had given her brother his copy of *Denken und Wirklichkeit* as a birthday gift. Nietzsche's published correspondence tells a different story: he ordered the work from his publisher on 2 February 1877 (KGB II/5, 219). He had bought a copy of *Forschung nach der Gewissheit* in 1872 and sold it to a Basel bookdealer in 1875; see Karl Schlechta and Anni Anders, *Friedrich Nietzsche: Von den verborgenen Anfängen seines Philosophierens* (Stuttgart-Bad Cannstatt: Friedrich Frommann Verlag, 1962), 161–66.
12   Spir, *Denken und Wirklichkeit*, Band 1, 363.
13   Otto Liebmann, *Kant und die Epigonen. Eine kritische Abhandlung* (Stuttgart: Carl Schober, 1865), 63–64 and 204–05.
14   Friedrich Nietzsche, *Philosophy in the Tragic Age of the Greeks*, sect. 10.
15   Friedrich Nietzsche, *Human, All-Too-Human*, sect. 18. See also KGB II/5, 466.
16   Ibid., sect. 16; see also sect. 18 and 131.
17   Friedrich Nietzsche, *Beyond Good and Evil*, sect. 10.
18   Spir, *Forschung nach der Gewissheit*, IV. Similarly in *Philosophy in the Tragic Age of the Greeks* Nietzsche attributes to Parmenides a prayer to the gods, beginning 'Grant me just one certainty...'; KGW III/2, 339.
19   Nietzsche, *Beyond Good and Evil*, sect. 36.
20   Friedrich Nietzsche, *Twilight of the Idols*, 'How the 'True World' Finally Became a Fable'.
21   Nietzsche, *Human, All-Too-Human*, sect. 6.
22   Ibid., sect. 31 and 32.
23   Nietzsche, *The Gay Science*, sect. 111.
24   Spir, *Denken und Wirklichkeit*, Band 2, 7 and 15.
25   Ibid., Band 1, 263.
26   Ibid., Band 2, 7.
27   Ibid., Band 2, 14.
28   KGW VIII/3, 259–60. Alphonso Lingis writes: 'Certainly there are pages – particularly in the unpublished notes – where Nietzsche subscribes completely to a Kantian conception of the subjective and a priori character of space and time': *Deathbound Subjectivity* (Bloomington-Indianapolis: Indiana University Press, 1989), 98–99. The reference here is unclear, but may be to Nietzsche's early notebooks, dating from

before his first reading of Spir; see, for example, KGW III/4, 52–55. Such passages are also cited by Alistair Moles in support of a reading of Nietzsche which sees him as denying a continuity of time; see his *Nietzsche's Philosophy of Nature and Cosmology* (New York: Peter Lang, 1990), 234–37. Yet the mature Nietzsche is a consistent and categorical supporter of absolute continuity, as the texts discussed below show.

29 KGW VII/3, 382. Cf. Nietzsche, *Beyond Good and Evil*, sect. 16.
30 Spir, *Denken und Wirklichkeit*, Band 2, 9. The passages referred to are in Johann Friedrich Herbart, *Sämtliche Werke*, ed. K. Kehrbach and O. Flügel (Aalen: Scientia Verlag, 1964), Band 4, 188–89 and Band 6, 227.
31 Spir, *Denken und Wirklichkeit*, Band 2, 9.
32 See Aristotle, *Physics*, trans. R.P. Hardie and R.K. Gaye, in *The Basic Works of Aristotle*, ed. Richard McKeon (New York: Random House, 1941)VI.2, 232a–233b. One could also argue that Zeno's paradoxes are relevant to these arguments, and that the 'Stadium' is important as a prototype of the kinematic argument discussed below.
33 Aristotle, *Physics*, VI.2, 233a.
34 Sextus Empiricus, *Against the Physicists*, II, 149–54, trans. R.G. Bury, Loeb Classical Library (London: Heinemann, 1960), Vol. 3, 286–89.
35 Moses Maimonides, *The Guide of the Perplexed*, I.73, trans. Schlomo Pines (Chicago: Chicago University Press, 1963), Vol.1, 197.
36 KGW V/2, 447.
37 When he wrote this passage, Nietzsche had just retrieved his copy of *Denken und Wirklichkeit* from the Zürich home of his friend Overbeck; see KGB III/1, 118.
38 Spir, *Denken und Wirklichkeit*, Band 2, 8. Similarly, Aristotle remarks that:

> when the state of our own minds does not change at all, or we have not noticed its changing, we do not realise that time has elapsed, any more than those who are fabled to sleep among the heroes in Sardinia do when they are awakened: for they connect the earlier 'now' with the later and make them one, cutting out the interval because of their failure to notice it. (*Physics*, IV.11, 218b.)

39 KGW V/2, 462.
40 Nietzsche, *The Gay Science*, sect. 112.
41 KGW V/2, 447.
42 KGW VII/1, 695 (*The Will to Power*, sect. 676).
43 KGW V/2, 411.
44 For a brief biography, see Jane M. Oppenheimer, 'Science and Nationality: The Case of Karl Ernst von Baer (1792–1876)', *Proceedings of the American Philosophical Society*, 134 (1990), 75–82.
45 KGW II/4, 268.
46 Ibid., 300.
47 KGW V/2, 398.
48 KGW VII/2, 106; cf. VII/3, 385. Nietzsche's authority for this claim seems to be Baudelaire's description of the effects of hashish smoking. See Charles Baudelaire, *Les Paradis artificiels*, ed. J. Crépet (Paris, Louis Conard, 1928), 34.
49 KGW V/2, 411.
50 KGW VII/3, 385. This critique has nothing to do with the theory of relativity, as suggested by Alwin Mittasch, *Friedrich Nietzsche als Naturphilosoph* (Stuttgart: Alfred Kröner Verlag, 1952), 54. Nietzsche is making a psychological observation about our inability to observe small intervals of time, and drawing conclusions from this about our conception of space.
51 Herbart, *Sämtliche Werke*, Band 4, 162.
52 Ibid., 171. In a footnote, Herbart justifies this third proposition by drawing an analogy with Newton's first law of motion:

> A circular course of things would demand something similar to a circular motion according to the familiar principles of mechanics, namely an external force apart from absolute becoming, in order to alter the direction of change again at every

moment. Without this effective force a continual flow of things would have to proceed in a straight line, and could never run back into itself.

This sort of metaphorical argument is typical of Herbart, as can be seen in his application of Newton's law of cooling to the contents of the mind; see ibid., 372.
53 Ibid., 173.
54 Ibid., 172. He cites Aristotle's assertion that the Heraclitean doctrine of becoming leads to contradictory statements about everything: see Aristotle, *Physics* I.2, 185b.
55 Spir, *Denken und Wirklichkeit*, Band 1, 270.
56 See, for example, KGW VII/3, 280 (*The Will to Power*, sect. 1062).
57 KGW VIII/2, 48 (*The Will to Power*, sect. 552). Nietzsche might therefore agree with Nelson Goodman's statement that 'a thing is a monotonous event; an event is an unstable thing': *The Structure of Appearance* (Cambridge, MA: Harvard University Press, 1951), 285.
58 KGW VII/1, 209.
59 KGW VI/1, 269.
60 KGW V/2, 397. One can find confirmation of this point in a modern philosopher's statement that 'There is a main type of event which can be regarded as an *ordered pair* of two states of affairs': G.H. von Wright, *Norm and Action: A Logical Enquiry* (London: Routledge and Kegan Paul, 1963), 27.
61 Nietzsche, *The Gay Science*, sect. 374; but cf. sect. 299, written five years earlier.
62 KGW VII/3, 95 (*The Will to Power*, sect. 625).
63 KGW VIII/2, 278 (*The Will to Power*, sect. 715).
64 The normal German word corresponding to 'event' is *Ereignis*, but Nietzsche tends to reserve this for especially notable episodes – see, for example, *Mixed Opinions and Maxims*, sect. 322, *The Gay Science*, sect. 125, and *Thus Spake Zarathustra*, 'On Great Events'. Nowhere to my knowledge does he use it in connection with eternal recurrence. Some commentators have debated whether the concept of an event rules out any possibility that an event might occur more than once; if I am correct, this is not directly relevant to the Nietzschean version of eternal recurrence.
65 Nietzsche does sometimes use the German word *Prozess* – as when he speaks of 'The separation of the "deed" from the "doer", of the event (*Geschehen*) from someone who produces events, of the process (*Prozesses*) from a something that is not process but enduring, substance, thing, body, soul, etc ...' KGW VIII/1, 134 (*The Will to Power*, sect. 631). As this passage indicates, the term seems to have the same meaning that *Geschehen* has for him. Cf. KGW VIII/1, 138 and VIII/2, 49 (*The Will to Power*, sect. 552). The same could be said of *Vorgang*, which Nietzsche uses very occasionally – for example, in *The Gay Science*, sect. 112, and *Beyond Good and Evil*, sect. 17.
66 Benjamin Lee Whorf, *Language, Thought and Reality,* ed. John B. Carroll (Cambridge, MA: MIT Press, 1956), 147.
67 See, for example, Donald Davidson, 'Events as Particulars', *Nous*, 4 (1970), 25–32; and Lawrence B. Lombard, *Events: A Metaphysical Study* (London: Routledge and Kegan Paul, 1986), 63–65.
68 W.V. Quine, 'Events and Reification', in Ernest LePore and Brian P. McLaughlin (eds), *Actions and Events: Perspectives on the Philosophy of Donald Davidson* (Oxford: Basil Blackwell, 1985), 162–71.
69 Cf. KGW V/2, 452.
70 The same term plays a prominent role in Spir's *Forschung nach der Gewissheit*. 'Each and every actuality', he writes, 'belongs under one of the two categories "being" and "occurrence"': ibid., 62. But these correspond respectively to the categories 'unconditioned' and 'conditioned', or 'reality' and 'appearance', so that all our experience belongs under the category of occurrence. See ibid., 86–87.
71 KGW VIII/1, 134 and VIII/2, 50 (*The Will to Power*, sect. 631 and 552).
72 KGW VIII/2, 202 (*The Will to Power*, sect. 639).
73 Ibid., Band 1, 264; cited in *Philosophy in the Tragic Age of the Greeks*, sect. 15. In his

lectures of the same period, Nietzsche attributed this argument to Democritus; see KGW II/4, 331.
74 KGW V/2, 451.
75 KGW VII/3, 280 (*The Will to Power*, sect. 1062).
76 Friedrich Nietzsche, *The Wanderer and his Shadow*, sect. 11.
77 KGW VIII/3, 127 (*The Will to Power*, sect. 478).
78 KGW V/2, 501.
79 KGW III/4, 177–81.
80 Ibid., 181.
81 On this point, one should note Zöllner's discussion of Helmholtz's claim (in his 1847 lecture 'Über die Erhaltung der Kraft') that science must look for ultimate causes which are unchanging if nature is to be completely intelligible. See J.C.F. Zöllner, *Über die Natur der Cometen. Beiträge zur Geschichte und Theorie der Erkenntnis*, 2nd edn (Leipzig: Verlag von Wilhem Engelmann, 1872), 316–18.
82 KGW III/4, 180.
83 Ibid., 177. See also 119.
84 Ibid., 181.
85 See, for example, ibid., 176–77.
86 Zöllner, *Über die Natur der Cometen*, 321. Zöllner refers here to Schopenhauer's *On the Fourfold Root of the Principle of Sufficient Reason*, pointing out that it anticipated Helmholtz's somewhat similar theory of perception.
87 J.C.F. Zöllner, *Principien einer elektrodynamischen Theorie der Materie. Erster Band* (Leipzig: Verlag von Wilhelm Engelmann, 1876), XXIX.
88 Carl Neumann, *Die Principien der Elektrodynamik. Eine mathematische Untersuchung* (Tübingen: Heinrich Laupp, 1868), 38; quoted by Zöllner in *Über die Natur der Cometen*, 338. Neumann's claim here, made with the approval of Wilhelm Weber, is that the causal influence of electrical charge radiates in space with a certain constant and finite speed, like light.
89 David Hume, *A Treatise of Human Nature*, ed. L.A. Selby-Bigge (Oxford: Clarendon Press, 1888), 76.
90 Ibid., 161.
91 KGW VIII/1, 29.
92 KGW VIII/3, 65 (*The Will to Power*, sect. 633). See also ibid., 67 (*The Will to Power*, sect. 551).
93 KGW VII/3, 338 (*The Will to Power*, sect. 1067).
94 Heraclitus, *Ecce Homo*, 'The Birth of Tragedy', sect. 3.

Chapter 2

Dühring and Time

So far we have looked at one side of Nietzsche's concern with the question about infinitude and time. Turning to the other, the question of a beginning or end to time, we encounter arguments directed against an infinity of past time which have given rise to many philosophical debates: for instance, between al-Ghazali and Averroes in the eleventh and twelfth centuries, or St Bonaventure and St Thomas Aquinas in the thirteenth. A similar debate occurring in the nineteenth century involved Dühring and Nietzsche; and, although they were not its only participants, their disagreement brings out the important features of the debate. In fact, it is Nietzsche's attack on the position taken by Dühring that is most instructive for an understanding of the issues, as well as for the light it throws on his own thinking about time.

That attack is closely related to Nietzsche's idea of eternal recurrence, which says that every event occurs not just once but an infinite number of times. The doctrine also says something about time or, rather, it implies certain theses about time which need to be accepted before any argument about the recurrence of events can be properly assessed. I think that we can readily state three such assumptions. First, time must be infinite, since nothing can occur an infinite number of times without taking an infinite time to do so, assuming a finite period of time between any one occurrence and any other occurrence. Second, time must be linear rather than circular in form, since a circular time would presumably be finite, in that no two occurrences within it could be separated by more than a certain period of time. Third, time must be distinct from the events within it, since there is no *recurrence* unless the same event occurs at different times. Anyone who holds that the concept of an event includes the specifying of a single time at which it occurs will comment that, on this definition, recurrence is simply impossible. However, I intend to set aside this objection, resting as it does either on an arbitrary stipulation about the term 'event', or on further arguments which would have to be considered at length.

Now, each of these assumptions can be identified in Nietzsche's writings. For instance, they include a number of passages in which he asserts that time is infinite.[1] The second point is harder to judge, in that the image of a circle abounds in Nietzsche's writings, and especially in relation to the doctrine of eternal recurrence.[2] Yet the claim that 'time itself is a circle' is explicitly rejected, if not by Nietzsche himself, at least by his spokesman Zarathustra.[3] It seems therefore that the image, as he uses it, represents the set of events that recur, not the time in which they do so. That Nietzsche considers time to be independent of the events within it is shown in another fact: his reasons for holding time to be infinite are quite separate from his reasons for holding that the course of becoming has no absolute beginning. No state can be the first, Nietzsche argues, because each is produced by what has gone before, so that a state not preceded by a different one would not in its turn have given rise to a succession of different states, but would have lasted forever.[4] This argument is neutral in relation to the alternatives of an infinite time and a finite but unbounded time: it sets out only to decide whether that time is wholly occupied by a changing course of events.

Nietzsche's approach to the question we have seen to be basic to these points, namely the problem of the infinity of time, is defined in relation to a particular argument advanced by several writers of his time. It is an argument which sets out to show that time cannot be infinite, at least in the direction of the past. The traditional consensus is that there is no particular problem in an infinity of future time, when this is expressed by the concept of an infinite progress from the present moment. But there has been disagreement over whether the notion of an infinite past can be accounted for adequately by an infinite regress from the present moment. For some, it has seemed that this concept is sufficient to supply the idea needed, but for others it has seemed just as evident that an infinite past must be understood as an infinite progress up to the present moment – a far more problematical concept, given a basic notion of infinity as a series which never comes to an end. The controversy between Nietzsche and Dühring occurs within this setting. They agree on what constitutes an acceptable concept of a future infinity and what constitutes an unacceptable concept of a past infinity. Their disagreement is over the status of the infinite regress from the present moment. Dühring argues that this cannot be taken as expressing a past infinity and concludes that it is an 'idle notion', in so far as it lacks such an application. Nietzsche accuses Dühring of having contradicted himself in the course of his argument. He concludes that no valid objection has been made against this way of understanding an infinity of past time. I will show that neither writer states his own case without making mistakes, and go on to argue that the real issue in the debate between Nietzsche and Dühring is an epistemological, rather than a logical, one. In a final section, I will return to the theme of eternal recurrence and discuss some problems concerning the relation of this doctrine to the infinity of time.

The Argument for Finite Time

How is Nietzsche's assumption that time is infinite in the direction of the past to be understood, and what reasons does he have for asserting it? His only argument is to be found in a defence of the idea against criticism by some recent writers.

> As little familiar as I am with what is philosophised these days amongst Germans: I have discovered, thanks to some fortunate accidents, that in Germany it is now in fashion to think, not of a creation of the world, but at least of a beginning: one resists an 'infinity behind' – But do you understand my

abbreviated formula? Mainländer, Hartmann, Dühring etc. all agree on this. The most objectionable expression for the opposite view, that the world is eternal, has been found by Mainländer, an apostle of unconditional purity, like Richard Wagner.[5]

Let us look in turn at the writers he mentions by name here, beginning with Dühring's discussion of time in his *Cursus der Philosophie*. Nietzsche was familiar with the writings of Dühring: he owned copies of many of Dühring's books, seems to have read some of them several times – including the *Cursus der Philosophie* – and refers to them in his notebooks on various occasions.[6] These references are usually not favourable. Nietzsche particularly disliked Dühring's abusive style of argumentation.[7] He described Dühring as 'a clever and well-informed scholar, but one who nevertheless betrays with almost every word he says that he harbours a petty soul and is tormented by narrow, envious feelings'.[8] But their philosophical outlooks were also quite different. Dühring's 'philosophy of reality' (*Wirklichkeitsphilosophie*) amounted to a dogmatic realism, allied to positivism and sharply opposed to the current revival of Kantianism. In several of his published works, Nietzsche (without naming Dühring) takes a firm stand against any such appeal to 'reality'.[9] In this connection, he is clearly influenced by F.A. Lange's condemnation of what he termed 'the cult of reality'.[10]

Here our concern, at least at this stage, is with Nietzsche's relation to another aspect of Dühring's philosophy, his finitism.[11] In view of Nietzsche's criticism, it is surprising to see the extent to which he is in agreement with Dühring's general views on infinity. Both Nietzsche and Dühring hold, for example, that the world must be finite in extent. In a typical text, Nietzsche insists that the world must be thought of 'as a certain definite quantity of force and as a certain definite number of centres of force'.[12] The terminology he uses suggests an application of what Dühring terms 'the law of definite number'. This expression is a new name for an old idea.[13] All it really means is that every number must be a determinate number. While one might not consider that to represent any new insight, for Dühring it is a premise which leads to some wide-ranging conclusions, especially when 'definite' is taken to imply 'finite'.[14] Its 'absolute' status means that is it not just a law of thought, but also a 'law of nature'.[15] Hence we can assert with certainty that everything in nature which has a magnitude must have a certain determinate magnitude. For example, the number of existing beings in the universe at a given time must be some definite number. In so far as things can be divided into parts, the number of their parts in existence at one time must also be a definite number. This is not to deny that a process of addition or division might go on without ever reaching an absolute limit, but that any further process is to be understood only as an ideal possibility, since it could never be fully completed. Hence Dühring concludes that the world must be regarded as finite in both of these respects.

The only acceptable concept of the infinite, in his view, is one that takes as its model the series of natural numbers. What is important about this series is not just that it goes on forever, but that it cannot be grasped as a unity. For that to occur, there would have to be a last number which would complete the series, and this is out of the question. He writes: 'The essence of the infinite consists in never ending and never being closed off.'[16] Dühring adds that his law of definite number also holds true for natural phenomena whose existence is successive. For instance, even if we knew nothing about the origin of the solar system, we would know that the earth has revolved around the sun a definite number of times. We might have no clue as to what number this may be, and yet we could be quite certain that there must be such a number. He writes:

> The infinity which is precisely thought in this way thus has only a single basic form with a single direction. Although it is of course indifferent for our thinking to project an accumulation of states in an opposite direction, the infinity that proceeds backwards is however just an idle notion. In reality it would have to be traversed in the inverse direction, and in that case it would have an infinite series behind it at each of its states. But that would involve committing the inadmissible contradiction of an infinite yet completely counted series, and so it proves to be senseless to assume a second direction for infinity.[17]

He goes on to state his conclusion: in so far as the world consists in a series of states which are similar to a series of numbers, 'some one state of this kind must be postulated at the first'.

Dühring was not alone in asserting the finitude of the world in past time. As we have seen, Nietzsche was aware of other versions of the same line of thought – for instance, the one presented by Eduard von Hartmann in his *Philosophie des Unbewussten*. Like Dühring, Hartmann begins from the assumption that the notion of a completed infinity is an absurdity. There is no problem, he says, in the notion of an infinite process going forward, provided that this infinity is understood as something ideal or postulated, rather than real. But it is a different matter for the other direction. He writes:

> *Thinking* can just as easily follow the path backwards from the given now as the path forwards, with the unrealisable postulate of endlessness; but that proves nothing at all for the *real* process, which pursues its course in an *inverse* direction to this thinking ascending in to the past. The infinity that remains an unsatisfiable ideal postulate for thinking backwards is supposed to be complete accomplished result for the process going forwards; and here occurs the contradiction that an infinity (if only one-sided) is supposed to be given as completed realisation.[18]

Both these writers present their argument in terms of a contrast between 'thinking' on the one hand and 'reality' on the other. Both argue that an infinite regress in time makes sense as far as thought is concerned, but that it is nevertheless impossible in reality. The contrast is central to this argument for a finite past. In one way it is readily acceptable, in that most of us would allow that thought and reality are not the same thing. Yet what can it mean to say that some proposition can be correct 'for thought' but not correct 'for reality'? It looks like the familiar claim that some idea is correct 'in theory' but not 'in practice'. From a logical point of view, such an assertion is quite confused. From a rhetorical point of view, it is defensible as a way of saying that some idea is plausible but wrong. It is this plausibility that is conveyed by saying that the idea is correct 'in theory'. If we set aside rhetorical devices, we find that the real contrast made in this formulation is not the contrast between theory and practice, but the contrast between a theory which is not confirmed in practice and another theory which is confirmed in practice. A similar point can be made about the apparent appeal to a contrast between thought and reality. We point out that one thought is wrong not by a substitution of reality for the thought, but by advancing *another* thought as correct in so far as it is borne out in reality. In short, the real contrast is not between thought and reality, but between one thought and another thought, or else between one reality, or intended reality, and another – which really amounts to the same thing.

How, then, can counting backward into an infinite past be correct for thought and yet wrong for reality? The answer seems to be that this procedure does not give us an accurate *description* of the process in question, because it does not represent a series of events or states in their real order. One might say that it gives a false picture of how the series came about, because it starts with what was in reality the ending and goes on to present each stage as taking place after the one which, in fact, it preceded. Now this objection is valid only if the procedure of counting is understood as saying something about the order of what is counted, so that anything less is taken to be an incomplete and, to that extent, misleading description. In effect, we are being asked for a *narrative*. Since narratives proceed from the past towards the future, it is reasonable to expect this in the most general description of the past existence of the world. A reply to this line of thought would be that, in using terms like 'finite' and 'infinite' in a mathematical rather than metaphysical sense, we are only concerned with counting and not with any more concrete description. And counting is always an abstract procedure which leaves out many features of what is counted, interesting though these are. Counting is not invalid for this reason, and nor are our concepts of quantity. So far, then, the argument seems to be quite arbitrary. We need a further reason for supposing that counting has to conform to a particular direction in time, and no such reason has been supplied. Having said that, I will set aside this question for the time being, returning to it once Nietzsche's criticism of Dühring has been examined.

Another problem faced by these philosophers concerns their need to postulate an initial state of the world. Dühring makes the surprising claim that he is not attributing a beginning to the world itself. Rather, he explains, his argument proves that we should not identify the world with any succession of states of affairs. Even though some such state is to be taken as the first, we need not deny that the world existed before the course of becoming began with a transition from this state. Yet it could not be a state of complete equilibrium, since that would never give way of its own accord to a succession of different states. In mechanical terminology, it could not be classified either as static or as dynamic. Clearly Dühring is in some difficulty here.

The solution which to a religious thinker would be obvious – that the world has its origin in an act of creation – is not available to him, since his realism also involves a firm commitment to atheism. Hartmann also has difficulty in explaining just what preceded the beginning of the series of events. He has already argued that the inner essence of reality consists in willing, but now claims that this willing may, under certain circumstances, be a 'non-willing'. So it is in this case. He treats the initial state as a potentiality without actuality, leaving unexplained the transition from potentiality to actuality – that is, from a 'timeless eternity' to time as we know it.

Mainländer, on the other hand, while he differs from the others by providing no real argument for a beginning of the world, is more forthcoming about its nature. The previous state of things, he says, cannot be imagined by us. However, we can think of it in terms of a notion of God, and accordingly of the transition as the *death of God*.[19] Only one act was possible for God – namely, a free act of self-annihilation. However, since it is not possible for an omnipotent being to accomplish this act all at once, it was necessary for the world to arise as a means for attaining that goal. Everything in the world, according to Mainländer, is an expression of a will to death, and as such is part of God's intention. The progress of the human race towards a perfect state is just a prelude to its voluntary self-annihilation. Mainländer's whole account is appropriately morbid in tone and dominated by a fascination with what he terms 'the sweet still night of absolute death'.[20] One can see why Nietzsche, who had his own ideas about the death of God, was not attracted to this transformation of the doctrine of creation into an apotheosis of suicide.

Nietzsche was also suspicious of the motives behind this insistence on a beginning of the world. He wrote: 'I have come across this idea in earlier thinkers: every time it was determined by other ulterior considerations (– mostly theological), in favour of the *creator spiritus*.'[21] This may not be accurate as applied to Dühring (a realist and materialist), or to Hartmann and Mainländer (essentially followers of Schopenhauer), but it is correct in identifying the tradition from which they borrowed their argument. In earlier thinkers such as al-Ghazali and St Bonaventure, the argument is presented as a demonstrative proof for God's creation of the world. Hence, among other reasons, Nietzsche's determination to expose it as a fallacious line of thought.

Nietzsche's Counterargument

> Lately one has sought several times to find a contradiction in the concept 'temporal infinity of the world *behind*': one has even found it, although at the cost of confusing the head with the tail. Nothing can prevent me from reckoning backward from this moment and saying 'I shall never reach the end'; just as I can reckon forward from the same moment into the infinite. Only if I made the mistake – I shall guard against it – of equating this correct notion of a *regressus in infinitum* with an utterly unrealisable concept of an infinite *progressus* up to

the present, only if I suppose the direction (forward or backward) to be logically indifferent, would I take the head – this moment – for the tail: I shall leave that to you, my dear Herr Dühring![22]

In so far as Nietzsche has any argument for an infinity of past time, it is found in his assertion that counting back from the present moment into infinity is just as possible as counting forward into infinity. Presumably it is up to everyone who denies this to show a difference between the two cases and, until that is done, we are entitled to believe that time is as infinite in the past as in the future. Nietzsche is, of course, aware that an objection has indeed been made against this presumption. However, he regards it as a misguided one, and in this passage tries to point out where its error lies. The objection, as stated here, is that the notion of a past infinity involves a 'contradiction'. His reply is that the argument which is supposed to prove this is itself guilty of the same fault, since it reaches it conclusion 'at the cost of confusing the head with the tail'. But to see how far this charge and countercharge are justified, we need to carry out a close analysis.

Nietzsche says that nothing can prevent him from counting back into infinity, just as he can count forward into infinity. It must be noted that Dühring fully agrees with this claim, since he allows that it is indifferent for our thinking whether we count forward or backward from the present moment. So this proposition is common ground. The difference is that Nietzsche takes it to be sufficient to account for the infinity of past time, whereas Dühring has a further argument which aims at ruling out that conclusion.

So, what is the charge made by Nietzsche against Dühring? He says twice that Dühring has mistaken the head for the tail, where 'the head' stands for the present moment. Although his language is figurative, it is clear that Nietzsche is here accusing Dühring of an inconsistency or contradiction. What he means is explained in an earlier note:

> – and whether I count backward or forward from the present, I hold the strip of infinity in hand and ... Fools say: 'But then an infinity would already have been completed': but one should be scrupulous in using different words and not call 'beginning' at one time what one calls 'end' at another time.[23]

I take it that this too refers to Dühring and makes the same criticism of his argument: that he goes from calling the present moment a beginning to calling it an end, and in so doing contradicts himself. There does seem to be one way in which the present moment can be a beginning and also an end. According to Aristotle, 'since the "now" is an end and a beginning of time, not of the same time however, but the end of that which is past and the beginning of that which is to come, it follows that, as the circle has its convexity and its concavity, in a sense, in the same thing, so time is always at a beginning and an end'.[24] It would be a contradiction to call the present moment the beginning and end of the *same* time, at least on the assumption that time is not circular in form. This must be the contradiction that Nietzsche is attributing to Dühring: that he treats the present as both the beginning and the end of past time.

We come now to the line of thought which, according to Nietzsche, leads Dühring into committing himself to this contradiction in terms. It involves three stages which Nietzsche simply states without explaining their relation to each other. He asserts that:

1. Dühring equates an infinite regress with an infinite progress up to the present moment.
2. Dühring supposes the direction (forward or backward) to be logically indifferent.
3. Dühring takes the head – this moment – for the tail.

Presumably Nietzsche considers that all three are mistakes, although it is only with (3) that the mistake emerges as a contradiction in terms. Presumably he also considers that (1) implies (2), which in turn implies (3). In that case, his aim is to show that Dühring can be forced into a contradiction on the basis of his own stated position.

In order to sort out these claims, we have to clarify some of the expressions Nietzsche uses. First, we need to grasp the link between the terms 'equate' and 'logically indifferent'. Fortunately, another entry made by Nietzsche in the same notebook is helpful in clarifying this relation. He writes:

> In fact, science has emptied the concept causality of its content and retained it as the formula of an equation, in which it has become at bottom indifferent on which side cause is placed and on which side effect. It is asserted that in two complex states (constellations of force) the quanta of force remain the same.[25]

Nietzsche is thinking of a scientific equation as an application of the law of conservation of force (or rather energy, in modern terminology) to a particular case. What it asserts is that the same quantity of force is present in two different forms. For instance, one side may represent force as heat, and the other, represent it as kinetic energy. Nietzsche would go further and say that the two sides represent the same force, which for him implies the same 'centres of force', in different states or arrangements. In much the same way, an equation in chemistry is an application of the law of conservation of matter, its two sides representing two different arrangements of the same material atoms. Nietzsche uses the word 'indifferent' to emphasize that an equation sets aside certain considerations. It does not, as he points out, say which state gives rise to the other. In other words, it treats any process as a reversible one, for which either side could be cause and the other effect. Elsewhere he notes another omission: as long as we are thinking in terms of equivalence, 'we have not the slightest inherent reason for assuming that one change must follow upon another'.[26] As a result, mechanism cannot rule out the prospect of a final standstill of force, a state in which no further change is possible. Such a state is, after all, quite consistent with the conservation of energy, and yet Nietzsche thinks that its impossibility is 'the sole certainty we have in our hands'.[27] In order to compensate for these omissions, Nietzsche advocates an addition to the mechanistic view of the world – an inner 'will to power' which acts as the source of all change and interaction.

We have seen that, for Nietzsche, to equate is to declare 'indifferent' in one or more respects which depend on one's standpoint: what is indifferent for a purely quantitative approach to the world would not be so for some other standpoint. What is it, then, to equate an infinite regress with an infinite progress up to the present moment? We might consider it as represented by the following equation:

$$(0, -1, -2, -3 \ldots) = (\ldots -3, -2, -1, 0)$$

Here it is not just the case that the two sets have the same number of members: they also have the same members. Although these members are arranged in a different order on the two sides, for the purpose of the equation their order is not taken into consideration. In other words, the sets are 'indifferent' with respect to order. But this still leaves the ambiguity between 'same members' and 'same number of members'. Which of these would Dühring or Nietzsche have in mind? Our earlier examples of physical and chemical equations suggest that they are probably thinking of an equation not in terms of 'equivalence' in the narrow sense, but as making a stronger assertion about the sameness of two sets. Does Dühring, in fact, equate an infinite regress with an infinite progress up to the present moment? He says of the infinity that is counted backward that 'in reality it would have to be run through in the inverse direction'. This 'it' indicates that the *same* set of states is in question. Every state which is counted in the regress is also counted in the progress, and vice versa. Thus, when Nietzsche says that Dühring 'equates' a regress into infinity with a progress from infinity, he is correct.

However, this regress and progress are different in several ways. For one thing, the present moment has a different meaning for them: it is the beginning in one and the end in the other. This is a logical difference. To overlook it is thus to take the present moment as the beginning and end of the same time, which is a contradiction in terms. Nietzsche attributes this contradiction to Dühring, and yet one could argue that his own position is open to a similar objection. For he seems to be taking the present as the beginning of the future *and* the beginning of the past. Is not this also a contradiction in terms? Nietzsche might reply that no contradiction is committed, in that the present does not figure in both of these roles at once. We can count forward or backward, but not both together. In so far as those are different operations, carried out on different occasions, there is no contradiction. But Dühring can make the same defence against Nietzsche's accusation. Is Athens the beginning or end of the road that extends between Athens and Larissa? Either answer is correct, depending on which way one is travelling. Someone who makes a round trip will take Athens first as the beginning, and later as the end. It would be unreasonable to say that this person is committing a contradiction – yet how does her case differ from that of Dühring in relation to past time?

Nietzsche makes things too easy for himself by trying to pin Dühring down in a contradiction. The problem is not to be solved by such logical considerations. It is true that Dühring also sometimes seems to be taking a short-cut, as when he calls the concept of a past infinity a 'contradiction'. But I think that his real argument is more subtle than this. Dühring does not say that the regress into infinity and the progress from infinity are logically indifferent. He says that the progress into infinity and the regress into infinity are 'indifferent for our thinking'. Now if this means there is some other way in which they *are* different, it can only be due to the difference between their directions in time. But if that is not a difference for thinking, what is it?

I think the answer must be that it is a difference for another source of knowledge – *intuition*. In other words, Dühring seems to be operating in terms of a Kantian distinction between a conceptual and an intuitive element in all knowledge. The intuitive component is especially important for Kant in considering the role of space and time in knowledge. We cannot, he claims, grasp the difference between 'left' and 'right' in terms of general concepts alone; this depends on our having an intuition of space.[28] The difference cannot be explained in conceptual terms, but has to be *shown*. It is the same with 'forward' and 'backward' as directions in time. Thinking by itself cannot enable us to grasp these concepts; for that we must appeal to an intuition of something particular – namely, time itself. Assuming that something like this is what Dühring has in mind, then Nietzsche is right in saying that he supposes the direction of counting (backward and forward) to be logically indifferent.

But there is more to be said, because we have to explain why Dühring holds that an infinite regress from the present moment is just an 'idle notion'. Here again a comparison with Kant supplies an answer. If the Kantian view concerning the two elements in knowledge is accepted, then an application of concepts involves their satisfying two kinds of conditions – not just logical requirements, but also whatever conditions apply to intuition. One of the latter would be that time has a certain *direction*, to which any temporal application of concepts must conform. This is where, in Dühring's opinion, a regress *in infinitum* is inadequate and is thus only an 'idle notion'. In effect, he is arguing that when we attempt to grasp the idea of an infinite past, we are faced with a dilemma. Whereas an infinite regress is acceptable for our thinking, it fails to satisfy the conditions of intuition. Trying to grasp past time through an infinite regress is like trying to put a glove made for one hand on the other hand. In contrast, an infinite progress up to the present moment is in accord with intuition, as far as the direction of time is concerned, but fails the test of thinking, in that it involves a logical contradiction.

If Dühring's objection to an infinity of past time does rely on a dilemma of this kind, then Nietzsche is wrong in saying that Dühring commits an inconsistency by calling the present moment both a beginning and an end.

Those two descriptions fall on different sides of the dilemma. Dühring goes from one to the other, but not in a way that involves their conjunction. Rather, he is saying that we must choose between them, and that neither alternative provides a satisfactory conception of a past infinity.

Nietzsche misdirects his criticism, I think, by misunderstanding the relation between an infinite regress and an infinite progress up to the present moment. There are two differences between them. One is the difference in direction: the regress proceeds backward in time, whereas the progress runs forward. The other is the 'logical' difference between a series which has a beginning, but no end, and one which has an end, but no beginning. Between a progress from the present and a regress from the present, there is only the first difference, and so they are logically indifferent, in that each has a beginning but not an end. When we equate an infinite regress with an infinite progress up to the present, however, we are ignoring *both* of these differences, and simply noting that the series have the same members. This has nothing to do with taking the direction to be 'logically' indifferent, since we are equally setting aside the other difference, which is a 'logical' one, between the two series. But, it seems, Nietzsche has in mind only this kind of indifference; perhaps he is thinking of this comparison along the same lines as the other one. Hence he assumes that Dühring is taking a series with only a beginning and one with only an end to be 'logically indifferent', and is thereby committing a contradiction.

Our assessment can be summed up as follows. Nietzsche is right in his first two statements about Dühring, but wrong in this third. Moreover, he is wrong in thinking that (2) is implied by (1), and in thinking that (3) is implied by (2). None of this means that Nietzsche was wrong to oppose Dühring's attack on an infinity of past time. After all, his doctrine of eternal recurrence does presuppose an infinity of both future and past time, which brings it into conflict with any position like that of Dühring. So let us see what Nietzsche *could* have argued on the point.

If, as I have argued, Dühring's position really relies on his epistemology, then Nietzsche's most adequate reply would also be an epistemological one. There is certainly a sharp contrast between their theories of knowledge. Dühring is a realist who supports a foundational epistemology, according to which knowledge depends on what is given to us by a real world. Nietzsche, by contrast, is a non-foundational thinker. As one of his best-known formulations puts it, 'Against positivism, which halts at phenomena – "there are only facts" – I would say: No, facts is precisely what there is not, only interpretations'.[29] On this view, even such basic features of the world as space and time must be regarded as our interpretations, rather than be seen as having some independent, let alone absolute status. They are certainly not *a priori* forms of intuition, in the Kantian sense. Indeed, it seems that, in Nietzsche's epistemology, the distinction between thinking and intuition loses any validity. If that is the case, the basis for Dühring's argument against a past infinity is absent.

We could sum up Nietzsche's own position on the infinitude of past and future in the following way. To say that each of them is infinite is just to say that I can count on and on, in either direction, without ever coming to an end. This is not an 'idle notion' as Dühring claimed, because it is not subject to the imposition of a further condition which expresses directionality as a property of time. What Nietzsche requires of concepts is that they be 'useable' in organizing our thinking. He rejects the concept of a progress *ex infinito* as an 'unrealizable' one, as we have seen. What does this mean? Nietzsche uses the same word elsewhere within the same notebook entry. He says: 'The concept "create" is today completely indefinable, unrealisable: merely a word.'[30] Presumably his objection to the progress *ex infinito* is along the same lines: it cannot be defined or used as a concept, whereas the regress *in infinitum* can be grasped in terms of an operation of counting which is readily imaginable. In this sense, it is as 'realizable' as the progress from the present moment into infinity. Hence, there is no genuine problem in an infinitude of past time.

Another Critical View

The debate we are discussing has not been altogether overlooked by commentators. An article by Oskar Becker, first published in 1936, gives an account of the issues and comes to conclusions which are different from those I have presented.[31] The scope of Becker's discussion is wider, in that he also looks into the arguments about a past infinity that Kant sets out in his First Antinomy, and the critical comments made by Schopenhauer on these arguments. After summarizing these contributions and those of Nietzsche and Dühring, Becker provides the following analysis.

> To make a serious judgment on the opinions cited, we have to bear in mind two basic distinctions:
>
> 1   A regress *in infinitum* and a progress *ex infinito* are not the same. Therefore we cannot argue from the possibility of the first to the possibility of the second.
> 2   Progress *in infinitum* and progress *ex infinito* are different; therefore we cannot argue from the absurdity of a progress *in infinitum* up to a certain limit (i.e. the present) to the impossibility of a progress *ex infinito* up to a certain limit (e.g. the present).
>
> Dühring does not in the least commit the first substitution, as Nietzsche unjustly charges. For he considers it possible 'to project an accumulation of states in an opposite direction' (regress *in infinitum*) but 'the infinity that proceeds backwards' is according to him 'an idle notion' (but not an impossible one), since 'this infinity would in reality [i.e. in real time] have to be traversed in the inverse direction', thus as a progress *ex infinito*. On the other hand, he certainly does make himself guilty of the second substitution and its faulty conclusion...
>
> Nietzsche, to conclude, goes wrong in his critique of Dühring, as already remarked. He opposes the regress *in infinitum* to the infinite progress up to the present, which leaves it unclear whether this means the progress *ex infinito* up to the present or the (unthinkable) progress *in infinitum* up to a limit, i.e. the present. That is, he accuses Dühring of a substitution, namely (1), which Dühring

has not committed at all, and places himself on point (2) in the same confusion as Dühring, even though Schopenhauer had put an end to precisely the confusion in this second point.[32]

Becker's general aim in this analysis is to offer an answer of his own to the question of a past infinity. But before considering this, I will review his review of the debate, or that part of it which refers to Dühring and Nietzsche. We must note that the vocabulary used by Becker in his analysis is a very restricted one. He relies on a simple contrast between the terms 'same' and 'different', omitting any consideration of the term 'indifferent', as used by both Dühring and Nietzsche. He arrives at a sweeping conclusion: since everything is different from everything else, we cannot learn anything about the progress *ex infinito* from a comparison either with the progress *in infinitum*, or with the regress *in infinitum*. That the object of the exercise *is* to understand a past infinity as a progress *ex infinito* is taken for granted. This assumption is especially odd in relation to Nietzsche's position, because Becker has to explain Nietzsche's refusal to follow this line of inquiry as a failure to bear in mind the distinction, emphasized by Schopenhauer, between beginninglessness and endlessness. Yet an insistence on this distinction – expressed in terms of 'head' and 'tail' – is precisely what Nietzsche takes to be the decisive feature of his reply to Dühring's argument. These omissions tell against Becker's analysis. But it is inadequate in other ways, simply because it restricts itself to logical points like these. If the opposition between Dühring and Nietzsche is epistemological, then dealing with the concepts they apply to a past infinity is only a first step; we need to get to the basis on which the appropriateness of any such concept is assessed.

In the aftermath of his disposal of all previous contributions, Becker suggests that the only way to grasp an infinity of past time is through the concept of *eternal recurrence*. This fact, he says, amounts to a proof of the doctrine which has been overlooked by readers of Nietzsche. Indeed, 'it is doubtful whether Nietzsche was fully clear about the meaning of this line of proof, although he often mentions it'.[33] Becker cites various passages which support the first part of his assertion, rather than the second part, in that none of them contains anything like the argument just stated. Yet one text *not* cited by him does present the same idea. In a notebook entry of 1883, Nietzsche writes: 'An infinite process cannot be thought at all other than as periodic.'[34] This is just the argument for eternal recurrence that Becker considers far more straightforward, and less dependent on debatable premises, than those arguments which have so far attracted the attention of commentators. What is more, he adds, it provides a solution to Kant's First Antinomy, along 'immanent' rather than 'transcendental' lines. It does this by proving that validity of the antithesis – something that Schopenhauer attempted but, according to Becker, failed to achieve.

The argument turns out to centre on, once again, the relation between the regress into infinity and the progress from infinity up to the present moment. The problem for Becker is in getting from the first to the second, because it is only through such a manoeuvre that we can gain a clear idea of a progress from infinity. Without retracting his previous assertion that the two are 'not the same', Becker argues that this proposition is 'no longer fully valid' when a periodic process is in question.[35] The transition from infinite regress to infinite progress is simply an inversion, but the difficulty is that this operation depends on grasping the series as a *whole*, which it is assumed is impossible for an infinite series. Now Becker argues that a periodic process *can* be inverted without this requirement. For it consists of finite periods, each of these can be reversed by itself, and this task is only a finite one. But, one might object, what advantage is there in replacing an infinite task with an infinite number of finite tasks? Becker is perhaps aware of this objection, for he immediately proceeds to appeal to an idea of time which is indeed finite – the idea of time as a circle.

He begins by attributing this view to Nietzsche ('as Nietzsche says') on the basis of the words uttered by the spirit of gravity in *Thus Spake Zarathustra*. He then points out, quite correctly, that it solves the problem by removing infinity from the concept of time:

> The time-manifold is thus closed without infinitely distant points. The inversion of the *in infinitum* into the *ex infinito* is ultimately made possible, therefore, because it is not really a question of an *infinitum* at all, but of something finite returning into itself, whose circular direction is simply reversed.[36]

It appears that Becker's motive for this move involves an objection to infinite time which he has not so far mentioned, and which is not answered by his model of an infinite series of reversible finite periods. It is the claim that, in an infinite time, there would be past moments at an infinite distance from the present moment, and that the problem of accounting for the transition from those moments to the present is an insoluble one. The objection was first raised by St Bonaventure, and has been repeated by many later critics of infinite time.[37] Yet it was effectively answered by Aquinas, who pointed out that an infinite time, whether past or future, does *not* have to include such moments.[38] After all, the infinity of the natural numbers does not imply that one or more of them is an infinite number. Becker, it seems, simply takes the validity of this objection for granted. But with this appeal to a circular model of time, his own ingenious notion of reversing an infinite series of finite periods is reduced to irrelevance. On the circular model, there is just one finite period. It does not appear that we need to go through any reversal of direction to grasp that concept.

Apart from this, it seems that Becker is now committed to a relational view of time, and he claims to find a surprising affinity between Nietzsche and Aristotle on this point. By a 'relational' view is meant the approach in which it makes no sense to separate moments of time from the events or states of affairs that occupy them. Aristotle was well aware of one direct consequence: 'Is time then always different or does the same time recur? Clearly time is, in the same way as motion is. For if one and the same motion sometimes recurs, it will be one and the same time, and if not, not.'[39]

But if the same motion occurs at the same time, why speak of recurrence, either of the time or the motion? This argument seems to provide a simple refutation of Nietzsche's doctrine of eternal recurrence. Whether one appeals to a principle of the identity of indiscernibles or to a relational account of time, the outcome is the same: recurrence is nothing more than occurrence.

Why the two should appear to be different involves the idea of a circular time. This need not be taken as depending on a relational concept of time: some philosophers have taken time to be circular for reasons having nothing to do with the course of events, although it must be admitted that these are not very convincing. If any argument for a circularity of time is worth considering, it is a line of thought which has two stages. It first establishes a cyclical course of events, and then appeals to an identification of moments of time with events to conclude that time itself is circular in form. Perhaps it is because this second step is so taken for granted by many writers that they refer to 'cyclical time'. In fact, that phrase is not just a misnomer, but an incoherent expression. It is events that may be cyclical, not the time in which they occur. The mistake is to overlook the fact that the outcome of the first stage of the argument – a cyclical course of events – is *cancelled* by the second stage. For that reason, it is inappropriate to carry over the earlier terminology into the conclusion of the argument as a whole. But whatever its cause, use of the phrase 'cyclical time' (or 'cyclical theory of time') is a sign of confusion.

In any case, the idea of eternal recurrence is not the same as the idea of a circular time. Indeed, the two appear to be inconsistent with each other. If we assume that, in a circular time, some finite period of time would be the longest possible interval between events, then any one state could recur only a finite number of times. All this is, or ought to be, quite straightforward. Yet one often encounters remarks such as 'The doctrine of eternal recurrence amounts to the assumption that time is a vast circle'.[40] The symbolization of eternal recurrence in a circle is a very natural one, but one should bear in mind what is symbolized and what is not. The events or states of affairs that recur eternally are represented by the circle, which allows us to see at a glance that they occur both before and after each other. What the circle does *not* show, however, is that its circumference is traversed again and again. That belongs to our use of the model, not to the model itself. Only by appealing to a relational theory of time can we make the further step towards understanding the model as representing time itself, but in that case we are, as before, moving from a concept of eternal recurrence to a concept of finite but closed time.

The notion that a circular model of time implies a doctrine of eternal recurrence relies on a similar error. In this case, it consists of a kind of reluctance to allow that time has been represented within the diagram. The same thing happens, of course, when time is represented as an infinite line. Someone who wants to have time not only in the model but also, as it were, present in person, imagines that it consists in the movement of a point, which symbolizes the present moment, along the line. But, in thinking this way, we are committing ourselves to a doubling of time without any theoretical basis for such a move. Again, the problem is to grasp what is represented in the model and what is not represented, but belongs instead to the use we make of it.[41] Someone adopting a circular model of time may be puzzled by the following question. What happens when a point representing the present moment travels around the circle and arrives back at its starting place? Does it come to a halt there, or does it travel around once again? The question is based on a misconception of the kind already described. But it shows how easily a temptation arises to identify circular time with eternal recurrence.

We can conclude this chapter with a brief discussion of a related problem. Nietzsche's own statement concerning the infinity of time draws on a traditional notion of potential infinity. He considers that time is infinite in so far as one can go on *counting* either forward or backward without ever coming to an end. Now, a procedure of counting, if properly carried out, requires not only leaving nothing out, but also never repeating oneself. But is not this inconsistent with eternal recurrence? If it is the case that every event occurs not just once but again and again, then at some future time I will repeat the counting I am performing at present. The possibility of counting on forever is ruled out by the doctrine of recurrence, according to this argument, and so therefore is the infinity of time, as Nietzsche has explained it. Yet recurrence can hardly be eternal unless time is infinite. What is more, Nietzsche in some places appeals to the infinity of time as an assumption in an argument designed to establish a doctrine of eternal recurrence. In a standard version of the argument, it is also assumed that, if time is infinite, every possible event must have happened already. It follows that the present moment, which is also a possible one, must have occurred before and must occur again an infinite number of times. So, once again, the doctrine of eternal recurrence presupposes the infinity of time.

Let us make sure the problem has been understood. Eternal recurrence is supposed to be inconsistent not so much with infinite time, as with *one* way of understanding infinite time. Is it a certain concept of infinity, or a certain concept of time, that is supposed to be inconsistent with eternal recurrence? The paradox just set out lies in a conflict between eternal recurrence and the notion of potential infinity. As such, it is very different from an objection often made against Nietzsche – that eternal recurrence is inconsistent with a relational view of time. This has the advantage of being a valid argument, but in the absence of evidence that Nietzsche subscribes to a relational concept of time, it is not an *ad hominem* objection, but relies on some justification of the relational view in its own right. In contrast, the other objection we are considering refers to Nietzsche's own use of the concept of potential infinity.

The question is whether the doctrine of recurrence rules out an understanding of infinite time in terms of the possibility of counting on forever. In what sense must this be possible if we are to say that time is infinite? The question brings us back to the 'law of definite number' and its relation to potential infinity. Nietzsche claims that the world can contain only a finite number of elements. From that premise he infers that the number of possible combinations or arrangements of these elements must also be finite, so that the same states must eventually come into being again, and succeed one another in the same order as before. The important point to note, however, is that the period of recurrence must be finite at any given time, although always open to increase. So a procedure of counting, while it may always reach only a finite number, is still potentially infinite, as long as the absence of a limit leaves open this possibility of increase. Since that is the case, an argument for eternal recurrence based on the 'law of definite number' is able to make use of the concept of the potential infinite. In other words, there is neither an inconsistency nor a paradox in linking the doctrine of recurrence with infinite time.

Notes

1 See, for example, KGW VII/1, 637 and VII/3, 285 (*The Will to Power,* sect. 545).
2 *Thus Spake Zarathustra,* 'The Seven Seals' and 'The Convalescent'.
3 Ibid., 'On the Vision and the Riddle'.
4 See, for example, KGW V/1, 432.
5 KGW VII/2, 250. I have not managed to find any 'objectionable expression' in Mainländer's discussion. Dühring seems a far likelier candidate for such a charge, given his frequent use of harsh language. And in fact, Nietzsche did later remark disapprovingly on Dühring's description of the Kantian view of space and time as belonging to 'the mind that sees the peak of wisdom in the self-mutilation of its procreative power': letter of 23 July 1885, in KGB III/3, 69. So he may simply be confusing the two in this intended reference to Mainländer.
6 See especially the long summary and critique of Dühring's *Der Werth des Lebens* in KGW IV/1, 207–57.
7 A collection of typical examples can be found in Friedrich Engels, *Herr Eugen Dühring's Revolution in Science (Anti-Dühring),* in Karl Marx and Friedrich Engels, *Collected Works* (London: Lawrence and Wishart, 1975 –), Vol. 25, 30–32. Nietzsche apparently did not know this work, but he would have appreciated Engels' characterization of Dühring as 'a Richard Wagner in philosophy – but without Wagner's talents': ibid., 107.
8 KGW VII/3, 274 (*The Will to Power,* sect. 792).
9 See *Thus Spake Zarathustra,* 'On the Land of Education', and *Beyond Good and Evil,* sect. 10.
10 KGW VII/3, 173. See F.A. Lange, *The History of Materialism and Criticism of its Present Importance,* trans. E.C. Thomas, 3rd edn (London: Routledge and Kegan Paul, 1925), vol. 3, 332.
11 On this aspect, see Henri Bois, 'Le finitisme de Dühring', *L'Année philosophique,* 20 (1909), 93–124.
12 KGW VIII/3, 168 (*The Will to Power,* sect. 1066).
13 It goes back to Zeno of Elea: 'If things are many, they must be as many as they are and neither more nor less than this. But if they are as many as they are, they must be finite': Fragment 3, in Kathleen Freeman, (ed. and trans.), *Ancilla to the Pre-Socratic Philosophers* (Oxford: Basil Blackwell, 1948), 47.
14 It is worth noting that Cantor agreed entirely with this basic principle, insisting that his transfinite numbers were just as determinate as finite numbers. See Georg Cantor, *Gesammelte Abhandlungen,* ed. Ernst Zermelo (1932) reprint edn, Hildesheim: Georg Olms, 1962), 390.
15 Eugen Dühring, *Cursus der Philosophie als streng Wissenschaftlicher Weltanschanug und Lebensgestaltung* (Leipzig: Erich Koschny, 1875), 64.

16　Ibid., 18.
17　Ibid., 19.
18　Eduard von Hartmann, *Philosophie des Unbewussten*, 3rd enlarged edn (Berlin: Carl Dunckers Verlag, 1871), 772. This passage is not found in earlier editions. Hartmann also uses a different argument for a beginning of the world, claiming that 'it would be inconsistent with the concept of development to attribute an infinite duration in the *past* to the world-process, since then every thinkable development would have been run through, which after all is not the case'; ibid., 747. Nietzsche cites this passage with evident disapproval, but without specific criticism, in section 9 of *On the Uses and Disadvantages of History for Life*. In his own later arguments concerning eternal recurrence and a final state, he asserts more than once that whatever is possible must occur in an infinite time; see Chapter 6 for a discussion of this proposition.
19　Philipp Mainländer, *Die Philosophie der Erlösung* (Berlin: Verlag von Theobald Grieben, 1876), 108.
20　Ibid., 216.
21　KGW VIII/3, 167 (*The Will to Power*, sect. 1066).
22　Ibid. Note the correction of 'finite *progressus*' to 'infinite *progressus*'.
23　KGW VII/1, 547.
24　Aristotle, *Physics* IV.13.222a–b, trans. R.P. Hardie and R.K. Gaye, in *The Basic Works of Aristotle*, ed. Richard McKeon (New York: Random House, 1941), 297. Elsewhere Aristotle argues that this analogy between points of time and points of space breaks down, in that taking a point as an ending and a beginning implies *pausing* to count it twice, which in the case of time is impossible. Hence we must think of the present moment as dividing time not actually, but only potentially. See ibid., IV.11.220a; and VIII.8.262a–b.
25　KGW VIII/3, 67 (*The Will to Power*, sect. 551). The link between *Gleichnissformel* and *gleichgültig* is lost in English translation.
26　Ibid., 92 (*The Will to Power*, sect. 688).
27　Ibid., 167 (*The Will to Power*, sect. 1066).
28　See, for example, Immanuel Kant, *Prolegomena to any Future Metaphysics that will be able to present itself as a Science*, trans. Peter G. Lucas (Manchester: Manchester University Press, 1953), 42, sect.13.
29　KGW VIII/1, 323 (*The Will to Power*, sect. 481).
30　See also KGW VII/1, 706.
31　Although neglected by English-language writers on Nietzsche, Becker's article has been discussed in Wolfgang Müller-Lauter, *Nietzsche: Seine Philosophie der Gegensätze und die Gegensätze seiner Philosophie* (Berlin and New York: Walter de Gruyter, 1971), 164–80; Klaus Spiekermann, 'Nietzsches Beweise für die ewige Wiederkehr', *Nietzsche-Studien*, 17 (1988), 497–504; and Dirk L. Couprie, '"Hätte die Welt ein Ziel, […] so wäre es […] mit allem Werden längst zu Ende." Ein Beitrag zur Geschichte einer Argumentation', *Nietzsche-Studien*, 27 (1998), 107–18.
32　Oskar Becker, *Dasein und Dawesen: Gesammelte philosophische Aufsätze* (Pfullingen: Verlag Günther Neske, 1963), 55–56.
33　Ibid., 52.
34　KGW VII/1, 507.
35　Becker, *Dasein und Dawesen*, 57.
36　Ibid., 58.
37　See, for example, F. Van Steenberghen, *Thomas Aquinas and Radical Aristotelianism* (Washington, DC: The Catholic University of America Press, 1980), 24–26.
38　He writes, 'A passage is always from one limit to another limit. But whatever day from the past we pick on, between that and the present day there is only a finite number of days, which can be traversed. Yet the objection proceeds as if, given two extremes, there are infinitely many things in between': Thomas Aquinas, *Summa theologiae*, 61 vols, (London: Blackfriars, 1965–81), 1a q.46 art.2.
39　Aristotle, *Physics* IV.13.222a, in *The Basic Works of Aristotle*, 297.
40　Rudy v.B. Rucker, *Infinity and the Mind* (Brighton: Harvester Press, 1982), 13.

41 A related problem arises about representing the process of inference from premises to conclusion. See Lewis Carroll, 'What Achilles said to the Tortoise', *Mind*, 4 (1895), 278–80.

Chapter 3

Teichmüller and Perspective

The relation between Nietzsche's thought and the philosophy of Gustav Teichmüller (1832–1888) was noted quite early in the history of Nietzsche scholarship, in a 1913 article on 'perspectivism' by Hermann Nohl.[1] Yet this important link has since been generally overlooked. The reason may be simply that Teichmüller has not been remembered for most of the twentieth century. He was first and foremost a historian of ancient Greek philosophy, a student under Adolf Trendelenburg who specialized in Aristotelian scholarship. At a later stage, Teichmüller developed his own metaphysical system, presented at length in his major treatise, *Die wirkliche und die scheinbare Welt*.[2] His approach to philosophy combined an austere and uncompromising metaphysical doctrine with a sweeping dismissal of the philosophies of his time – none of which, he asserted, had advanced as far as Plato in his *Parmenides*.[3] These features no doubt ensured him a marginal position in philosophy, but they were not necessarily an objection for Nietzsche. On the contrary, it was just such writers who often appealed to him, and either stimulated or provoked the more original aspects of his own thinking – a policy in accordance with a favourite remark of Goethe: 'Anyway, I hate everything that merely instructs me, without increasing or immediately enlivening my activity.'[4]

Nietzsche and Teichmüller had some personal acquaintance. Teichmüller had been professor of philosophy at the University of Basel for a year when Nietzsche took up his chair in classical philology in 1869. There were two chairs in philosophy at Basel, one occupied since 1855 by Karl Steffensen and the other filled by a succession of younger scholars, usually for short periods.[5] Teichmüller left Basel in 1871 to go to Dorpat (the German name for Tartu, in Estonia) where he remained until his death. On his departure, Nietzsche made an approach to the university authorities, asking to be transferred to the chair in philosophy, and to be replaced as professor of classical philology by his friend Erwin Rohde.[6] Writing to Rohde, Nietzsche predicted that a main obstacle to his plan would be opposition from the conservative Steffensen, though conceding that lack of evidence for his expertise in philosophy might be a reasonable concern.[7] The university made its decision while Nietzsche was on his Easter vacation in Lugano, and awarded the vacant chair in philosophy to Rudolf Eucken, a philosopher very similar to Teichmüller in his academic background, and recommended by him. Nietzsche expressed himself irritably to Rohde: 'In my absence they have discovered a young talented Aristotelian, carrying the torch of Trendelenburg, so I am once again occupying my chair as a humble philologist ....'[8]

It is noticeable that Nietzsche made no attempt to gain Teichmüller's support for his scheme. Despite their proximity in Basel during the two years between Nietzsche's arrival and Teichmüller's departure, it is doubtful whether the two men had come to know each other well. Nietzsche's closest colleague in Basel was Franz Overbeck, the professor of theology, who remained a lifelong friend. Nietzsche's admiration for Schopenhauer, soon to be displayed in *The Birth of Tragedy*, would not have recommended him to academic philosophers. For his part, Nietzsche may have found some interest in the study of Aristotle's aesthetics that Teichmüller had already published.[9] However, it was only after this time that the more original works which he found important appeared. Ten years later, Nietzsche's appreciation of his former colleague was to grow considerably. By then, his preoccupation with Schopenhauerian themes had been replaced by a broader outlook, which included a better appreciation of positive science and its mode of thinking, encouraged by his friendship with Paul Rée. In addition, his own writing was dealing more directly with questions of epistemology and metaphysics, to which the theses of *Die wirkliche und die scheinbare Welt* were of direct relevance.

Nietzsche's first encounter with Teichmüller's philosophy seems to have been indirect, an outcome of background reading during the summer of 1881. One of the books he studied then was a collection of philosophical essays by the neo-Kantian Otto Caspari which included a long review of Teichmüller's 1877 work *Darwinismus und Philosophie*. Caspari is a hostile and somewhat condescending critic, describing Teichmüller as a dogmatist who misunderstands Kant, and as an 'Eleatic' who denies the reality of change, despite the testimony of experience.[10] Yet he does give an account of the book's contents which quotes some of Teichmüller's more striking assertions, such as the claim that 'time is like a circle', and that 'time is the perspectival appearance of the timeless world-order'.[11] The review may have made little impression on Nietzsche at the time. He went to the trouble of ordering several other books reviewed or mentioned by Caspari, but not this one, as far as we know. No work of Teichmüller is listed in Nietzsche's personal library. Nevertheless, a notebook entry from early 1883 shows that he had been reading the recently published *Die wirkliche und die scheinbare Welt*.[12] Further, Nietzsche's correspondence indicates that he borrowed two volumes of Teichmüller from his friend Franz Overbeck, probably during a visit to Basel in October 1883, and returned them in November 1885.[13] The direct influence of Teichmüller's ideas on Nietzsche can thus be located fairly precisely in time, and this is borne out by the various notebook entries which refer to Teichmüller, either directly or indirectly. During these years Nietzsche was working on *Beyond Good and Evil* and Book Five of *The Gay Science*, as well as producing the last two parts of *Thus Spake Zarathustra*; so it is also clear where we are likely to find signs of Teichmüller's influence in Nietzsche's published works.[14]

Nietzsche was certainly familiar with *Die wirkliche und die scheinbare Welt*, but it is less easy to identify the other books of Teichmüller that he was reading from 1883 onwards. One notebook entry of this period refers to the volume of Teichmüller's *Neue Studien zur Geschichte der Begriffe* which is on Aristotle's theory of practical reason.[15] In addition, Nietzsche wrote to Overbeck that Teichmüller's work had made him realize '*how little* I know Plato – and *how much* Zarathustra πλατονιζει [platonizes].'[16] On the other hand, Part Three of *Thus Spake Zarathustra*, written at the beginning of 1884, contains several passages that suggest a familiarity with *Darwinismus und Philosophie*. An allusion to the notion that 'time is a circle'[17] may be explained by the appearance of this proposition in Caspari's article on Teichmüller. However, Zarathustra's suggestion that 'God is a thought that makes crooked all that is straight'[18] looks like a version of Teichmüller's description of the finite perspective as one 'in which the crooked must appear straight and the straight appear crooked'.[19] So the full extent of Nietzsche's familiarity with the philosophical works of Teichmüller is unclear. One thing is certain: he was very familiar with *Die wirkliche und die scheinbare Welt*; and so any assessment of Teichmüller's influence must explore the themes of this work in some detail.

Teichmüller's Metaphysical System

Teichmüller begins *Die wirkliche und die scheinbare Welt* by distancing himself from contemporary thinkers – although he praises Trendelenburg for his scholarship, and Lotze for his literary style. Modern philosophy, he asserts, is caught in the polarities of thinking and being, spirit and nature, building its theories on one or other of these concepts: but all such metaphysical systems 'are projective presentations of the content of our knowledge and, since knowledge is necessarily from the point of view of the subject, merely perspectival pictures'.[20] In contrast, Teichmüller proposes a doctrine which escapes such limitations by finding the only exception to this rule. All experience, he explains, is a function of the immediate and singular self (*Ich*).[21] Inner and outer phenomena are *projections* of the contents of inner and outer senses: that is, we combine these contents, using various relational forms such as space and time, to produce pictures of things. So where is being to be found in all this? The being of 'so-called things' is, Teichmüller argues, merely inferred.[22] How do things arise? An altering and yet relatively stable complex of sensations is grasped as a unity and projected (*hinausgeworfen*) from our consciousness out into so-called actual space and there acknowledged as a being and designated with the name 'thing' or 'object'.[23] The unity of the object cannot be found in the object itself; it is just a projection of our own point of reference. The object itself is thus just a projection, or a perspectival picture.

Being is not to be found in awareness of our own mental activities either, Teichmüller argues, for what these have in common is just their relation to an *external* point, in that they are all activities of the self, which provides the point of view for relating them to one another. The concept of being, he concludes, can only be located in an intellectual intuition of the self which transcends and encompasses the multiplicity of sensed elements.[24] That is the source of the concept of reality which we then use for objects outside ourselves, and it is to this prototype that all our definitions of being, either as subject or as substance, must refer. Ideal being (the 'what' of things) and real being (the 'that' of things) are both relative to this substantial being: one expresses the content and the other the occurrence of the self's activities. It is these derivative forms of being that are given an absolute status by idealism and realism.

The being of the self is thus the only immediate knowledge we have, Teichmüller concludes. All other knowledge is merely 'semiotic' – that is, a kind of sign language. On this account, everyday experience is an illusion. It is as if we are looking at the world in a mirror and taking the objects seen there as reality. Amongst these is our own image, and it seems that we identify ourself with this image, forgetting the real person who is seeing all these phenomena. Only upon attaining a metaphysical understanding do we realize that 'it is our self, our substantial being, that is best known and certain and inexpressible, whose picture we glimpsed in the mirror of objects'.[25]

We rely on semiotic knowledge in everyday life when we infer the mental states of others from their behaviour, Teichmüller argues. For example, blushing indicates shame, but remains distinct from the feeling itself. We could not recognize shame in others if we had not felt it in ourselves and been able to correlate the feeling with its outer signs. But do we really know our own feelings and moods? Teichmüller now makes a further claim: these, too, are instances of semiotic knowledge. There is no privilege attaching to experience of our mental states, as contemporary thinkers such as Brentano had asserted. Even what is usually called self-consciousness is just semiotic, in Teichmüller's view.[26] Idealists are mistaken on this point, because they identify the self with thinking. In fact, thinking is just one of its various activities, and despite its wide range (numbers, for example, have no limit to their application) thinking has no privileged status in relation to the self. Descartes is a target of criticism on this score, owing to his uncritical invocation of the concept of being and his belief in the immediate certainty of thinking. Teichmüller stresses that he is not devaluing conceptual knowledge, only pointing out that it is 'not the essence of the matter'.[27] We have to see through to the experiences of feeling and willing out of which this knowledge is constructed semiotically.

Without the distinction between semblance (*Schein*) and actuality (*Wirklichkeit*), Teichmüller writes, Heraclitus and Protagoras would be right: the only world would be the world as it appears to the individual at some moment.[28] Even common sense acknowledges that things are not always as they seem, and science enforces the distinction systematically in constructing its theories – for example, it separates the apparent motion of the planets from their real motion. But for philosophy, Teichmüller insists, even this objective knowledge is only perspectival. Natural science is a sign language which does not describe the real essence of things, 'any more than written letters as such can give us an inkling of audible sounds and the ideas that accompany them, though it is harder to realise this with one's mother tongue because of habitual association'.[29]

Teichmüller now sets himself the task of showing how time, space and causality are schemata used by us to organize the content of experience, and not *a priori* forms of knowledge. The case of time occupies him in some detail. An empiricist derivation of time from experience is inadequate, he argues, since children perceive change and succession, yet live in the present and have no consciousness of time. Only the activity of the self, comparing ideal contents by means of memory, sensation and expectation, provides such an awareness. Hence, the self (or soul) transcends these distinctions and is indifferent to past, present and future. It is an eternal being, lying outside the time order and imposing the temporal perspective on its ideal content.

This theory of time as a perspectival construction had been advanced five years earlier in Teichmüller's *Darwinismus und Philosophie*, and he refers back to that essay in *Die wirkliche und die scheinbare Welt*, summarizing its main propositions. Despite its title, *Darwinismus und Philosophie* is only partly about the origin of biological species. Teichmüller disagrees strongly with the materialism of leading evolutionists such as Darwin and Haeckel, who derived higher forms of nature from lower forms and explained their emergence in terms of chance variation and natural selection. The assumption of materialism is that atoms are combined by external forces, but Teichmüller asks how an unchangeable atom could allow itself to be acted upon, and concludes, 'We must thus admit in them something *inner*, which undergoes influences and reacts to them of its own accord.'[30] In our own case this is just the soul, only a small part of whose functioning is conscious. Thus, there is no sharp distinction between living and dead matter. Indeed, there is no dead matter on Teichmüller's view. He proposes an alternative theory of 'metamorphosis' based on inner causes, but he also puts forward a metaphysical doctrine which makes the usual question about origins seem inadequately formulated.

The idea of an absolute beginning is absurd, Teichmüller argues, but so is the idea of an endless regress. Their common error is a search for causes in the past alone. In fact, every state of affairs is conditioned just as much by the future as by the present and past.[31] For science, the world is a timeless structure: 'All science has to do with timeless and unchanging elements and explains from them the phenomena changing in time.' Yet it is unavoidable that we see the world from our own finite standpoint; that is why we take the past and future to be different in kind, one fixed and determinate, and the other open and indeterminate. An infinite being, having the absolute consciousness that we attribute to God, could grasp the whole sequence of world phenomena at once as a completed totality, but our limited consciousness restricts us to one part of it.[32] Hence, our conception of time is perspectival, and to that extent false.

Teichmüller treats space similarly, as a construction commencing from our own perspectival standpoint. The target of his criticism is again the Kantian theory of *a priori* intuition, and his solution to problems about space is to treat its properties as questions for conceptual analysis. For example, the proposition that a straight line is the shortest distance between two points is just a definition, not an axiom – in other words, straightness is not a matter of intuition, but simply the least length.[33] Like time, space implies infinitude. This is not because of the nature of space itself, as Kant supposed, but because the concepts we employ in relating and connecting can be extended indefinitely. Commenting on Kant's antinomies, Teichmüller argues that the world as a whole has no magnitude, 'because there is no standard of measure outside the world by which one could measure its size'.[34] Any units we use are arbitrary, and anything can be finite or infinite depending on the unit chosen.

All knowledge of the world as it appears to the senses, then, is perspectival. Indeed, every sense has its own kind of perspective. In one of the most interesting chapters of *Die wirkliche und die scheinbare Welt*, Teichmüller explores the sign languages which correspond to different senses. Coordination between the senses does not show that their different characters are reducible to one or other – all are equally semiotic in status, although the sense of sight has traditionally been accorded a privileged place, even by philosophers. Touch is its nearest competitor, responsible for the idea of impenetrability and hence for the concept of matter. Teichmüller writes: 'If humanity were to lose these two senses, touch and sight, then the world of the senses would be posited by empirical science under forms of understanding which would have nothing to do with space, corporeality and matter.'[35] This is hard to imagine, he concedes. Even blind people still have the sense of touch, so their conception of the world is not so different from others. 'But now the ideas of space and movement are specific to sight and touch; hence one commits a logical error if one asserts the validity of these forms for *all* the senses.'[36] One task for a true philosophy, Teichmüller suggests, would be to overthrow the 'dictatorship of sight' and establish a democracy of the senses.

Summarizing his system, Teichmüller emphasizes that materialism and idealism are both inadequate. All these *Weltanschauungen* are perspectival. They fail to get beyond the world-picture to the activity out of which it arises. 'As a result, we find ourselves in a *seeming* world, as if we were looking at the world merely in a mirror and over the objects seen there, including our own mirror image, quite forget ourselves as a real person, who sees and lives here.'[37] When we ask where this picture comes from, 'then the whole perspectival world of ghosts vanishes and we come back to ourselves and wake up as from an anxious dream. We see then that it is our self, our substantial being, that is best known and certain and inexpressible, whose picture we glimpsed in the mirror of objects.' For, as we saw, this is the source of our concept of substance, which we then use for objects outside ourselves. This new metaphysics is not his invention, Teichmüller insists; other religions teach idealism, but Christianity has already presented this view in its own way, in that it teaches a personal god and emphasizes the importance of the individual self.

Nietzsche's Reaction to Teichmüller

What do we find in Nietzsche's writing that points to his reading of Teichmüller? First of all, we can discern a frequent use of such key words as 'projection', 'sign language' (or 'semiotic') and above all, 'perspective'. There can be no doubt that the idea of perspective is the clearest and most frequent debt of Nietzsche's thinking to Teichmüller. But to give some content to this claim, we need to see how his use of this metaphor changes and develops as a consequence of his encounter with Teichmüller's system. In Nietzsche's early writings it is associated with optical phenomena such as mirror images, and with the illusions that arise from them.[38] The theory of perception advanced by Helmholtz and Lange, and inspired largely by the scientific study of vision, is a source for this vocabulary. Knowledge, Nietzsche writes in 1881, involves 'necessary optical errors – necessary, since we generally want to live – errors, since all laws of perspective must be errors in themselves'.[39] At this stage, perspective is given a negative valuation by being identified with error and illusion.

A more figurative usage of the same period associates perspective with *distance*. Nietzsche speaks of *long* perspectives (and similarly of *broad* perspectives) as the best means of knowledge. He praises both religion and art, especially drama, for providing us with ways of seeing ourselves from a great distance.[40] In these discussions, his concern is with ways of correcting or improving our powers of observation. He asserts that some perspectives are better than others and that, apart from this, having access to a number of perspectives is better than being confined to a single perspective, or 'corner'. This idea is not so uncommon, but it may be borrowed from Helmholtz, who had recommended looking at things upside down in order to free oneself from the influence of habitual and unnoticed interpretations.[41] These theses have little or nothing in common with Teichmüller's concept of perspective, for he emphasizes that all empirical knowledge is equally semiotic and equally concerned with semblance rather than reality, and so discriminations like these do not achieve any advance towards what could be considered genuine truth.

How does Nietzsche's use of the notion of perspective change with his reading of Teichmüller? There is no sharp division, it must be allowed, and some of the applications we have noted can be found in later works such as *Beyond Good and Evil*. In any case, although Teichmüller makes no reference to Helmholtz and Lange's theories of perception, it is possible that his approach to empirical knowledge was informed by their works. Nevertheless, there are some developments in Nietzsche's ideas. His appeal to the concept of perspective becomes more systematic and more centred on its application to epistemology. In effect, 'perspective' becomes a technical expression for him.[42] Finally, towards the end of his writing career, Nietzsche takes a further step in formulating a doctrine of universal perspectivism: everything has a perspective for everything else, and this is what the being of things consists in.[43] That is, the world as it appears from a particular standpoint, the world of perspectival appearance, is the only one. As it happens, Nietzsche uses the word *Perspektivismus* in only a few places, and in none of these does it refer to any philosophical doctrine.[44] Rather he takes it to be synonymous with *Perspektivität*, which clearly refers to the property of being perspectival.[45] It is this that Nietzsche attributes to all forms of human knowledge, and to all objects of human knowledge.

An important feature of Nietzsche's epistemology is his claim that our knowledge of our mental states is no more certain than our knowledge of the external world. He describes this as 'the phenomenality of the inner world', because it means that thinking, willing and feeling are phenomena in the same sense as physical objects. If that is true, then the epistemic privilege attached to introspection or self-awareness by many philosophers is a myth. In *Beyond Good and Evil*, Nietzsche names only Descartes as a supporter of this proposition, but a preparatory note criticizes Spir for following Descartes in assuming the evident character of inner experience – and cites Teichmüller's rebuttal of this error.[46] Between these two metaphysicians, then, Teichmüller emerges as more consistent in his rejection of common opinion.

In the course of his survey of philosophy in the First Article of *Beyond Good and Evil*, Nietzsche writes:

> The eagerness and subtlety – I might almost say, shrewdness (*Schlauheit*) – with which the problem of 'the real and the apparent world' is today attacked all over Europe makes one think and wonder; and anyone who hears nothing in the background except a 'will to truth', certainly does not have the best of ears.[47]

Here the title of *Die wirkliche und die scheinbare Welt* is used as a label for the ideas of several contemporary thinkers. None is named, but references to the ideas of Teichmüller, Spir and Lange are conspicuous in what follows. The first instance is a 'puritanical fanatic of conscience' who demands certainty above all other things, an attitude Nietzsche takes to be one of despair and renunciation of life itself. Clearly this is Spir, identified along similar lines in a contemporary notebook as a 'fanatical logician' who acknowledges only 'the absolute authority of the goddess "Reason".'[48] Such an attitude is nihilism, Nietzsche comments, using that term for the first time in his published writing. He goes on to draw a contrast with less destructive versions of metaphysical thinking, attributable to 'stronger and livelier thinkers who are still eager for life'. One characteristic of these figures is that 'they side *against* appearance, and speak of "perspective" with a new arrogance'. Another is that they are prepared to doubt the reality of even their own bodies – that is, they are prepared to give up the securest possession anyone could have. These are references to Teichmüller and Lange, identified respectively by a main concept and by a provocative conclusion.

Crucial to Nietzsche's critique of Teichmüller is his attack on the assumption that every mental act is the activity of a subject. Memory, he writes, does not imply 'a "soul" which reproduces, recognizes etc. timelessly'.[49] Rather, it is just a process that occurs for any of various reasons. So is thinking itself: 'a thought comes when "it" wishes, not when

"I" wish, so that it is as falsification of the facts of the case to say that the subject "I" is a condition of the predicate "thinks".'[50] Even using the impersonal 'it' here, Nietzsche adds, would amount to an interpretation which is only a prejudice. 'One infers here according to the grammatical habit: "thinking is an activity; every activity requires an agent; consequently – ".' In consequence of this analysis, Nietzsche rejects Teichmüller's claim that an absolute self is our paradigm case of 'being': 'If our "self" is the sole being (*Sein*) for us, in accordance with which we can understand anything or make it exist: very well! Then it is very pertinent to doubt whether there is not a perspectival illusion here – the apparent unity which encompasses everything as in a horizon line.'[51] Nietzsche's argument is that Teichmüller's reification of the subject as 'substantial being' is unjustified. He goes on to suggest that 'the evidence of the body' points to an enormous multiplicity as the starting-point for explaining simpler and more abstract phenomena, rather than vice versa.

This revision of Teichmüller's doctrine is typical of Nietzsche's attitude to the metaphysical thinkers he praises in *Beyond Good and Evil*. It is the same tactic that we noted in his relation to African Spir. These thinkers have eliminated the concept of being from everyday experience, but retained it as an abstraction. For Teichmüller, being is identified with the absolute self, while for Spir it is not only unconditioned but unconditioning, and so has no connection with plurality and change. As noted earlier, Nietzsche considers that such a minimal concept of reality is 'an idea which is no longer good for anything, not even obligating – an idea which has become useless and superfluous'.[52] Hence, it should be abolished, leaving only the world of appearance which, however, should no longer be called by that name, since it implies a contrast with some 'true world'. In this way, the metaphysical venture, when taken to its final consequence, eliminates its own content and is thereby replaced by its opposite, a vindication of the senses. In other words, by completing this detour through the outer fringes of idealism we arrive at 'sensualism', an acknowledgment of the essential contribution of sensory experience to all conceptual knowledge. This theme will be discussed in some detail in Chapter 9.

It is thinkers like Teichmüller, then, who enable Nietzsche to come full circle to his early identification of his standpoint as an 'inverted Platonism' which attaches greater worth to semblance than to 'true being'.[53] He is no longer limited by the framework within which that assertion had been made, primarily owing to what some commentators have described as a 'positivist' phase in his development – that is, the emphasis on useable concepts and empirical knowledge displayed most clearly in *Human, All-Too-Human*.

Teichmüller's Perspectival Account of Time

Having looked into the general relation between Teichmüller's metaphysical perspectivism and Nietzsche's thinking, we can focus on an area which extends the discussion of the last two chapters. The theme of time is of special interest, because Teichmüller elaborates it in ways that are closely linked with Nietzsche's approach, especially in *Thus Spake Zarathustra*. For Teichmüller, time is a concept which allows us to organize the 'ideal' content of experience. In particular, it enables us to reconcile contradictory, yet equally true, judgements by separating their locations and setting them in a certain order.[54] 'The sun is overhead' and 'The sun is on the horizon' can both be true if they are taken as being true at different times. This introduces differences which are not present within the content or nature of what is experienced, but consist in its links with our own activity. We organize our ideas according to their various degrees of intensity, and interpret this as the relation between present and past reality. Young children are unable to make such comparisons, because they live wholly in the present, absorbed by its pleasures and pains. The same is true of animals, and even of an adult person who is wholly absorbed by a single thought. The ordering of contents into past, present and future is perspectival, since it depends on the standpoint of the subject. Teichmüller concludes:

> Ideal objects are transferred by us into time and form the temporal. *But for anyone who lives wholly in the temporal, there is no time at all.* We need the *timeless standpoint* to grasp the perspectival image of the temporal, to grasp the differences between the 'light rays' of our activities as intervals and through this situation perceive a chronological ordering.[55]

He insists that it is completely wrong to derive a concept of time from external events. For the successions we observe in nature – between sunrise and sunset, spring and autumn, the ages of human life, and even cause and effect – all depend on comparisons of ideal content for their temporal form. Children and animals experience change and succession, yet they live in the present and have no consciousness of time. In some pathological cases, people lose this ability to tell the difference between past and present. Teichmüller says he knew someone whose mind was wholly occupied with the violent events of 1848 and who imagined them to be still taking place.[56] Or people may confuse fantasies of future possibilities with present reality. So, while we certainly cannot take awareness of these dimensions of time for granted, we should not suppose that such awareness arises from the content of experience alone. Rather, it requires the activity of the subject to compare and relate the ideal content of experience, interpreting its mental acts as perception, memory or fantasy, and their objects accordingly, as actual or not actual. This subject itself is indifferent to memory, sensation and expectation, and therefore to past, present and future. That means it must be timeless, since it is what creates time in general. Teichmüller sums up: 'Time is thus a perspectival order established by an eternal being lying outside this order, or grasping it in itself, in relation to its ideal content.'[57]

On this view, what counts as the present is determined by the comparative strength and clarity of the content of consciousness. The present is just the most intensive point of consciousness, the past and future being relatively *un*conscious, except for the pathological cases just mentioned.[58] The concept of the future is accounted for by our power of fantasy, which gives us the idea of the possible as distinct from the actual, and from feelings such as fear and hope; if we were purely knowing beings it would be impossible to acquire the idea of the future as what we imagine coming to – or rather, as it presents itself in experience, as what is coming towards us. Teichmüller considers an objection to his account: in thinking of past and future as 'projected' perspectivally, is not he reducing them to the present? He replies that our idea of them is in the present, since this is where we carry out the correlation of contents of consciousness. But the result of that operation is just the constitution of perspectival time, at first for a single subject, and then as an objective ideal order which is common to every subject.

Is time infinite and infinitely divisible? Teichmüller's answer is that it is both, but for different reasons from those given by Kant. Time by itself has no duration, and therefore is not infinite in magnitude, for it is just as much present in the shortest period. He rejects Kant's objection to a finite past existence of the world as mistaken on the grounds that the infinitude of past time has nothing to do with temporal phenomena themselves, but is just our conceptual operation.[59] To determine the magnitude of duration, or anything else, we need to establish a unit of measurement. The choice of this unit will be arbitrary and made on pragmatic grounds. Teichmüller refers here to von Baer's description of the relative character of subjective impressions of duration: for living beings with different metabolic rates and lifespans, the process of becoming must seem to be faster or slower. If we pick a small enough unit of measurement, anything will be infinite – after all, Homer calls the earth and sea infinite. Hence, it is illogical to say that the world is either finite or infinite in its duration or, for that matter, in its size in space. There is nothing outside the world as a whole, and so there can be no unit (*Masseinheit*) or standard of measure (*Massstab*) outside the world through which its magnitude could be measured.[60] Teichmüller insists that this holds true whether we understand the world in a dogmatic fashion, as the totality of things in themselves, or critically, as the totality of appearances. He presents his arguments as a criticism of Kant, although it might reasonably be said that his conclusion, in effect, endorses the point that Kant wanted to make through his antinomies.

Teichmüller concludes that the concept of time contains within itself infinitude in both directions, as well as infinite divisibility. Yet this is just as true of other kinds of series, such as any causal series, and expresses only the conventional character of measurement, not the nature of time in itself. So while it is true that time must be taken as infinite, this infinity is not a property of time by itself; it simply expresses what is common to all of the concepts we use for ordering and relating, the absence of any limit to their application. Whereas Kant derived the infinity of time and space from their unique status as the forms of inner and outer intuition, Teichmüller treats them as two of many concepts having similar functions, and concludes: 'so the infinity of time is not something special, on the contrary, nothing would be more surprising than if time or space or cause and effect or any general concept could be thought without this infinity.'[61]

As we have seen, Teichmüller's account of time relies on the distinction between an ideal order which is timeless, and the perspective of a finite subject which imposes the distinctions between past, present or future upon this ideal content. This theory had already been presented in his earlier work *Darwinismus und Philosophie*, and the account he gives in *Die wirkliche und die scheinbare Welt* is a more detailed elaboration of the same model. The objective time-order of events is like the series of all numbers: in each case, an infinite being could grasp the whole series at once; but our limited consciousness restricts us to one part of it:

> Taken absolutely one can and must regard the whole succession of worldly phenomena as complete, so that, to put it paradoxically, the future has already occurred and past and future are simultaneous. Such a view would however be possible only for the absolute consciousness that we attribute to God.[62]

Teichmüller notes that his theory accords with the traditional idea of God as a non-temporal being and, what is more, seems to lend support to the notion of destiny, in so far as that implies a single totality of past and future events.

Nietzsche's Temporal Perspectivism

It is not surprising that aspects of Teichmüller's theory of time should figure in *Thus Spake Zarathustra*, for Nietzsche's notebooks of 1882 and 1883 show that he was reading *Die wirkliche und die scheinbare Welt* and making notes on passages which deal with the nature of temporality.[63] If one looks for evidence of this influence within *Zarathustra*, it will be found in the central chapter entitled 'On the Vision and the Riddle'. In this speech, Zarathustra presents what he explicitly identifies as an enigmatic challenge to his hearers. Not surprisingly, therefore, its interpretation is not immediately clear.[64] It centres upon a narrative in which Zarathustra describes finding himself at a gateway standing between two long, endless lanes. The gateway at which they meet and, we are told, 'contradict' each other, is called 'Moment'. The two lanes are not named, but it is evident that they symbolize the past and future directions of time, for one is identified with what has happened or been done before, and the other with what is still to come. Zarathustra indicates that the coming together of these lanes is a forceful confrontation, and raises the question whether a similar situation is found along each of the lanes themselves; and in a later passage he advances a bold argument for the proposition that all those who run on the lanes must do so again and again, 'out there'.

The gateway is the standpoint from which an observer looks forward into the future or backward into the past. So far, this seems to be close to Teichmüller's conception of the present as a perspectival standpoint. From this gateway, two paths extend in opposite directions, and we are told that 'no one has yet followed either to its end'.[65] That description leaves open the possibility that time may be closed rather than linear in form, since in that case it would still be endless. However, this idea is raised only to be dismissed by Zarathustra. As we have seen, Nietzsche maintained the infinitude of time against the arguments of several contemporary writers. But does rejecting a finite time mean rejecting a closed time as well? One might well think so, and yet Teichmüller manages to hold not only that time is infinite but also that it is 'like a circle'. Let us look at what he has in mind by this second thesis, and see how it compares with the claim that seems to be summarily rejected in *Thus Spake Zarathustra*.

In *Darwinismus und Philosophie*, Teichmüller had argued for a circularity of time on the grounds that only this conception can enable us to escape from a dilemma posed by the search for causes which leads back, further and further into the past. The idea of an absolute beginning to this series is ruled out by the principle of sufficient reason, as well as the absurdity of any notion of an empty time preceding the beginning of the world. On the other hand, an endless regress of causes is no more satisfactory. The linear model of time is to blame, he suggests, for leading us on this futile chase in one direction.

> Times are firmly co-ordinated only when one has taken one point as beginning, thus through making a comparison; however nothing is in time by itself. One can thus see that time is like a circle. A circle has no beginning and no endpoint; nevertheless, one can choose any arbitrary point as the beginning and from then on follow the curve forwards or backwards. But since each point is only chosen arbitrarily, since none can claim the privilege of being the beginning, one must therefore, by following the curve, necessarily come back to the starting point again, i.e. concede that this point was not the beginning, but can just as much be treated as the middle and end.[66]

That time seems a straight line to us is an illusion, like the apparent flatness of the earth's surface. In both cases, reason reveals the truth: that the earth is a sphere, and time a circle. The important point that Teichmüller uses this metaphor to make is not that becoming is a circular process, but that events are conditioned as much by the future as by the past. More generally, he believes that scientific explanations are timeless, because they are directed towards a reality which is indifferent to distinctions between past, present and future. Hence, his alternative to Darwinism appears to be a theory of Platonic ideal types which, although they are instantiated within the realm of living things, have their own timeless being. While that theory is not expounded in *Die wirkliche und die scheinbare Welt*, Teichmüller does repeat his claim about circular time, and recalls that something similar was said by Aristotle who, however, seems to have been thinking only of the natural cycles of nature and 'had no notion of a deeper meaning to this metaphor'.[67]

In *Thus Spake Zarathustra*, a circular model of time is introduced, only to be rejected out of hand. When Zarathustra challenges his opponent in debate, the dwarfish spirit of gravity, to say whether the two lanes contradict each other eternally, he is met by the reply: 'All that is straight lies ... All truth is crooked; time itself is a circle.' He becomes angry and accuses the dwarf of 'making things too easy' for himself. Commentators on this passage have been made uneasy by a suspicion that Zarathustra is here condemning his own doctrine of eternal recurrence. That notion can be disposed of: the identification of closed time with eternal recurrence is a confusion, as we noted earlier.[68] The question remains: how similar is the metaphorical conception presented in 'On the Vision and the Riddle' to Teichmüller's perspectival model of time? Are there aspects to Nietzsche's account which take it in a different direction altogether? I think that closer examination will show that this is indeed the case.

Nietzsche's aim is to symbolize what he takes to be the character of existence in time. That involves the distinctions between past, present and future, but it also involves the reality of becoming, which he regards as a fact of experience that is far more certain than any interpretation. Hence, any model of past and future in their relation to the present is plausible only when one adds that the present is not always the same, and that what is future at one time is past at another. In other words, past and future are relative to the present, and this is a point which is not fixed in location, but rather occupies later and later positions in the succession of events. In Nietzsche's metaphor, this is symbolized by the movement of travellers on the lanes. Those on one lane are approaching the observer in the gateway, while those on the other lane are moving away from the observer. Teichmüller's static image of time includes nothing corresponding to a flow of becoming. Nor does he relate time with feelings or practical concerns. It is true that he links the future with hope and fear, but these merely provide the occasion for classifying some ideal content as imaginary rather than actual. In contrast, what Nietzsche is describing is a predicament within which such feelings are inseparable from the experience of temporality.

Arguably, we cannot imagine a time without supposing that we are ourselves located within that time; however, whether or not the same is true of space is another matter. If this is accepted, it follows that 'perspectivism' has greater relevance to an understanding of time than to an understanding of space. That is a surprising thesis, given that the notion of perspective is originally a visual and hence a spatial one. But the line of thought presented by Teichmüller gives some support to the idea. His account of the 'perspectival illusion' which leads us to perceive time as a straight line rather than a curved one relies wholly on its appeal to a spatial model, within which a conception in which no one point is identified as 'now' (or rather, as 'here') is not problematical. If it is true that to grasp time *as* time, we must locate ourselves within it, then Nietzsche's refusal of this move is quite justified. He does not regard space and time as corresponding in all their properties – for example, he categorically asserts the finitude of space and the infinitude of time – but in this respect they are presumably alike. In fact, one does not have to agree with this view of space to accept the point about time.

Zarathustra's gateway figures as a perspectival point of view, and yet past and future are not *just* perspectival concepts in his account. He is concerned to include the element of becoming in his account of temporality. The metaphors he uses for that purpose have two aspects, which could be labelled as 'kinematic' and 'dynamic'. The first has to do with motion, and the second with force. On the two sides of the gateway are 'lanes' along which travellers are said to walk or run. Their walking or running is, however, a highly constrained movement. It has a single direction, from future to past, and also seems to have a single speed, implied in Zarathustra's statement that all things are firmly 'knotted together', and that each 'draws after it' all those that are to come. As Nietzsche makes clear elsewhere in *Thus Spake Zarathustra*, this predicament is experienced as a lack of freedom and power which gives rise to frustration and anger.[69] In addition, he refers to the gateway as a scene of conflict, apparently between the two lanes themselves. How that is to be understood is not easy to grasp, but it too points to something beyond a perspectival model. In one late note, Nietzsche makes a distinction between 'becoming', which implies conflict and contradiction, and 'change', a weaker concept indicating only a succession of states.[70] In that terminology, we could say that the kinematic model of perspectivism accounts for change, but fails to account for becoming.

A kinematic conception fits in quite well with the notion of a perspectival standpoint, as we can see in presentations of the theory of special relativity. To this extent, the symbolizing of becoming is not by itself a departure from perspectivism, provided that it uses a visual vocabulary. But forces are not seen, they are felt. Moreover, it seems that they are felt when – and only when – they come into conflict with one another. For Nietzsche, the reality of time can be expressed only in these terms. A purely perspectival picture of past and future is, for this reason, not sufficient for his purpose. Its static and contemplative character suits Teichmüller's intentions well by predisposing the reader towards belief in a timeless reality. His circular image adds to this effect, because it implies an elimination of temporal directionality, as typified in the asymmetry of cause and effect. But Nietzsche wants to understand temporality as a place of tension, conflict and overcoming. When this is taken into account, his approach to time is more complex than Teichmüller's. It includes a range of metaphors, somewhat along the lines of Teichmüller's notion of a multiplicity of sign languages corresponding to different senses. Whether it is helpful to call these perspectives is questionable, for the term becomes vague if removed too far from its original meaning. For Teichmüller, perspective is the limitation of a finite standpoint, and Nietzsche is still a perspectivist in this sense, since he does not believe in absolute knowledge; yet his account of time contains elements that are inconsistent with the visual version of perspectivism.

Nietzsche's version of perspectivism does not have the metaphysical bias of Teichmüller; he repudiates any 'true' or 'real' world over and above the world of perspectival appearance. He insists that we have no concepts that could be used to describe any such world, and that it is merely an empty fiction. Teichmüller asserts that we have an intellectual intuition of a 'self' which is the unique source of all those organizing activities that constitute cognition, and that our concept of absolute being is based on this certainty.[71] Nietzsche denies any such intuition, and any such self. His perspectivism is thus far more radical in its implications than Teichmüller's. It frees the construction of a conceptual framework from the constraints that a 'real' world would presumably impose. No doubt our concepts depend on the kind of beings we are. This, it seems to Nietzsche, is why we must think of space as Euclidean space.[72] It is also why we must think of time as having a certain direction, whereas, for all we know, other beings could experience time as proceeding 'backward'.[73] But the kind of beings we are also depends on our concepts: Nietzsche holds out the possibility of a transformation of the self through an 'incorporation' of certain concepts, such as the thought of eternal recurrence. Still, we are able to grasp the world only in terms of our own human interpretation – for the time being.

Notes

1 Hermann Nohl, 'Eine historische Quelle zu Nietzsches Perspektivismus: G. Teichmüller, die wirkliche und die scheinbare Welt', *Zeitschrift für Philosophie und philosophische Kritik*, 149 (1913), 106–15.
2 Gustav Teichmüller, *Die wirkliche und die scheinbare Welt* (Breslau: Verlag von Wilhelm Koebner, 1882).
3 Ibid., XIV.
4 Quoted by Nietzsche in his Foreword to *On the Uses and Disadvantages of History for Life*, this is from a letter of Goethe to Schiller, dated 19 December 1798. See Johann Wolfgang von Goethe, *Briefwechsel mit Friedrich Schiller*, ed. Ernest Beutler (Zürich: Artemis-Verlag, 1949), 666–67.
5 See Curt Paul Janz, *Friedrich Nietzsche Biographie* (München: Deutsche Taschenbuch Verlag, 1981), Band 1, 402.
6 KGB II/1, 174–76 (letter of January 1871).
7 Ibid., 189 (letter of 29 March 1871).
8 Ibid., 192 (letter of 10 April 1871). In the event, Eucken also stayed in Basel for only a few years, moving to Jena in 1874. He was in turn followed by Max Heinze, whose writing on Heraclitus is the target of repeated criticism in Nietzsche's lectures on pre-Platonic philosophy: see KGW II/4, 251, 280 and 281.
9 Gustav Teichmüller, *Aristotelische Forschungen*, 3 vols (Halle: G.E. Barthel, 1867–73).
10 Otto Caspari, *Der Zusammenhang der Dinge: Gesammelte philosophische Aufsätze* (Breslau: Verlag von Eduard Trewendt, 1881), 144–45 and 158.
11 Ibid., 166 and 169. See Gustav Teichmüller, *Darwinismus und Philosophie* (Dorpat: Verlag von C. Mattiesen, 1867–73), 41 and 49.
12 KGW VII/1, 300 refers to and quotes from *Die wirkliche und die scheinbare Welt*, 204.
13 See KGB III/1, 449, and III/3, 109 (letters of 22 and 27 October 1883, and 12 November 1885).
14 To this list should be added the 1886 Preface to *Human, All-Too-Human*, which refers to 'the perspectival and its injustice'; and the 'Attempt at a Self-Criticism' added to *The Birth of Tragedy* in 1886, which asserts 'the necessity of perspectives and error' (sect. 5).
15 KGW VII/1, 624. These references are to Gustav Teichmüller, *Neue Studien zur Geschichte der Begriffe*, Band 3 (Cotha: F.A. Perthes, 1879), 55 and 65.
16 KGB III/1, 449 (letter of 22 October 1883).
17 Friedrich Nietzsche, *Thus Spake Zarathustra*, 'On the Vision and the Riddle'.
18 Ibid., 'Upon the Blessed Isles'.
19 Teichmüller, *Darwinismus und Philosophie*, 43. This is not quoted by Caspari in his review of *Darwinismus und Philosophie*, nor is it repeated by Teichmüller in *Die wirkliche und die scheinbare Welt*.
20 Teichmüller, *Die wirkliche und die scheinbare Welt. Neue Grundlegung der Metaphysik* (Breslau: Verlag von Wilhelm Koebner, 1882), XVI.
21 Ibid., 17.

22 Ibid., 24.
23 Ibid., 333.
24 Ibid., 32.
25 Ibid., 346.
26 Ibid., 104.
27 Ibid., 110.
28 Ibid., 183.
29 Ibid., 331.
30 Teichmüller, *Darwinismus und Philosophie*, 8.
31 Ibid., 39.
32 Teichmüller, *Die wirkliche und die scheinbare Welt*, 227.
33 Ibid., 282.
34 Ibid., 261.
35 Ibid., 323.
36 Ibid., 324.
37 Ibid., 346.
38 See, for example, Friedrich Nietzsche, *Daybreak*, sect. 121 and 243.
39 KGW V/2, 535.
40 Friedrich Nietzsche, *The Gay Science*, sect. 78. See also, for example, *Daybreak*, sect. 485 and *Beyond Good and Evil*, sect. 129, an earlier version of which appears in an 1882 notebook: KGW VII/1, 59.
41 'It may even happen that with the head upside down the clouds have the correct perspective, whereas the objects on the earth appear like a painting on a vertical surface, as the clouds in the sky usually do': Hermann von Helmholtz, *Helmholtz's Treatise on Physiological Optics*, ed. J.P.C. Southall (New York: Dover Publications, 1962), Vol. 3, 9 (sect. 26).
42 It is easy to overestimate the occurrence of the word 'perspective' in Nietzsche's later writings if one is using the English versions of Walter Kaufmann, since the German word corresponding to his 'perspective' is often *Optik* rather than *Perspektive*. See, for example, Friedrich Nietzsche, *Ecce Homo*, "Why I am so Wise", sect. 1, "The Birth of Tragedy", sect. 1 and "Why I am a Destiny", sect. 5; also KGW VIII/2, 48 and 216 (*The Will to Power*, sect. 552 and 544); and KGW VIII/3, 55, 59, 100 and 149 (*The Will to Power*, sect. 444, 569, 288 and 811). Kaufmann also translates *Blick* as 'perspective' in *Ecce Homo*, "Why I am so Clever", sect. 1, and "The Case of Wagner", sect. 2.
43 KGW VIII/3, 371 and 373 (*The Will to Power*, sect. 567 and 636).
44 See KGW V/2, 275; VIII/1, 311 and 323; and VIII/3, 165.
45 KGW VII/3, 381. A similar remark could be made about Nietzsche's use of *Phänomenalismus* and *Phänomenalität* as interchangeable expressions; see KGW V/2, 275; VIII/1, 295; VIII/3, 126 and 252–53.
46 KGW VII/3, 372.
47 Friedrich Nietzsche, *Beyond Good and Evil*, sect. 10.
48 KGW VII/3, 373. The link between the demand for certainty and nihilism (or fanaticism) is also made in *The Gay Science*, sect. 347.
49 KGW VII/1, 376.
50 Nietzsche, *Beyond Good and Evil*, sect. 17.
51 KGW VIII/1, 104 (*The Will to Power*, sect. 518).
52 Friedrich Nietzsche, *Twilight of the Idols*, 'How the "True" World Finally Became a Fable'.
53 KGW III/3, 207.
54 Teichmüller, *Die wirkliche und die scheinbare Welt*, 191. Cf. Kant: 'Only in time can two contradictorily opposed predicates meet in one and the same object, namely, *one after the other*': Immanuel Kant, *Critique of Pure Reason*, trans. N. Kemp Smith (London: Macmillan, 1929), B48–49. This point is also emphasized by Spir in *Denken und Wirklichkeit, Versuch einer Erneuerung der kritischen Philosophie* (Leipzig: J.G. Findel, 1873), Band 2, 5 and 11.
55 Teichmüller, *Die wirkliche und die scheinbare Welt*, 192.

56 Ibid., 201.
57 Ibid., 206.
58 Ibid., 198 and 220.
59 Ibid., 211.
60 Ibid., 213 and 261. In a similar way, Nietzsche argues (in refutation of pessimism) that since the value of the world cannot be measured against anything, 'it has no value at all': KGW VIII/2, 277–78 (*The Will to Power*, sect. 708).
61 Teichmüller, *Die wirkliche und die scheinbare Welt*, 207.
62 Ibid., 227.
63 See, for example, KGW VII/1, 219, 300 and 318.
64 For a closer reading, see Robin Small, 'Zarathustra's Gateway', *History of Philosophy Quarterly*, 15 (1998): 79–98.
65 Nietzsche, *Thus Spake Zarathustra*, 'On the Vision and the Riddle'.
66 Teichmüller, *Darwinismus und Philosophie*, 42.
67 Teichmüller, *Die wirkliche und die scheinbare Welt*, 239. This is apparently an allusion to Aristotle's *On Generation and Corruption*, II.11.
68 The same mistake is made by Wilhelm Wundt in an 1877 article on 'the cosmological problem', where he writes:

> If time does run back into itself, then every event proceeds between states of affairs that repeat themselves in eternal uniformity. There would be no real progress in the world and, for that matter, no permanent regress. The present state of affairs has already existed in exactly the same way, a very long time ago, and will exist again after an equally long time. The same action I am now performing, I have already performed countlessly many times, in precisely in the same circumstances, and will do again infinitely many times in the ceaseless course of time. (Wundt, 'Ueber das kosmologische Problem', *Vierteljahrsschrift für wissenschaftliche Philosophie*, 1 (1877), 115).

This article is discussed at length by Caspari in *Der Zusammenhang der Dinge*, 199–237.
69 See, for example, Nietzsche, *Thus Spake Zarathustra*, 'On Redemption'.
70 KGW VIII/3, 134 (*The Will to Power*, sect. 778).
71 Teichmüller, *Die wirkliche und die scheinbare Welt*, 346.
72 KGW VIII/3, 126 (*The Will to Power*, sect. 515).
73 Nietzsche, *The Gay Science*, sect. 374.

Chapter 4

Zöllner and Space

A number of commentators have remarked on a possible influence of the physicist Friedrich Zöllner on Nietzsche's thinking about natural science, and in particular on his notion of space.[1] On a wider level, Nietzsche's ideas about the methodology of science may bear a relation to Zöllner's scientific programme.[2] Apart from this, however, there is a question about Nietzsche's own opinion of Zöllner, which underwent a startling change in the eleven years between his several published references to Zöllner. The contrast is not to be explained in terms of any personal quarrel or broken friendship, since there is no evidence that the two men ever met, although they were indirectly linked through several intermediary figures.

In this chapter I will bring out some of these links in tracing the parallel paths of Nietzsche and Zöllner, and at the same time explore the questions that arise concerning their ideas on scientific and other matters. As we shall see, the link throws some light on certain passages in Nietzsche's *Thus Spake Zarathustra* which commentators have found obscure. My discussion, then, traces some remarkable changes in Nietzsche's attitudes, and makes an attempt to correlate these with other aspects of his development. It also examines the relation between Nietzsche and one of his contemporaries who, although prominent and controversial in his time, is seldom mentioned today.

Nietzsche and the Zöllner Scandal

Friedrich Zöllner was born in 1834, the son of a Berlin factory owner. From his birth, he suffered from a severe malformation of the spine, which failed to respond to medical treatment. In an autobiographical sketch, Zöllner later remarked on the suffering that his 'asymmetry' occasioned throughout his childhood, and no doubt into adult life as well.[3] His disciple and literary executor, Moritz Wirth, remarked on Zöllner's striking appearance, and a surviving photograph tends to bear this out.[4] It seems very likely that some of the unusual features of Zöllner's character were due to this misfortune, but another factor may also have been at work – a tendency to mental instability which appeared in several of his siblings, as his later critics were to point out.

After studying physics in Berlin, Zöllner moved to Basel to complete his doctorate and, in 1866, became professor of astrophysics in Leipzig, where he remained until his death in 1882. Zöllner's achievements in science were of a very practical kind: he devised a new instrument for measuring the brightness of stars, and went on to develop a new kind of spectroscope. However, Zöllner considered himself a theoretician as well as a practical scientist, insisting on the inseparability of speculative and empirical thinking in science. He made this aspiration clear in his inaugural address, in which he tried to derive the law of conservation of energy from a more general law of causality; yet his first years in Leipzig were spent in continuing his practical work in devising and using spectroscopic methods for measuring the rotation of the sun. It was not until 1872 that Zöllner became a public figure and a centre of controversy, with the publication of his book *Über die Natur der Cometen*.[5]

This is not quite the straightforward scientific treatise that its title might suggest. The subtitle is an indication of the book's intended significance: 'Contributions to the History and Theory of Knowledge'. Only a few of the many items included in the work deal with comets and, of those that do, several are reprinted papers of Olbers and Bessel. Other chapters deal with the philosophy of space and time, the theory of unconscious reasoning, morality and religion, and the life of Kant. One chapter on the relation between the physical universe and space will later be discussed in detail. For the moment, however, it is the controversial nature of *Über die Natur der Cometen* that concerns us. What attracted the attention of readers, first and foremost, was Zöllner's extraordinary preface, a 67-page manifesto of scientific methodology – and also a declaration of war against the scientific establishment. This preface bears the date 27 December 1871, the anniversary of the birth of Johannes Kepler, to whose memory the work as a whole is dedicated. Kepler, Zöllner explains, understood the need for a scientific reliance on the logical powers of the understanding, as well as on empirical observation. Unfortunately his example has been neglected: 'The majority of current representatives of the scientists of today have never bothered to study the first principles of epistemology, and instead rely on a one-sided accumulation of empirical facts.'[6]

Warming to this theme, Zöllner identifies several cases in point. It is no accident that his main targets are English scientists, since he postulates a fundamental difference between the intellectual talents of the English and those of the Germans. The English, it appears, are empiricists by nature, and so use inductive rather than deductive reasoning in formulating their theories. Darwin and Wallace, for instance, advanced the principle of the continuity of organisms on this empirical basis, whereas German commentators have achieved a far more comprehensive account, from the standpoint of epistemology rather than that of immediately observed facts.[7] Zöllner picks on a recent speech of Sir William Thomson as illustrating 'the primitive state of epistemology amongst the leading representatives of the exact sciences in England'.[8] The scientific scene in England could hardly be less healthy, Zöllner says, dominated as it is by an inductive tradition and by a popularizing tendency which has corrupted scientific integrity. Worse still, the *Theoretical Physics* of Thomson and P.G. Tait had recently appeared in a German edition, under the sponsorship of Hermann von Helmholtz. What especially offended Zöllner about this work was a passage which criticized the theories of his colleague, Wilhelm Weber. Thomson and Tait argued that Weber's theory of electricity was inconsistent with the conservation of energy.[9] Helmholtz supported their view, rather than rallying to the support of his fellow German. In Zöllner's opinion, Helmholtz had shown 'thoughtlessness' and a 'lack of tact' in condoning this attack on an older colleague.[10]

Zöllner's preface introduces another theme which figures prominently in other sections of his book – the question of *priority* in scientific discovery. He finds that Stokes was anticipated by Kirchhoff, Thomson by Lippich, Wallace by Schopenhauer, and almost everyone by Kant. His method of establishing these conclusions is to present relevant passages from the writers in question in parallel columns. Inevitably the reader gains an impression of plagiarism, although Zöllner avoids saying so explicitly. Apart from British authors his main target here is Helmholtz, whose theory of perception, according to Zöllner, bears a strong resemblance to the one put forward fifty years earlier by Schopenhauer. To assist the reader in seeing this resemblance, Zöllner uses his standard method of displaying corresponding passages alongside each other.[11] It is not surprising that Helmholtz later refused to accept Zöllner's somewhat disingenuous explanation that he had only intended to be helpful. Towards the end of the preface, Zöllner indicates that he expects his book to meet with a hostile response: 'According to the usual opinion of the crowd, I will do myself enormous harm by this book, by antagonising the English and creating whole crowds of bitter opponents in Germany. – So much the better!'[12] But, he adds, no such difficulties can alter the fact that a new age of deductive reasoning in science is about to dawn, and that 'Germany alone is called to become the bearer and showplace of this epoch'.[13]

If opposition was what Zöllner wanted, he was not to be disappointed. On its publication, *Über die Natur der Cometen* aroused a storm of controversy, mainly because of its attack on Helmholtz, the dominating figure in German science. As well as objecting to Zöllner's attacks on the British scientists with whom he maintained friendly relations, Helmholtz was, understandably, deeply offended by the personal tone of Zöllner's remarks about him. His official response took the form of a brief answer to the scientific objections raised by Zöllner against William Thomson and P.G. Tait, ending with a magisterial reproof:

> Mr Zöllner is without question a man of talent and knowledge, who did most promising work before he fell into metaphysics, and even now shows acuteness and the faculty of invention whenever he is limited to the field of the actual, e.g. in the construction of optical instruments and the devising of optical methods.[14]

The British response was comparatively mild. An anonymous reviewer in *Nature* adopted a strategy of apparent good humour, describing the book as 'a work of exceptionally high merit as a mere literary composition', and referring to its 'hundreds of racy passages' and 'numberless sources of amusement'.[15] He explained that the work dealt not only with the nature of comets, but also with many other subjects, including 'the inferiority of British to German physicists, and the grave offence of which a German is guilty when he sees anything to admire except at home'.[16]

According to his own account, Zöllner returned to Leipzig after the Easter vacation in 1872 to find that *Über die Natur der Cometen* had become a subject of contention.[17] His disregard for the conventions of academic debate had gained him many enemies. He soon realized that he had mortally offended the most powerful men in German science – Hermann von Helmholtz and Emil du Bois-Reymond. Rumours of Zöllner's committal to a mental institution were circulating in Leipzig, and he was soon convinced that their source lay in the Berlin scientific establishment which he had attacked. By now, the first printing of the book had been completely sold out; Zöllner issued a second edition, containing an appendix in which he defended himself against the charge of behaving badly towards his scientific colleagues. However, the controversial passages in the text were left unaltered, and the unrepentant tone of Zöllner's explanatory remarks merely gave further offence.

It is at this point that Nietzsche enters the picture. One may wonder whether Nietzsche had encountered Zöllner during his time as a student in Leipzig. It appears that he did not, or at least there is no evidence that he had ever set eyes on Zöllner – apparently a striking enough figure to be readily remembered. But, then, Zöllner was not widely known during those years. By the time the furore over his book broke out, Nietzsche had left to become professor of classical philology in Basel. In November 1872 Nietzsche wrote to his friend Erwin Rohde, who had taken up a similar post in Kiel:

> Have you heard of the Zöllner scandal in Leipzig? Have a look at his book on the nature of comets; there is an amazing amount *for us* in it. This honourable man has, since this deed, been as much as excommunicated in the basest way in the republic of learning, his closest friends dissociate themselves from him and he is everywhere decried as 'crazy'! That is the spirit of the Leipzig scholarly ochlocracy![18]

Clearly Nietzsche was strongly in sympathy with Zöllner, whose book he had recently borrowed from the Basel University library.[19] As his letter indicates, one reason was a belief that Zöllner had been treated unjustly by his university colleagues. Nietzsche had his own reason for sensitivity on this score, since he was fighting for his own scholarly reputation after criticism of *The Birth of Tragedy*. There were closer parallels as well: both men were able to identify their opponents as belonging to Berlin academic circles – in Nietzsche's case, Ulrich von Wilamowitz-Möllendorff, in Zöllner's, Hermann von Helmholtz and Emil du Bois-Reymond. Both could have felt that their university positions were under threat: five years earlier, Eugen Dühring had been deprived of his right to teach at the University of Berlin on account of his personal attacks on colleagues.[20] Admittedly, Dühring had only been a *Privatdozent*, but there was still some worry over the long arm of Berlin. Nietzsche did, however, have active allies in Richard Wagner and Erwin Rohde, both of whom came to his defence in published replies to Wilamowitz.[21] In contrast, Zöllner was on his own.

Anni Anders suggests that Nietzsche may have felt that Zöllner was trying to do for natural science what his own efforts aimed at for the humanities.[22] Earlier in 1872 he had delivered a series of lectures on 'The Future of Our Educational Institutions', calling for a reform of the university in accordance with genuine principles of scholarship. Unlike Zöllner, Nietzsche prudently ensured that criticism of his colleagues was kept general and impersonal. Still, there are noticeable overlaps between their attitudes. For instance, Nietzsche's criticism of vocational education resembles Zöllner's attack on the 'scientific proletariat'. Nietzsche's insistence on a revival of the 'genuine German spirit' and rejection of cosmopolitan culture finds an answering note in Zöllner's highly patriotic tone. More importantly, Nietzsche does seem to have regarded Zöllner's views on scientific methodology as similar to his own on related matters. In his *Untimely Meditations* he referred approvingly to Zöllner's condemnation of 'the senseless excess of experimentation' in modern science.[23] This theme is one that continues in *Thus Spake Zarathustra*, where the figure of the 'leech-gather' is held up for ridicule as an example of excessive dedication to the gathering of trivial facts.[24] Nietzsche's notebook entries show that he wanted to apply Zöllner's claim to his own discipline. 'It is the same in philology,' he noted.[25] And, again, 'What Zöllner complains about, the unending experimentation and the lack of logical-deductive force, is just as much to be seen in the historical disciplines'.[26]

The other theme that Nietzsche picked out of Zöllner's book for repeated mention in his notebooks was the notion of *unconscious inference* as a component of human perception of the external world. He was critical of this expression as biased towards thought rather than imagery. Nietzsche was sympathetic to the claim that hidden mental processes are present in human knowledge, but suggested that instead of being logical operations, these might better be seen in terms of tropes such as metaphor and metonymy.[27] This idea was developed at greater length in an unpublished essay of 1873 entitled 'On Truth and Lies in an Extra-Moral Sense'.[28] There Nietzsche describes truth as 'a mobile army of metaphors, metonyms, and anthropomorphisms', suggesting a historical dimension which is missing from Zöllner's account of unconscious reasoning: 'Truths are illusions about which one has forgotten that this is what they are; metaphors which are worn out and without sensual power; coins which have lost their pictures and now matter only as metal, no longer as coins.' The idea that familiar concepts have a hidden background, a long history which is also an unconscious presence, remained a central theme for Nietzsche throughout his writing career.

Before long Nietzsche found an opportunity to make a public declaration of his support for Zöllner. In the first issue of the Leipzig periodical *Im neuen Reich* for 1873, he read a leading article by the editor Alfred Dove, a professor of history at the University of Breslau, entitled 'A New Year's

Word to the German Intellectuals'. In reviewing the German intellectual scene during the previous year, Dove remarked with apparent approval on two controversial books which had appeared in 1872. One of these was *Über die Natur der Cometen*. Dove reported that 'the notable physicist Zöllner' had delivered an earnest summons to his colleagues in science, calling them to reflection and a return to the older simplicity of their ways. He described *Über die Natur der Cometen* as 'a truly amazing book'.[29] But Dove went on to mention another book, Theodor Puschmann's *Richard Wagner: Eine psychiatrische Studie*. In this short work, Dove said, Puschmann had 'sought in brief to demonstrate practically and analyse theoretically Richard Wagner's megalomania'. He concluded that both books, although they might be offensive to some readers, were valuable as powerful warnings and likely to have useful effects.

Infuriated by Dove's praise of an anti-Wagnerian book, Nietzsche immediately prepared a public reply in the form of a letter to the editor of the *Musikalisches Wochenblatt*, the Wagnerian periodical published by Ernst Wilhelm Fritzsch, whom Wagner had persuaded to accept *The Birth of Tragedy*.[30] Nietzsche began by protesting against the linking of 'the noble name of Zöllner' with the far from noble name of Puschmann, and went on to abuse both Puschmann and Dove as guilty of scandalous behaviour.[31] The style of polemic is not very worthy of Nietzsche, or of anyone else: as an outburst of only partially coherent sarcasm, it is possibly the worst piece of writing that Nietzsche ever published. His main rhetorical thrust is that Dove's praise of Puschmann is an indictment of the readers of *Im neuen Reich*. Puschmann's book appeals to a public which has a 'mania for scandal'; the question whether that might also be the case for Zöllner's book is not raised. Much of the letter is a series of fierce questions which Nietzsche says 'are not intended to be rhetorical'. Why, Nietzsche asks, did Dove feel the need to seize upon and shake the hand of Puschmann? What pressure was exerted on him? Dove and Puschmann, he asserts, are plainly comrades and brothers and cater to 'unnatural tastes'.

Nietzsche was well satisfied with his letter; in writing again to Rohde he described it, accurately, as 'a furious attack on Alfred Dove'.[32] The extent of his newly acquired taste for public polemic became evident in his next published work, the first of the *Untimely Meditations*, in which David Friedrich Strauss is pursued up hill and down dale with a similar mixture of elaborate sarcasm and pious high-mindedness. One should bear in mind that the manner is the conventional one of the time; it is not too different from that of Zöllner himself.[33] In his next 'untimely meditation', *On the Uses and Disadvantages of History for Life*, Nietzsche repeated the performance with regard to Eduard von Hartmann.[34] To his credit, it must be acknowledged that Nietzsche soon tired of, or outgrew, this genre in its narrow form.[35] His later polemics against Wagner are quite different in kind and, for that reason alone, of greater interest. There, for the time being, Nietzsche's involvement with Zöllner rested. It was not for another ten years that it revived, and in a very different context. In the meantime much had happened, with both Zöllner and Nietzsche.

Here I break off a chronological account to look at the passage in Zöllner's book which probably constitutes its one claim to scientific significance. Zöllner was one of the first scientists to make use of the Riemannian concept of a finite but unbounded space, and to suggest that real space could be understood as Riemannian. The argument which supports this view is developed in a chapter entitled 'On the Finitude of Matter in Infinite Space'.[36] Zöllner begins with a discussion of matter as presented in Newtonian physics. He points out that a finite mass of vapour or gas cannot have a stable form within an unbounded space. If we take vaporization to be a universal property of matter above zero temperature, then even the greatest masses must disperse over the course of time. Yet experience tells us that no such universal dispersal has occurred in the world as we know it, and that more or less dense concentrations of matter are present. Zöllner now states his argument in terms of four assumptions:

1 The quantity of matter constituting the world is a finite one.
2 The space in which this matter is located is unbounded Euclidean space.
3 The time during which matter is located in this space is infinitely great.
4 Matter possesses, as well as the usual general properties, that of vaporising at every temperature above absolute zero.[37]

He sets out the reasons supporting the truth of the first premise: if matter were infinite in quantity, the *pressure* upon each place occupied by matter would be infinite. But since it is an empirical fact that this is not the case, we must conclude that the totality of matter is finite. What about the other assumptions? To imagine a boundary for Euclidean space or for time is to make an ad hoc decision which merely raises further questions about the origin of this boundary. Zöllner's objection is epistemological; the laws of the understanding, as expressed in the principle of sufficient reason, are inconsistent with any such assertion. As for the fourth premise, this has been shown in an earlier section of the book to follow from standard assumptions about the properties of matter.

Yet the properties of space, Zöllner argues, are empirical in nature. Whether space is Euclidean remains an open question, even though its boundedness has been rejected. Recent geometers such as Gauss and Riemann have explored the possibility of non-Euclidean geometries. Zöllner quotes Riemann as saying that:

> The unboundedness of space possesses a greater empirical certainty than any other external experience. But the infinitude of space in no way follows from this, rather, if one assumes independence of bodies from place, and thus attributes a constant curvature to space, then space is necessarily finite, as long as this curvature has any positive value, however small.[38]

In Zöllner's view this passage provides the solution to the cosmological problem. Riemannian space, he insists, is no harder to grasp than Euclidean space, at least from the conceptual point of view.[39] For once, Zöllner is prepared to relax his preference for invoking laws of the understanding to solve scientific problems, and to leave the choice to empirical considerations. He concludes by drawing out some consequences of the Riemannian model:

> In such a space, the parts of a finite quantity of matter, moving apart with a finite speed, could never reach infinitely distant points. After finite intervals of time, whose magnitude would depend on the speed of the motion and on the curvature of space, they would converge again, and in this way transform kinetic energy into potential energy by convergence and divergence, as periodic as a pendulum.[40]

Later he says that we must attribute 'a certain dynamic property' to a Riemannian space: 'For in such a space a moving body, left to itself, would describe a curved line returning into itself, rather than a straight line.'[41] One could comment that this statement involves a naive use of the terms 'curved' and 'straight': it is characteristic of Riemannian space that 'straightest' lines do return into themselves. Zöllner is still thinking in terms of a Euclidean model of space in describing such lines as 'curved'. As a consequence, he supposes that Newton's first law of motion would not hold true in a curved space; this is wrong, at least for a space whose curvature is constant.

The cosmological problem that exercises Zöllner in this chapter is one that Nietzsche was deeply interested in – the problem of a final state. Usually this was raised as a question arising from the second law of thermodynamics, and the consequence drawn from it by William Thomson, that the universe would eventually reach a standstill of force. Zöllner's version of the final state problem is not quite that of Thomson and others such as Helmholtz, who posed the problem of a thermal equilibrium as an implication of the second law of thermodynamics. It has some affinities with Olbers' paradox, which suggests that the darkness of the night sky is inconsistent with an infinite universe.[42] One could even compare it with Einstein's 1919 paper 'Cosmological Considerations on the General Theory of Relativity', which argued for a finite but unbounded space as the only alternative to insoluble problems concerning the density of matter at infinity.[43]

Nietzsche explored aspects of these problems in a number of notebook entries, sometimes mentioning the problem posed by Zöllner. In a note of 1882 he writes: 'Only with the false assumption of an infinite space, in which force evaporates, so to speak, is the final state an unproductive dead one.'[44] This formulation is clearly borrowed from *Über die Natur der Cometen*. Various other passages link the impossibility of a final state with the question of the shape of space: 'That a state of equilibrium has never been reached proves that it is not possible. But in an indeterminate space it must have been reached. Similarly in a spherical space. The *shape* of space must be the cause of eternal motion, and ultimately of all "incompleteness".'[45] However, we also find Nietzsche denying the possibility of *empty* space.[46] This is a consequence of his preference for a dynamic physical theory, in which 'centres of force' replace the solid particles of traditional atomism. On this view, space is entirely occupied by interacting fields of force, so that the problematical concept of action at a distance can be discarded from scientific thinking. Here

Nietzsche is, in effect, supporting a *relational* concept of space. While that is consistent with the idea of space as finite and closed, it is not a theme one can find in Zöllner, who believes in action at a distance, and whose sympathy for a conception of *absolute* space comes out explicitly in his later writings. So while some influence of Zöllner can be found in Nietzsche's views on space, it is mixed with quite different standpoints.

Transcendental Physics and the Fourth Dimension

In 1877 Zöllner developed a new interest, one which was soon to make his name known far beyond the academic circles within which the controversy over *Über die Natur der Cometen* had occurred. He became a convinced spiritualist, and for the next few years was extremely active in sponsoring séances conducted in Leipzig by some of the leading mediums of the day. By this time, the vogue for spiritualism was on the wane, and embarrassing exposures of fraud had damaged the reputation of several of the movement's leading figures. Zöllner, however, was quickly and permanently convinced of the reality of the spirit world and added his own theoretical contribution to spiritualism by arguing that spirit manifestations were to be explained as interventions from a fourth dimension of space. The idea of a fourth dimension was not entirely new, and had been used for other purposes.[47] Because of Zöllner, however, its association with spiritualism quickly became widely known and discussed.

Zöllner's experiments with spiritualism were designed to demonstrate the reality of the fourth dimension, and he claimed that he had succeeded, although he was never able to convince the scientific community. His first medium was the American Henry Slade, usually referred to as 'Doctor' Slade, although his claim to this title was doubtful, to say the least. Slade's successful career in Britain had been interrupted by legal proceedings taken out against him by Professor Ray Lankester, professor of zoology at London University and a militant opponent of spiritualism. Slade was convicted in the Bow Street Magistrates' Court under a vagrancy act, and sentenced to three months' imprisonment with hard labour. He was freed on bail while the sentence was appealed. Although his appeal was successful, on the grounds that the act's wording had been wrongly entered into the court record, Slade heard that a new charge was in preparation and decided to shift his activities to Europe. After travelling through several countries, he arrived in Leipzig on 15 November 1877 and was introduced to Zöllner by some friends. Zöllner was sufficiently impressed by Slade to arrange a séance at his residence on the following evening, and invited a number of senior colleagues from the university to attend. All were convinced by what they saw, and Zöllner arranged a second session two days later, this time including as a participant the philosopher Wilhelm Wundt – an invitation he may have later regretted. After repeating his performance, Slade left for Berlin, but returned in December for a more systematic series of experiments which continued into 1878.

In his published report on the proceedings, Zöllner reported that Slade had produced a number of varied manifestations of spirit activity, including writing on slates, impressions of hands and feet, flying objects, a broken wooden bed-screen, tying knots in an endless cord and, at one point, a personal encounter between Zöllner and a visiting spirit. A materialized hand had appeared and rung a hand bell. Zöllner seized the opportunity, as he later wrote:

> I hereupon expressed the wish to be allowed to hold that hand once firmly in my own. I had scarcely said this when the hand appeared once again out of the opening, and while I now covered and held fast both of Slade's hands with the palm of my left hand, I seized the hand protruding from the opening with my right hand, and with a hearty laugh thus shook hands with a friend from the other world. It had a fully living warmth, and returned my grasp so heartily that, thinking of certain experiences with my learned 'friends' in this world, I felt the greatest desire to let myself be led by that hand into the fourth dimension, in the hope of encountering more honesty and love of truth amongst the intelligent beings in *that* world than here.[48]

After this experience, Zöllner was fully convinced of the reality of the fourth dimension. He set about publicizing his discoveries, as well as organizing further experiments to which he invited his university colleagues. He was disappointed to find that those who attended these sessions were not always convinced. Wilhelm Wundt was a case in point; on finding his name associated with the experiments, he issued a public repudiation, which in turn led to new controversy.[49] Zöllner published a full report on his dealings with Slade in his collected papers, which appeared in four volumes – two in 1878 and the third and fourth in 1879 and 1881. The third volume, devoted to spiritualism, was also published under the title *Transcendental Physics*. An English translation of sections of this work soon appeared in both British and American editions, and has been reprinted in recent years to satisfy a renewed interest in spiritualism.[50]

The key concept in this book is the idea of a fourth dimension of space. Zöllner saw the reality of such an 'absolute' space as demonstrated by spiritualist phenomena. The spirits appearing in séances were visitors from another dimension, and what participants observed was merely an aspect of a higher reality, like the shadows in Plato's 'cave' allegory. Now, one important property of a space of four rather than three dimensions concerns the theme of *symmetry*. Kant's famous example of left- and right-handed gloves serves to illustrate the point at issue. Kant observes that there are no differences 'that the understanding could think' between them, and yet a glove made for one hand will not fit the other hand.[51] Later writers such as the mathematician A.F. Möbius pointed out that a left-handed glove *could* be turned into a right-handed one by means of rotation in a space of four dimensions – if such a thing were possible. Zöllner believed that such operations were not only possible, but could be achieved by a medium such as Slade. Accordingly, he designed a series of experiments which were carried out with what was claimed as almost complete success. Closed and sealed knots were transformed into their mirror images. Although Slade failed to achieve similar results with snail-shells, Zöllner reported that the snail-shells did at least pass through a solid table, thus demonstrating an interpenetration of matter by means of motion in a fourth dimension. These and other feats, such as the linking of solid wooden rings to a table leg with a larger base, were taken by Zöllner as a scientific demonstration of the reality of a fourth dimension.

Even before these experiments, Zöllner had found a reason to postulate another dimension of space, using a purely epistemological argument.[52] He begins by suggesting that our notion of space develops progressively in order to provide explanations for phenomena encountered in experience. Its only *a priori* element is, in fact, the law of causality; everything else is empirical. Even the idea of a third dimension first arose, Zöllner argues, to account for various phenomena which would otherwise have remained puzzling. We explain why things often change in their apparent size and shape, or seem to disappear temporarily, by postulating that they move about within a three-dimensional space and present varying appearances to observers in accordance with laws of perspective. Again, a third dimension enables changes in intensive magnitudes to be explained in terms of changes in extensive magnitudes, as when the fading of a light is attributed to its increasing distance from the observer. However, the phenomenon which Zöllner considers most instructive is that of symmetry. The problem he identifies here is that phenomena which are identical for conceptual thinking are not identical for intuition, so that the process of explanation remains incomplete. However, there is a solution: the symmetry of two-dimensional objects is explained by a third dimension, which enables them to be interpreted as different orientations of the same object, and as mutually interchangeable through a process of rotation within three-dimensional space.

The same question concerning symmetry arises for three-dimensional objects, as in the case of left- and right-handed gloves. The fourth dimension solves this problem (assuming it is a problem) in an analogous way. As Möbius pointed out, rotation in a four-dimensional space allows such objects to be brought into similarity with each other. Thus, Zöllner concludes, if three-dimensional objects are to satisfy the requirements of knowledge, there must be a fourth dimension of space, so that they can be understood as partial views of four-dimensional objects. Hence, our present intuition of space as having three dimensions must be regarded as a merely provisional one, likely to be overtaken by a further development. Now, one objection to Zöllner's epistemological argument is that an analogous problem must arise for four-dimensional objects. If asymmetry occurs there, the demand for an intuitive correlate to every conceptual identity would presumably force us to resort to a fifth dimension of space, and so on to an infinity of dimensions. Zöllner is aware of this point, and answers it by emphasizing that the existence of symmetrical objects cannot simply be assumed, but must be verified in experience.[53] Yet, since he gives no reason for supposing that asymmetry would be any less present in a four-dimensional realm of objects than in a three- or two-dimensional realm, the objection seems quite a strong one.

One could well argue that the idea of a fourth dimension represents a kind of regression in Zöllner's thinking about space, for he suggests that the hypothesis of four-dimensional space enables us to understand how there can be several infinite three-dimensional spaces, and adds that we ourselves are located in one of these infinite spaces.

> The idea of the *juxtaposition* of different, infinitely extended regions of space (*Raumgebiete*) necessarily presupposes the idea of the next higher region of space. Thus, a two-dimensional being would certainly be able to perceive any number of parallel, infinite straight lines, i.e. infinitely extended one-dimensional regions of space; but it would it only be able to imagine *in a single way* the infinite plane in which it moves, as we with our bodies move in an infinitely extended three-dimensional space, whereas we as three-dimensional beings know that there can be any number of infinitely extended parallel planes which can be juxtaposed in a perpendicular direction (i.e. in the third dimension).[54]

This is hardly consistent with his earlier advocacy of a finite and closed three-dimensional space. Nowhere does Zöllner argue for a fourth dimension on the basis of his earlier hypothesis of a curved three-dimensional space. Such an argument would, in any case, have been invalid. It is often supposed that curved three-dimensional space and a fourth dimension go together, but this is a straightforward error.[55] A believer in a fourth dimension has no need to regard either three- or four-dimensional space as finite in extent, as Zöllner's own opinion shows. More difficult to appreciate is the fact that a curved space does not of itself imply a fourth dimension. The method commonly used to make Riemannian space more accessible takes the surface of a sphere as a simplified model – that is, a finite but unbounded two-dimensional surface within three-dimensional Euclidean space. This is a useful approach, but it has one drawback. It often happens in science that a model is confused with what it represents, so that its further features are carried over into the resulting idea of reality. When this occurs in regard to the third dimension within the spherical model, it leads to the false assumption that a closed three-dimensional space must be located within a four-dimensional space. However, it does not appear that Zöllner was guilty of this line of thought.

Did the idea of a fourth dimension have any influence on Nietzsche? It is true that in one 1884 notebook we can find Nietzsche mentioning four dimensions of space. In expressing his view that what we take to be *a priori* truths are really only conditions of our own existence, he writes: 'Therefore other beings could make other basic assumptions, e.g. 4 dimensions.'[56] Earlier in the same note, there is a reference to Zöllner: his opposition to vivisection, Nietzsche suggests, is one of several signs that 'he does not belong to us'. Is this coincidence, or did Nietzsche have Zöllner in mind in speculating on the possibility of an experience of four dimensions? Perhaps he did. But this may be a false trail, for there is another possible source for the remark. A similar speculation is found in an author whose influence on

Nietzsche was greater and longer-lasting, F.A. Lange. In his *History of Materialism* Lange offers an epistemology in which the forms of knowledge are identified as structures of our human constitution.[57] As an illustration he offers our idea of space, and suggests that 'in the same way beings are also conceivable with spatial intuitions of more than three dimensions, although we cannot possibly represent anything of the kind to ourselves'.[58] Lange's general outlook appealed to Nietzsche, so it is not surprising that he used the same example in making the same general point. This seems to be confirmed by a nearby note which indicates clearly that Nietzsche had been reading the revised edition of Lange's book.[59]

Zöllner continued his experiments in 1879 and 1880 with other spiritualist figures passing through Germany, such as Carl Hansen, a Danish practitioner of animal magnetism, and two other mediums, Elizabeth d'Espérance and William Eglinton. Unfortunately, Zöllner's sudden death in April 1882 prevented him from reporting on these last experiments. In his last few years, he had put all his considerable energies into waging campaigns on an astonishing number of fronts. He produced four large volumes of collected papers, one of which is in two parts, as well as a series of polemical works dealing with subjects such as vivisection, social democracy and Bismarck's *Kulturkampf* against the Catholic Church.[60] His targets became more numerous and his attacks more unbalanced. Most noticeable was his involvement in the anti-Semitic movement, which became a preoccupation in 1880. Zöllner had become involved in undignified wrangles with members of the Leipzig student philosophy society over his spiritualist activities. He came to suspect that some Jewish students had supplied information about him to the foreign press for use in anti-spiritualist articles.[61] After issuing defamatory statements about these individuals, Zöllner set to work on a full-length book, attacking the Jewish influence in German universities.

At about this time, another incident which provides an indirect link to Nietzsche occurred. Zöllner heard of the anti-Semitic petition, addressed to Bismarck, being circulated around Germany by a Berlin teacher, Bernhard Förster. One of its most ardent supporters was Nietzsche's sister Elisabeth, who went even further a few years later by marrying Förster and emigrating with him to South America. It appears that Zöllner had the unusual distinction of being the only German professor to sign this petition.[62] His unfinished book extends to 747 pages, consisting of the usual attacks on enemies old and new, along with biographies of eminent German figures. Apparently Zöllner was just getting into his stride when a fatal stroke removed him from the fray. Even then, he was pursued by controversy, with rumours going round that he had taken his own life in an onset of madness. His biographer Moritz Wirth assures us that these are without foundation. Zöllner's deep religious convictions, his proven high ethical sense and devotion to his scientific work would have ruled out suicide.[63] As for the perennial charge of insanity, Wirth rebuts this by reporting that Zöllner was talking of resuming his work in astrophysics at the time of his death.[64] By this time, Zöllner had become something of an embarrassment to the spiritualist movement, and its regret at losing a prominent champion may have been mixed with a certain relief.

Nietzsche as Spiritualist?

We come now to an incident in Nietzsche's life which his biographers have only mentioned in passing – his attendance at a séance conducted in Leipzig in October 1882. The evidence suggests that the medium was the same Elizabeth d'Espérance who had been successful there a few years earlier. Before looking into this episode, then, we should find out something about this mysterious figure.

Despite her French name and title, Madame d'Espérance was born and raised in the East End of London. Her real name was Elizabeth Hope.[65] In her autobiography, entitled *Shadow Land or Light From the Other Side*, she describes her early experiences as a 'sensitive' child, given to visions of 'shadow friends'.[66] Introduced to a spiritualist circle as an adult, she soon emerged as a medium, beginning with clairvoyance and automatic writing and going on to more dramatic accomplishments. One later writer has described Madame d'Espérance as 'better known for her looks than for her phenomena'.[67] This is an unfair comment, since she practised the most spectacular form of spiritualism, materialization, in which the visiting spirit takes on material form and may be seen, heard and touched by participants, while the medium is in a trance and remains seated inside a separate closet. The spirit guides who appeared in person during her séances included a Spanish child, an Arab girl, an Egyptian priestess and various other personages. Sometimes ferns and roses were materialized on request, and even large flowering plants not ordinarily grown in Europe. Later in her career Madame d'Espérance engaged in experiments which aimed at taking photographs of materialized spirits, with results that can be seen in her autobiographical volume. Clearly the possibility of exposure as a fraud is a real one under these circumstances. Many practitioners of materialization were accused of impersonating visiting spirits, and Madame d'Espérance was no exception; she records several painful experiences at the hands of sitters attempting to seize hold of the materialized spirit. Her earnest and sincere account of her life is remarkable for its candid expression of confusion over these incidents, and of a persistent uneasiness over the reality of the visiting spirits. Often she had the feeling that they were expressions of her own 'subliminal consciousness', acting independently of her will.[68] At length she came to the conclusion that the materializations were genuine, yet only an imperfect representation of the spiritual reality.[69]

Why did Nietzsche take an interest in spiritualism at this stage in his life, and what was his attitude towards participating in a séance? The answer is to be found in his relationship with Lou Salomé. The interest in spiritualism was hers, and Nietzsche wanted them to go together to a séance, for reasons more closely linked with her than with spiritualism itself. Nietzsche had met Lou in Italy in April 1882 and developed an immediate friendship with her, complicated by the presence of their common friend Paul Rée. In July Lou travelled with Elisabeth Nietzsche to the Bayreuth Festival, where the first performances of *Parsifal* took place. Among the Wagner circle were a number of spiritualists, and Lou found that she had not only an interest but also, as she claimed, a certain talent in spiritual phenomena. In August she spent several weeks with Nietzsche and his sister at Tautenberg, a village not far from Jena. There she and Nietzsche had long philosophical discussions and confirmed what seemed to be a close affinity – one that, on Nietzsche's side at least, had also become an intense emotional attachment. On 14 August Lou wrote in her diary, 'To the horror of Elisabeth (who incidentally is hardly ever with us) my room is immediately visited by "ghostly knocks" when Nietzsche enters, much to our amusement. We must have even this cursed ability in common.'[70] Shortly after, the stay in Tautenberg came to an end. Lou went off to visit Rée's family in West Prussia, while Nietzsche established himself in Leipzig, waiting for their joint return on 2 October. Meanwhile, he arranged to attend the séance, and used his notebook to sketch out his own ideas on the subject.

> Towards an explanation of so-called 'spiritualistic phenomena'. Part of the intellectual functions of the medium occur without his knowledge: here his state is hypnotic (separation of a waking and sleeping intellect). The nervous force concentrates on this unconscious part. – There must be an electrical current taking place between the persons whose hands are linked, towards the medium, by which the *thoughts* of each person are transmitted to the medium. Such a current of thoughts is no more amazing than the current from the head to the feet, in the case of stumbling, within a single person. The questions are answered by the intellects of the persons participating; and in the process memory often succeeds in producing something that *ordinarily* appears to be forgotten. Result of nervous emotion. – There is no forgetting. – Even unconscious fraud is possible: I mean that a fraudulent medium operates with all sort of fraudulent manipulations, without knowing it: his kind of morality expresses itself instinctively in these actions. – Ultimately it is *always* like this with all our actions. What is essential occurs unconscious to us, and the rogue is unconsciously a hundred times more a rogue, and more often, than he is conscious of.[71]

Nietzsche's speculations on a natural explanation for spiritualistic phenomena are of some interest in their own right, and on the same track as other scientific approaches. While his notion of an electrical current passing around the circle of participants is mere speculation, his ideas about unconscious mental processes represent a theory which has become quite familiar.[72] Most modern commentators suggest that a dissociation of personality provides an explanation of the phenomenon of materialization which is consistent with the sincerity of the medium. Such a theory seems particularly appropriate in the case of Madame d'Espérance, given her description of her own confusion over the distinct identities of her spirit guides.

Nietzsche arranged to attend at the séance on the evening of Lou's arrival. Earlier on that day, he wrote to his friend Heinrich Köselitz in high anticipation, explaining that the séance promised to be an important event, with materialized spirits due to appear in person, including 'the Russian nun' and 'the child'. What was more, he said, 'there are six people who are looking forward in excitement to what I will say about it'.[73]

So, what happened when the lights went out? We do not know exactly, but the next day Nietzsche wrote again to Köselitz:

> My dear friend, spiritualism is a miserable swindle, which gets boring after the first half hour. And this Professor Zöllner let himself be fooled by *this* medium! Not another word about it! I expected something different and was set up in advance with three fine physiological–psychological–moral theories – but I didn't *need* my theories at all![74]

Köselitz, who shared Nietzsche's sceptical attitudes, replied in a told-you-so vein: 'That people have tried to involve you too in spiritualism amused me greatly; I said to myself in advance that you would find it repulsive.'[75] Zöllner, he went on to remark, had been generally regarded as 'not in his right mind' in later years. Köselitz was clearly not aware of the context which made this incident important for Nietzsche. It had been an opportunity to demonstrate to Lou Salomé his superior abilities as a psychologist, thereby gaining a decisive advantage in his intense, if not openly acknowledged, rivalry with Paul Rée for her allegiance. But Nietzsche's prepared theories had been made superfluous by the failure of the medium to give a performance with enough *prima facie* plausibility to require a psychological explanation. The disappointment was a bad start to the period in Leipzig, and the next few weeks did not improve matters as the comradeship of Tautenberg failed to reappear. When Nietzsche parted from Lou at the railway station on 5 November, it was for the last time. Before long, the violent hostility of his sister Elisabeth towards Lou had led to a complete estrangement, from whose painful effects Nietzsche recovered only gradually, as he turned to the writing of his next work, *Thus Spake Zarathustra*.

A chance encounter provides an unexpected footnote to these events. At the beginning of 1884, Nietzsche was staying in Nice for the first of the five winters he was to spend there. He had made the acquaintance of Joseph Paneth, a Viennese physician living in nearby Villefranche, and their frequent meetings led to long discussions on a wide range of topics. Paneth made detailed notes on these encounters to send to his fiancée back in Vienna, and these were eventually published. On 15 February, Paneth recorded, the conversation had turned to spiritualism.

> He told me that he had once attended a séance in Leipzig, where the same medium that so deceived Zöllner performed, and everything was obviously the crudest sort of trickery: he had noticed the pronunciation of certain consonants on the part of the medium, and then recognised them again in the speech of the spirit. The medium had presented a child and shown him a hand through a curtain, which he grasped and so convinced himself that it was the hand of an adult ....[76]

The subject of spiritualism may have been on Nietzsche's mind at the time. Just a month earlier, he had finished writing the third part of *Thus Spake Zarathustra*. In one chapter, entitled 'On the Apostates', he had taken the opportunity to settle scores with former friends and allies. The 'apostates' here are those who 'have become pious again'. Zarathustra says that they have formed 'little hidden communities' in which they 'sit together for long evenings'. They are engaged in a kind of hunt, he says; but it is not a daring expedition into the unknown, as with the bold 'searchers and researchers' praised in an earlier chapter. Instead, it is a cautious and prayerful strategy, one that sets mousetraps to catch a 'soulful' prey. Zarathustra goes on to suggest that 'they learn to shudder from a scholarly half-madman who waits in dark rooms for the spirits to come to him – so his spirit will flee completely'. The reference is plainly to Friedrich Zöllner, the leading academic defender of spiritualism in Germany. It seems that Nietzsche now directed the blame for what had happened, or failed to happen, in Leipzig in 1882 on to Zöllner.

I do not want to claim that this chapter has any great importance within *Thus Spake Zarathustra*: no doubt the commentators are justified in passing over it without much explanation. It is interesting to note, however, that many features of Part Four of the work can be linked with 'On the Apostates'. The 'higher men' who figure in its final chapters are closely related to the 'apostates' of Part Three, and they too form a circle in which new forms of religious observance are devised.[77] It may seem strange that spiritualism should be a recurring theme in *Thus Spake Zarathustra*. It does serve as an instance of the phenomena that Nietzsche was keen to identify and attack as lingering versions of traditional religious belief. But just as importantly, it enabled Nietzsche to come to terms with an experience in which his personal hopes had been disappointed. It was for this reason that he turned his anger against the man he had once defended in public as a 'noble' and unjustly criticized figure.

Nietzsche's relation to Zöllner is one of those broken links that figure so much in his development. His stormy relation to Wagner is the most important of these, but the Zöllner case shows a surprisingly similar pattern, beginning with a strong sympathy, along with a characteristic exaggeration of the extent of common interests and a common direction, giving rise to a public declaration of support and leading in due course to disillusionment and denunciation. What is disappointing about the Zöllner case is how little Nietzsche learned from it, in contrast to the Wagner episode, which led him into profound reflections on art and style. For the qualities he had admired in Zöllner's book *Über die Natur der Cometen* were just those which threw doubt on Zöllner's claim to be making a serious contribution to science. Zöllner's distrust of experimentation, and his attempts to answer scientific questions by appealing to epistemological considerations, put him out of touch with the real scientific advances of his time. His criticisms of current attitudes towards scientific research quickly turned into futile exchanges of recriminations. If I am right, however, the changing phases of Nietzsche's engagement with Zöllner were largely driven not by these questions, but by concerns of a far more personal kind.

Notes

1. See Oskar Becker, 'Nietzsches Beweise für seine Lehre von der ewigen Wiederkunft', in Becker, *Dasein und Dawesen: Gesammelte philosophische Aufsätze* (Pfullingen: Verlag Günther Neske, 1963), 46–49; Günter Abel, *Nietzsche: Die Dynamik der Willen zur Macht und die ewige Wiederkehr* (Berlin: de Gruyter, 1984), 397–400; Alistair Moles, 'Nietzsche's Eternal Recurrence as Riemannian Cosmology', *International Studies in Philosophy*, 21 (1989), 21–35; and George J. Stack, 'Riemann's Geometry and Eternal Recurrence as Cosmological Hypothesis: A Reply', ibid., 37–40.
2. See Karl Schlechta and Anni Anders, *Friedrich Nietzsche: Von den verborgenen Anfängen seines Philosophierens* (Stuttgart and Bad Cannstatt: Friedrich Frommann Verlag, 1962), 122–27.
3. J.C.F. Zöllner, *Zür Aufklärung des deutschen Volkes über Inhalt und Aufgabe der wissenschaftlichen Abhandlungen von Friedrich Zöllner* (Leipzig: Commissionsverlag von L. Staackmann, 1880), 148–49. Further biographical details are given in Zöllner, *Wissenschaftliche Abhandlungen*, Band IV (Leipzig: Commissionsverlag von L. Staackmann, 1881).
4. See Fanny Moser, *Der Okkultismus: Täuschungen und Tatsachen* (München: Verlag von Ernst Reinhardt, 1935), Band 1, Tafel 4.
5. J.C.F. Zöllner, *Über die Natur der Cometen. Beiträge zur Geschichte und Theorie der Erkenntnis*, 2nd edn (Leipzig: Verlag von Wilhelm Engelmann, 1872). The title is often cited as *Über die Natur der Kometen*.
6. Ibid., VIII.
7. Ibid., XXIII.
8. Ibid., XXIX.
9. William Thomson and P.G. Tait, *Treatise on Natural Philosophy*, sect. 385. This passage was omitted in the second English edition of 1879. For the German version, see William Thomson and P.G. Tait, *Handbuch der theoretischen Physik*, trans. H. von Helmholtz and G. Wertheim (Braunschweig: Druck und Verlag von Friedrich Vieweg und Sohn, 1874), sect. 385, 350–51.
10. Zöllner, *Über die Natur der Cometen*, LXII.
11. Ibid., 345–50.
12. Ibid., LXIX.
13. Ibid., LXX.
14. 'Helmholtz on the Use and Abuse of the Deductive Method in Physical Science', *Nature*, 14 January 1875, 212. This is a translation of Helmholtz's Vorrede to the second German edition of Thomson and Tait, *Handbuch der theoretischen Physik*, V–XIV.
15. *Nature*, 14 July 1872, 177. The British world of science was preoccupied with other things at the time, such as the news of David Livingstone brought back from Africa by Henry M. Stanley, and a dispute over the management of Kew Gardens; thus, Zöllner's work did not attract much attention. However, Zöllner took note of the review and quoted it in later books, hinting darkly that coaching from a German source could be detected in the author's apparent familiarity with German literature: Zöllner, *Wissenschaftliche Abhandlungen* (Leipzig: Commissionsverlag von L. Staackmann, 1878–81), Band IV, 794.
16. Six years later, P.G. Tait was less tolerant when reviewing the first volume of Zöllner's *Wissenschaftliche Abhandlungen* in *Nature*, 28 March 1878, 420–22.
17. Zöllner, *Zur Aufklärung des deutschen Volkes*, 72–73.
18. KGB II/3, 86. Rohde, in reply, was puzzled: 'What is this about Zöllner? Write me something clearer': KGB II/4, 127.
19. He borrowed it in November 1872, in March and October 1873, and in April 1874; and he later bought his own copy of the second edition.
20. Zöllner considered that Dühring deserved sympathy 'from a purely human standpoint', but was not pleased by his dismissal of the fourth dimension as 'apparent nonsense', 'mystical bizarreness' and 'a bad joke'. See Zöllner, *Beiträge zur Deutschen Judenfrage*

mit academischen Arabesken als Unterlagen zu einer Reform der Deutschen Universitäten (Leipzig: Verlag von Oswald Mutze, 1894), 592–94; and Eugen Dühring, *Cursus der Philosophie* (Leipzig: Erich Koschny, 1875), 67–68. Zöllner regarded the cause of Robert Mayer, discoverer of the law of conservation of energy, as a more serious one, especially since it gave him an opportunity to criticize Helmholtz for mentioning Joule, but not Mayer, in his 1847 essay 'Über die Erhaltung der Kraft', *Beiträge zur Deutschen Judenfrage*, 564–65 and in many other places.

21 See Karlfried Gründer, *Der Streit um Nietzsches 'Geburt der Tragödie'* (Hildesheim: Georg Olms Verlagsbuchhandlung, 1969); William Musgrave Calder III, 'The Wilamowitz–Nietzsche Struggle: New Documents and a Reappraisal', *Nietzsche-Studien*, 12 (1983), 214–54; and Jaap Mansfeld, 'The Wilamowitz–Nietzsche Struggle: Another New Document and Some Further Comments', *Nietzsche-Studien*, 15 (1986).
22 Karl Schlecta and Anni Anders, *Friedrich Nietzsche: Von den verborgenen Anfängen seines Philosophierens* (Stuttgart and Bad Cannstatt: Frederich Frommann Verlag, 1962), 123. Cf. Charles Andler, *Nietzsche, sa vie et sa pensée*, 3rd edn (Paris: Librairie Gallimard, 1958), Vol. 1, 456.
23 Friedrich Nietzsche, *On the Uses and Disadvantages of History for Life*, sect. 6.
24 Friedrich Nietzsche, *Thus Spake Zarathustra*, 'The Leech'.
25 KGW III/4, 39.
26 Ibid., 243. See also the comments on Ranke in ibid., 280.
27 Ibid., 42, 53 and 75.
28 KGW III/2, 369–84.
29 Zöllner was pleased by Dove's remarks, and quoted them at length as evidence of the favourable reception of the book in Germany: *Wissenschaftliche Abhandlungen*, Band II, Zweiter Theil (Leipzig: Commissionsverlag von L. Staackmann, 1878), 959–60, and *Zur Aufklärung des deutschen Volkes*, 152. On the other hand, Dove had by then come out as an opponent of spiritualism, publishing a critique in *Im neuen Reich* to which Zöllner responded with personal attacks; see, for example, Zöllner, *Zur Aufklärung des deutschen Volkes*, 89 and *Beiträge zur Deutschen Judenfrage*, 24.
30 The book had been turned down by Wilhelm Engelmann, publisher of *Über die Natur der Cometen*.
31 KGW III/2, 289–91.
32 KGB II/3, 120.
33 It is also reminiscent of Wagner's defence of *The Birth of Tragedy* in his 'Open Letter' of 1872; see Gründer, *Der Streit um Nietzsches 'Geburt der Tragödie'*, 57–64.
34 Hartmann was one of Zöllner's few allies, sharing his views on matters such as the defects of the English character. Zöllner defends Hartmann against the impression of pessimism given by his writings, pointing out as evidence to the contrary the fact that Hartmann had married not just once but several times; see Zöllner, *Wissenschaftliche Abhandlungen*, Band IV, 766.
35 Nietzsche may have been somewhat embarrassed when his friend Heinrich Köselitz tried his hand at a similar exercise in an article entitled 'Musikalische Philister', also published in the *Musikalisches Wochenblatt* in 1877. See Frederick R. Love, *Nietzsche's Saint Peter: Genesis and Cultivation of an Illusion* (Berlin and New York: de Gruyter, 1981), 13–14. The Köselitz article can be found in Curt Paul Janz, *Friedrich Nietzsche Biographie* (München: Deutscher Taschenbuch Verlag, 1981), Band 3, 246–55.
36 Zöllner, *Über die Natur der Cometen*, 299–312.
37 Ibid., 300.
38 Ibid., 308. The quotation is from Riemann's lecture 'Über die Hypothesen, welche die Geometrie zugrunde liegen', delivered in 1854 but not published until 1867.
39 Arguing against the Kantians who maintained the *a priori* status of Euclidean geometry, Helmholtz insisted that non-Euclidean space could be *imagined*, and not just conceptualized. Others considered this an unnecessary concession; see, for example, Bertrand Russell, *An Essay on the Foundations of Geometry* (New York: Dover Books, 1956), 73.
40 Zöllner, *Über die Natur der Cometen*, 308–9.

41 Ibid., 339.
42 See Stanley L. Jaki, *The Paradox of Olbers' Paradox* (New York: Herder and Herder, 1969); esp. pp. 158–64. A note on Olbers' paradox appears in Nietzsche's notebook of early 1884: 'According to Fr Secchi space cannot be unbounded, because nothing composed of particular bodies can be infinite, and because an infinite firmament populated by innumerable stars would appear as bright as the sun across its entire extent': KGW VII/4/2, 69. The rest of the note has to do with astronomy, including references which Nietzsche used in sect. 196 and 243 of *Beyond Good and Evil*.
43 Albert Einstein, H.A. Lorentz, H. Weyl and H. Minkowski, *The Principle of Relativity* (New York: Dover Publications, 1952), 177–88.
44 KGW VII/1, 11. Cf. Zöllner: 'Thus if one takes vaporisation as a general property of matter above absolute zero, then on the above assumptions even the greatest masses, as long as they are finite, must gradually evaporate in an unbounded empty space to the point of vanishing': *Über die Natur der Cometen*, 92.
45 KGW VII/3, 258 (*The Will to Power*, sect. 1064).
46 KGW VII/2, 250 and 264; also VII/3, 158, 289, and 338–39 (*The Will to Power*, sect. 1064, 618 and 1067).
47 See, for example, H.P. Manning (ed.), *The Fourth Dimension Simply Explained* (New York: Mum and Co., 1910); Alfred M. Bork, 'The Fourth Dimension in Nineteenth-Century Physics', *Isis*, 55 (1964), 326–38; Roland W. Weitzenböck, *Der vierdimensionale Raum* (Basel and Stuttgart: Birkhäuser Verlag, 1956); Linda Dalrymple Henderson, *The Fourth Dimension and Non-Euclidean Geometry in Modern Art* (Princeton, NJ: Princeton University Press, 1983); Rudy v.B. Rucker, *The Fourth Dimension and How to Get There* (Harmondsworth: Penguin Books, 1985).
48 Zöllner, *Wissenschaftliche Abhandlungen*, Band III, 274. A certain naïveté on Zöllner's part can also be seen in his obtaining a notarized declaration from Signor Bellachini, official conjurer to the court in Berlin, to the effect that Slade's performances could not have been achieved by manipulation: ibid., 197.
49 Wilhelm Wundt, *Der Spiritismus. Eine sogennante wissenschaftliche Frage* (Leipzig: Wilhelm Engelmann, 1879). This was a reply to an article by the Halle spiritualist Hermann Ulrici, 'Der sogennante Spiritismus. Eine philosophische Frage', *Zeitschrift für Philosophie und philosophische Kritik* (1878), 239–71. Ulrici responded with *Der sogenannte Spiritismus. Eine wissenschaftliche Frage* (Halle: Pfeffer, 1879), and Zöllner, not content to remain on the sidelines, also replied to Wundt in the third volume of his *Wissenschaftliche Abhandlungen*, giving the debate a more personal turn with his title, 'Der Spiritismus und die sogennanten Philosophen'.
50 J.C.F. Zöllner, *Transcendental Physics* (1888), trans. C.C. Massey, 4th reprint edn (New York: Arno Press, 1976).
51 Immanuel Kant, *Prolegomena to any Future Metaphysics*, trans. Peter G. Lucas (Manchester: Manchester University Press, 1953), 42.
52 J.C.F. Zöllner, *Principien einer elektrodynamischen Theorie der Materie. Erster Band* (Leipzig: Verlag von Wilhelm Engelmann, 1876), LXVIII–LXXXV.
53 Zöllner, *Wissenschaftliche Abhandlungen*, Band I, 246.
54 He goes on to extend the analogy to introducing causal interactions between regions of space:

> All these planes can represent infinitely extended two-dimensional worlds, whose processes in every spatial region are completely separate from those in others. If there were under certain anomalous circumstances a two-dimensional being in one plane causally linked with other two-dimensional beings of other planes, so that this being could create effects in the two-dimensional space of its own plane by movements in the third dimension, this would appear just as miraculous to the beings moving in this plane as the effects in the neighbourhood of Mr Slade appear to us. (*Wissenschaftliche Abhandlungen*, Band II, Erster Theil, 348).

55 A defence of this idea can be found in Hermann Lotze, *Metaphysic*, ed. B. Bosanquet,

56   2nd edn (Oxford: Clarendon Press, 1887), Vol. 1, 293–303. For an effective rebuttal see Russell, *An Essay on the Foundations of Geometry*, 101–8.
56   KGW VII/2, 86.
57   A somewhat similar theory was advanced by Hermann von Helmholtz in his *Handbuch der physiologischen Optik*, which Nietzsche borrowed from the Basel University library in 1873.
58   F.A. Lange, *The History of Materialism and Criticism of its Present Importance*, trans. E.C. Thomas, 3rd edn (London: Routledge and Kegan Paul, 1925), Vol. 3, 227. In a footnote, Lange points out that this sentence appeared in the first edition of his work, published in 1865, and thus preceded the publication of the non-Euclidean speculations of Helmholtz and Riemann.
59   KGW VII/2, 90. For a discussion of Nietzsche's reading of the revised edition of *The History of Materialism*, see Jörg Salaquarda, 'Nietzsche und Lange', *Nietzsche-Studien*, 7 (1978), 240; and G.J. Stack, *Lange and Nietzsche* (Berlin and New York: de Gruyter, 1983), 13.
60   The oddest of these productions is *Das Deutsche Volk und seine Professoren. Eine Sammlung von Citaten ohne Commentar. Zur Aufklärung und Belehrung des deutschen Volkes zusammengestellt von Friedrich Zöllner* (Leipzig: Commissionsverlag von L. Staackmann, 1880), consisting of 86 very diverse items collected by Zöllner from newspapers and other sources.
61   One of these was 'Spiritualism in Germany', *The Nation*, 12 February 1880, 113–14. This article by an American visitor to Leipzig contains some factual errors: Slade had not been imprisoned in London, and Dühring had not been dismissed from a professorial chair in Berlin; but the writer was correct about the history of insanity in Zöllner's family.
62   See Moritz Wirth's introduction in Zöllner, *Beiträge zur Deutschen Judenfrage*, XXII.
63   Ibid., XVI.
64   Worth adding here is Nandor Fodor's answer to the claim that Zöllner was insane: 'As he filled his chair up to the moment of his sudden death, this charge cannot be seriously supported': see Fodor, *Encyclopaedia of Psychic Science* (New York: University Books, 1966), 416.
65   See 'd'Espérance, Mme. Elizabeth', ibid., 83–85.
66   Elizabeth d'Espérance, *Shadow Land or Light From the Other Side* (London: George Redway, 1897).
67   Ronald Pearsall, *The Table-Rappers* (London: Michael Joseph, 1972), 100.
68   d'Espérance, *Shadow Land*, 351. It seems significant here that she reports episodes of sleep-walking in childhood. Ibid., 42.
69   Ibid., 379–81.
70   Ernst Pfeiffer (ed.), *Friedrich Nietzsche Paul Rée Lou von Salomé: Die Dokumente ihrer Begegnung* (Frankfurt-am-Main: Insel Verlag, 1970), 183. This diary was written to be read by Rée, who knew about Lou's interest in spiritualism, and had already been told about the 'ghostly knocks'; see ibid., 177.
71   KGW VII/1, 12–13.
72   Of special interest here is Nietzsche's passing remark that an explanation of these strange mental phenomena might be just applicable to the mental processes we regard as 'normal' and not in need of any such explanation.
73   KGB III/1, 268–69.
74   KGB III/1, 269.
75   KGB III/2, 299.
76   KGW VII/4/2, 22.
77   The similarity extends to the reappearance of earlier expressions, such as *Dunst von Bet-Brüdern* in 'The Ass Festival'.

Chapter 5

Mechanism and Beyond

One of Nietzsche's most common criticisms of modern science is that it displays none of the *esprit* of its ancient counterpart. It is a business, not an adventure. It uses measuring and calculating as routine procedures, not as experimental hypotheses, let alone risky ventures. Accordingly the free spirit is replaced by the scientific worker, and the motive behind scientific research is no longer courage (as asserted by Zarathustra in one of his speeches[1]) but its opposite – fear of the unknown and a flight towards security. The genuine materialist is by nature an iconoclast and a 'free spirit'. Those that Nietzsche singles out by name as models for scientific research are the materialists of ancient Greece. Democritus is his most favoured example, and the subject of many notes and drafted discussions.[2] It is Democritus who stands at the other end of the scale from Plato as a representative of early philosophy. Their antagonism is the 'battle of the giants' described by Plato in his *Sophist*. Neither there nor anywhere else does Plato ever mention Democritus by name; according to one ancient tradition (which Nietzsche seems to accept) this is a sign of the same extreme hostility which led to the suppression of the writings of Democritus by his religious opponents. Yet there is one feature of Platonism which Democritean materialism shares – its scepticism concerning the senses. This is an aspect of Platonism that Nietzsche praises highly: he says that its resistance to the evidence of the senses showed it to be a 'noble' way of thinking.[3] But the same would apply to the statement of Democritus that the qualities of things are all due to convention, and that the only true reality is the atoms and the void within which they exist.

The revival of atomism by Gassendi and Boyle was a return to the doctrines of Democritus and Epicurus, yet it left out not only their resistance to the evidence of the senses, but also their use of imagination. The great poem of Lucretius demonstrates that the atomist account of the world as an eternal rain of corpuscles, with their crossing paths, interactions and vortices, is an image with as much poetic beauty as the most idealistic view of reality. But modern science is nothing if not prosaic in style, and in this respect it matches the philistinism of modern culture, against which Nietzsche aims many attacks. We can already see a tension within these criticisms. Is modern science too trusting in the senses, or is it not sensual (or sensualist) enough? What is Nietzsche's conception of the proper character of science, if it can be put to use in seemingly different ways? The first of these issues, the question of sensualism, will be dealt with later. This chapter will focus on Nietzsche's relation to the research programme I am labelling as 'mechanism'. Here we can find the apparent inconsistency just described, and the broader tension between a hostility which is often expressed in a fairly abusive manner (involving expressions like 'mechanistic doltishness'[4]) and a sympathy which extends into an announced intention to take over and 'complete' the programme of mechanism.

Science as Content and as Method

The starting-point for understanding Nietzsche's attitude is his assertion that what is essential about modern science is not its content but its method. Theories themselves may change from time to time without affecting the unity of their underlying research programme. Nietzsche writes: 'On the whole, scientific methods are at least as important a product of research as any other result: for the scientific spirit is based on insight into method, and if those methods were lost, all the results of science could not prevent a renewed prevalence of superstition and nonsense.'[5] What is this method which has given rise to a scientific outlook dominated by mechanism? In *Beyond Good and Evil*, Nietzsche says that method 'must be essentially economy of principles'.[6] Elsewhere he writes: 'The mechanistic world-explanation is an ideal – to explain, i.e., put into formulae, as much as possible with as little as possible.'[7] There is a certain irony in this remark, because he does not believe that to put something into formulae is to explain it: in fact, that is a point on which he attacks mechanism as it stands. His real point here concerns the definition of mechanism as a thinking which is guided by an ideal – that is, a goal which, although it can never be attained, has a very important function in determining how we see the world. This regulative principle is defined in terms of the *relation* between the conceptual equipment embodied in a scientific theory and the range of phenomena which it encompasses. The best theory is the simplest and most efficient: it is the one which uses as few concepts and principles as possible, and at the same time takes account of as many phenomena as possible.

This view is not a particularly original one: it recalls ideas which go back at least as far as Ockham's razor. It was common enough among Nietzsche's contemporaries. In 1882 Ernst Mach delivered a popular lecture entitled 'The Economic Nature of Physical Inquiry' in which a similar approach was adopted. Natural laws, he explained, were just 'concise, abridged description', valuable in saving us the labour of compiling an indefinitely extensive catalogue of particular cases.

> More than this comprehensive and condensed report about facts is not contained in a natural law of this sort. In reality, the law always contains less than the fact itself, because it does not reproduce the fact as a whole but only in that aspect of it which is important for us, the rest being either intentionally or from necessity omitted.[8]

This can be called an economic tendency, because it reduces the expenditure of thinking to a single mental process. As Mach points out, the use of formulae and equations in modern science is the best example of the condensation of facts into their simplest form.

The economic model of scientific theory was promoted by other representatives of the positivist movement such as Richard Avenarius, whose book *Philosophie als Denken der Welt gemäss dem Princip des kleinsten Kraftmasses* was read by Nietzsche and summarized in several notebook entries.[9] What is different about Nietzsche's version of the economic interpretation is its link with a wider theme in his own philosophy – the doctrine of the will to power. He says:

> This 'will to power' expresses itself in the interpretation, in the manner in which force is used up ... That which constitutes growth in life is an ever more healthy and far-seeing economy, which achieves more and more with less and less force – as an ideal, the principle of the smallest expenditure –.[10]

What makes mechanism an expression of the will to power is not just the fact that it enables us to exert more control over our environment by putting our scientific knowledge to practical use. Our scientific knowledge is already a form of power in its own right, in so far as it is determined by the principle of economy. As Mach pointed out, it is a means for mastering the content of experience as this presents itself in our minds.

But if mechanism as a scientific ideal is determined by the will to power, how is that principle itself to be justified? What is the status of this will to power? In *Beyond Good and Evil*, Nietzsche suggests that the concept is a kind of experiment:

> In the end not only is it permitted to make this experiment; the conscience of *method* demands it. Not to assume several kinds of causality until the experiment of making do with a single one has been pushed to its utmost limit (to the point of nonsense, if I may say so) – that is a moral of method which one may not shirk today – it follows 'from its definition', as a mathematician would say.[11]

The method he is referring to is clearly the principle of economy. The purpose of the doctrine of the will to power is to reduce every causality to a single kind, and as such it is wholly in accord with the reductionist programme which this principle licenses.[12] Yet there is surely a circularity in Nietzsche's argument. The principle of economy is an expression of the will to power, and the theory of the will to power is itself an 'experiment' in accordance with this principle. Is this circularity really a fault, though? One could see it instead as a common feature of naturalistic approaches to epistemology, which claim as a point in their favour the fact that they are able to account for their own principles, rather than leaving them in need of some further kind of explanation.

We can now see why, for Nietzsche, mechanism is not just one scientific approach among others, but the most advanced and successful kind of science. Moreover there can be no way of setting any limit to the scope of mechanism; its tendency must always be to widen the range of phenomena which it tries to explain, because every advance represents a closer approach to its ideal. At the same time, it must always strive to use fewer and simpler concepts, in accordance with the same ideal. This is why mechanism dispenses with many of the concepts used in other kinds of science or, for that matter, in everyday thinking about the world. *Reductionism* is the essential strategy for this scientific programme; it is the key to its successes in the past and its prospects for the future.

The work in which Nietzsche's support for this programme appears most obviously is *Human, All-Too-Human*. In the opening section, he introduces one idea whose subsequent influence is seen in the psychology of the twentieth century – the concept of 'sublimation'. The term is a metaphor taken from the vocabulary of chemistry.[13] Nietzsche uses it to suggest that a scientific account of attitudes and motives must recognize the origins of altruism and disinterestedness in feelings which are commonly regarded as their opposite. His conclusion is a challenge to the assumption that moral values must have a 'higher' origin, for he claims that 'good actions are sublimated bad ones'.[14] This is a typical example of the way in which the programme of reductionism can bring about the overthrow of some of the most cherished illusions of our culture. Others can be found throughout *Human, All-Too-Human*. The elimination of teleology in favour of causal explanation is a frequent topic, especially in its application not only to biology but also to psychology. While it is true that other themes are present in this work, it is just as true that the same commitment to positive science often recurs in Nietzsche's later writings, however mixed it may be with his critical reflections on the mechanistic approach to natural phenomena.

In one late notebook entry, Nietzsche suggests that 'mechanistic theory must be considered an imperfect and merely provisional hypothesis'.[15] That sounds like a criticism; yet he is a strong advocate of provisional hypotheses as a form of thinking. Elsewhere he says: 'In place of basic truths I put basic probabilities – provisionally (*vorläufig*) assumed guides by which one lives and thinks.'[16] To adopt a certain *method* is to commit oneself for the time being to such a guideline.[17] Now this idea has to be seen in the context of Nietzsche's insistence on the need for an adventurous spirit in the search for knowledge. He wants researchers to venture beyond the safe limits of existing knowledge. It is significant that the literal meaning of *vorläufig* is 'running ahead'. A provisional guide is one that encourages us to run ahead of our present knowledge into what is still unknown. It is an act of anticipation, an attempt to extend the range of one's powers into a distant future. What Nietzsche calls 'untimeliness' is its most important feature in his eyes, and he often describes his own most original ideas in just these terms. The idea of the will to power, for example, is supposed to be only a first suggestion for a new interpretation of the world: 'in all fairness, only provisional and precursory, only preparatory and prospective, only a "prelude" to a serious one.'[18] But the modesty which is emphasized in this passage is itself not very serious since, for Nietzsche, the discoverer may be said to achieve more than the consolidation that others carry out later on.

As we have seen, Nietzsche identifies mechanistic materialism as arising out of a research programme which can be characterized in a way that enables us to assess the progress achieved by its current version, as well as to foresee the directions still to be undertaken. When he seems to be attacking materialism, it is usually on this basis: he is criticizing it for not (or not yet) realizing its own goals. In a number of passages he indicates guidelines for a new advance. Sometimes he offers predictions:

> The development of the mechanistic–atomic mode of thought is today still not yet aware of its necessary goal – that is my impression, having looked at its supporters through my fingers for long enough. They will end with the creation of a system of signs; they will give up all claim to explanation; they will give up the concept 'cause and effect'.[19]

Similar passages predict that mechanism will dispense with the notion of empty space, or for that matter of space itself.[20] When he describes mechanism as an ideal, Nietzsche continues: 'Still needed: the denial of empty space; thinking of space as determinate and limited; thinking of the world as eternally recurring.'[21] These speculations raise the issues that will concern us in the rest of this chapter – the questions of explanation and causality, of atoms and empty space, and finally of eternal recurrence.

Explanation and Causality

Let us begin with what Nietzsche thinks is modern science's mistaken idea of its own aims. It pretends to explain the processes of nature; but what it really does, and all it can ever do, is to describe or interpret them. The first of these expressions is used in *The Gay Science*: "Explanation" is what we call it, but it is "description" that distinguishes us from older stages of knowledge and science. Our descriptions are better – we do not explain more than our predecessors.'[22] In *Beyond Good and Evil* a similar point is made, this time drawing the distinction between explanation and interpretation:

> It is perhaps just dawning on five or six minds that physics, too, is only an interpretation and exegesis of the world (to suit us, if I may say so!) and *not* a world-explanation; but in so far as it is based on belief in the senses, it is regarded as more, and for a long time to come must be regarded as more – namely, as an explanation.[23]

The theme of reliance on the evidence of the senses is a broad topic which raises some issues that I will not deal with until Chapter 10. For the time being, let us ask the following question: how does belief in the senses lead one to see physics as an explanation rather than an interpretation of the world? I think Nietzsche takes an explanation to be a procedure in which the unfamiliar is turned into the familiar, or in which the concepts in the final account are those with which we have a close acquaintance. He continues: 'What is clear, what is "explained"? Only what can be seen and felt – every problem has to be pursued to that point.' What is wrong with this is not just that it is 'plebeian' rather than 'noble', but that it is a hasty and unjustified move. We assume that we have an understanding of what can be seen and felt, and an even greater understanding of the processes that constitute the contents of our own minds – those of thinking, willing and so on. Nietzsche objects that this is an illusion. No greater certainty can be attributed to these experiences than to any other. Even the simplest case for which immediate acquaintance might be claimed, the famous 'I think', contains, on closer examination, a number of assumptions which have not been read off from the experience itself – that there is something which thinks, that it is the cause of the process of thinking, that the character of this process is known, and so on.[24]

In speaking of cases like this, Nietzsche is fond of claiming the superiority of the science of philology (his own profession) in encouraging researchers to separate each text from its interpretations. This separation is the first stage of scientific research; the second one is the stage of careful analysis. In speaking of mental life, one of his examples is the case of *willing*. He says, 'Willing seems to me to be above all something *complicated*, something that is a unit only as a word.'[25] If we look more closely we can see that any process of willing involves various different processes. This is an important case, because it is the basis for Nietzsche's critique of the concept of causality. That and other scientific concepts are implicated by his attack on the notion of immediate certainty. His conclusion might be summed up as a belief that no part of the world is closer to us than any other part. The distinction between 'inner' and 'outer' is a false one: it remains in our thinking only as a hangover from older, pre-scientific modes of thought, just as in ancient atomism the distinction between upward and downward movement was retained, albeit as an anomaly, in its account of the universe.

The replacement of explanation by description and a 'system of signs' (akin to Teichmüller's concept of a 'sign language' or 'semiotic') is closely linked with the next of Nietzsche's predictions, the giving up of cause and effect. We saw earlier that his commitment to a Heraclitean doctrine of becoming led him to emphasize continuity in the processes of nature and to reject those conceptions of time which reify events as distinct individuals. This is one motive for scepticism about causality; another is suggested by his reading of the positivist philosophers who threw scorn upon the anthropomorphism of the common notion of causal efficacy. Avenarius argued that we have no experience of the effectiveness of force, because the feeling of force and the feeling of movement (even the movement of our own muscles) are 'completely heterogeneous', so that one cannot be inferred from the other. Nor do we experience the necessity of movement: 'What we experience is always only that one thing follows upon another – we experience neither compulsion nor freedom in their following one another.'[26] Avenarius concluded that the ordinary concept of causality, in so far as it includes these ideas, is a naïve and anthropomorphic picture of reality which differs only in degree and not in kind from the primitive fetishism that projects the human soul into inanimate external objects.

Nietzsche agrees with this analysis and brings it to bear upon materialism which, as he observes, has always used causality as its primary mode of thinking, going back to Democritus. In the systems of his immediate predecessors there are still vestiges of mythology: Anaxagoras makes *nous* the basic premise of his cosmology, while Empedocles appeals to 'love' and 'hate' in explaining the combining and separating of elements. In contrast, Democritus speaks only of processes which are visible and tangible, and which work through a single process of cause and effect.[27] The modern science that continues his tradition also claims to have eliminated teleology from its explanations. Yet Nietzsche argues that these are not alternatives, but just different versions of the same conception. For our idea of an efficient cause has the same origin as our idea of a final cause; both assume our understanding of our own willing as a process in which an intention can be seen to give rise to its outcome. Since Nietzsche denies the validity of that understanding, he removes the foundation on which its extension to phenomena outside ourselves depends.

Nietzsche was keenly interested in current philosophical discussions of causality. In August 1881 he wrote to his friend Franz Overbeck requesting copies of a number of works he had read about in Otto Caspari's *Der Zusammenhang der Dinge*. One of them was a essay on causality which Caspari had praised as 'epoch-making'.[28] This was Adolf Fick's *Ursache und Wirkung*.[29] Fick was a versatile writer on physiology and other areas of science, as well as on social issues such as prohibition. In this thirty-page philosophical essay he argued for a reconceptualization of causality, not only eliminating any association with ideas of compulsion but also, more controversially, redefining the causal link as a relation between simultaneous rather than successive events.[30]

Fick begins with a provocative suggestion made by the physicist Robert Kirchhoff in the Foreword to his 1876 *Lectures on Mathematical Physics*. Kirchhoff had attacked the notion of mechanics as the science of forces, understood as the causes which produce motion, or at least 'strive' to produce motion. These concepts, he argued, were so unclear that we should rather see the task of mechanics as one of *describing* the motions observed in nature, as completely and simply as possible. Fick comments that Kirchhoff overstates his own case in proposing to replace explanation with description, since the propositions of mechanics state how a point *must* move, and not just how it does move. They lay down rules which admit of no exceptions, and so imply an element of necessity. On the other hand, Fick is strongly in sympathy with Kirchhoff's desire to eliminate the obscure notions of pushing and pulling (*Zug oder Druck*) from an understanding of causal interaction, and agrees that identifying force with a 'tendency' to motion is an arbitrary interpretation. If it is objected that we can experience this tendency directly – for example, as a sensation of pressure when holding a piece of iron and feeling the force of its attraction to a nearby magnet – Fick replies that what one feels here is just the pressure of the iron on the hand, and that is not the force attributed to the magnet.

Cause and effect are common notions, Fick observes, but used in many ways. We use words loosely when speaking of 'the' cause of the warm air in a room, since that is a complex of millions of processes, each having its own cause. What is the cause of a body's falling? There are various answers and, more generally, the cause of something may be a substance, a present or past event, a state of affairs and so on. He thinks that this is a confusion which needs to be cleared up. Certainly, cause and effect have to do with *changes* in phenomena. Kant says that they refer to laws governing the temporal succession of phenomena but, if constant conjunction were sufficient, Fick objects, day would be the cause of night.[31] Again, consider an object moving in a straight line at a constant speed. For Kant, each part of this motion must be the cause of the next, since that follows by necessity and according to a definite rule. But this, too, does not accord with our ordinary usage.

After these criticisms, Fick presents his own analysis along the following lines. Effects are changes in a thing which would not occur without the presence of another thing. Not all changes are like this: uniform motion in a straight line has no such necessary condition. But the formula states a basic concept of our understanding, the idea of the influence of one thing upon another. This is not the concept of a lawlike succession of phenomena, because it applies to single events, taken by themselves. Schopenhauer was right in claiming that, without such an *a priori* concept of causal influence, we would not even be able to infer an external world from our sensations.[32] Only later is the same principle used to establish relations between external things themselves. What is it that brings about a change in something? Not the mere presence of another thing, but rather a *change* in the relation between them. For instance, only when an object is moving does its speed increase owing to gravitation. In other words, the alteration is an effect when, and only when, it depends on another alteration. Hence, on Fick's account, an effect requires three things:

1   another thing
2   a nexus between the two (which we call 'force')
3   a change in the relation between the two things.

In everyday language, any one of these may sometimes be called 'cause', but Fick recommends using the word for (3) alone, to avoid confusion.[33]

The surprising part of Fick's essay is its rejection of the idea that cause and effect stand in a temporal succession. Kant seems to concede some cases of simultaneity, but Fick goes further: 'Cause and effect in the sense of our definition are always *simultaneous* occurrences.' After all, how could a change in the relations between things *fail* to produce a change in their states? And how could a past change which no longer exists produce such a change? Fick repeats the case against action at a distance, noting that it agrees with the philosophical maxim, *cessante causa cessat effectus*. If temporal succession were essential to causality, it would be the other way around, *cessante causa incipit effectus*. He sums up:

> The causal nexus is on our account only the conditionedness of the alterations in velocity by simultaneous changes in state of masses. It therefore does not join

successive occurrences, but only the two sides of one and the same occurrence. The reason why one occurrence follows upon another rests on a completely different principle from that of causality.[34]

For example, motion would continue even if causality were abolished. It would only be uniform motion, and yet it would have a sufficient reason, and therefore could be assigned an explanation. We would presumably say that the state of a body is the reason for its motion, but Fick thinks it is better not to speak of cause and effect here.

Since space is only the form of relations between things, Fick argues, it cannot be filled with matter.[35] Hence, the elementary parts of matter are unextended points and all change is reducible to their motion, in various directions and with various speeds.[36] Particles change their position and also their speed, but the second sort of change is just an effect of the first, brought about by interaction with other particles. If there were no other masses, the motion of a particle would continue indefinitely; it is the presence of other masses that brings about alterations in its speed or direction. Whether this law (in effect, Newton's first law of motion) is an *a priori* truth is debatable; Kant thought so, but Fick is less certain and does not commit himself. He concludes that mechanics does not need the 'obscure' notion of force to give a mathematical description of the state of things and to posit an interdependence of changes in this situation.

One can see why this programme of conceptual reform would have appealed to Nietzsche. Despite his early theory of 'time-atoms', he agrees with Fick in rejecting any causal link between distant events: 'that would mean making their effective capacity leap from 1 to 2, to 3, to 4, to 5.'[37] He also agrees that there must be some reason why one event follows another. As it happens, science does not address this issue, because it concentrates on establishing equivalences in accordance with the principles of conservation of mass and energy. As he goes on to say in the same note: 'In fact, science has emptied the concept causality of its content and retained it as the formula of an equation, in which it has become at bottom indifferent on which side cause is placed and on which side effect.' An equation does not say which state of affairs gives rise to the other: in effect, it treats any process as if it were reversible. In another note Nietzsche repeats this point, and adds: 'we observe only results, and we consider them equivalent in content of force. We spare ourselves the question of the *causation* (*Verursachung*) of a change ....'[38] Empirical science sets this question aside and contents itself with measuring and calculating mass or energy, a strategy which has proven very successful in getting valid and useful results.

If causality cannot explain the course of events, what can? Fick seems to be suggesting that something like Newton's laws of motion might fill the gap. As we saw in Chapter 1, Nietzsche has another proposal. He writes:

> It is a question of a struggle between two elements of unequal power: a new arrangement of forces is achieved, according to the measure of power of each of them. The second condition is something fundamentally different from the first

(not its effect): the essential thing is that the factions in struggle emerge with different quanta of power.[39]

Although it is never spelled out in detail, this points to his conception of a principle which is consistent with absolute Heraclitean becoming in a way that cause and effect was not – but which is also consistent with the commitment to calculability which is a main strength of modern science.

The Rejection of Atomism

Causality is only one of the concepts Nietzsche wants to eliminate from mechanistic theory. Another is the notion of material substance. In traditional materialism, reality is thought to consist of atoms and void. These atoms are permanent and indivisible particles whose various interactions and combinations constitute the phenomena of nature. Nietzsche argues that this is another mistake, due again to the supposed evidence of immediate experience. The paradigm case of substantial being is the self – the permanent and self-identical 'thing' that is present throughout all our experiences, and the subject to which we attribute thinking, perception, feeling and willing. But all this is denied by Nietzsche. He identifies the motive for a belief in substance as the desire to find a place for the category of being within a world of becoming. The pretext for satisfying this 'atomistic need' is supplied by the experience of the self.[40] As with causality and the will, the concept is then given an application to the 'outer' world: the substantial atoms of materialism assume the role of agents and causes in much the same way as the subject of experience.

It is not evident that science can dispense with the concept of matter, but Nietzsche supports his claim by invoking the 'dynamic' approach to physical theory, in which the properties of matter are explained in terms of the properties of force. Within Newtonian mechanism, matter and force remain categories which are separate yet interdependent: forces act upon objects, and objects exert force, both concepts together giving a complete account of the interaction of bodies. In the eighteenth century, however, a simpler scheme was suggested by the natural philosopher Roger Joseph Boscovich (1711–1787). In his theory substantial atoms are replaced by 'points of matter', and properties such as impenetrability and inertia defined by a complicated law of force. Nietzsche was strongly influenced by a reading of Boscovich during his time in Basel, and later wrote:

> When I think of my philosophical genealogy, I feel in agreement with the anti-teleological, i.e. Spinozistic movement of our time, but with this difference, that I hold even the 'aim' and 'will' *within us* to be an illusion: similarly with the mechanistic movement (tracing all moral and aesthetic questions back to physiological ones, all physiological to chemical ones, all chemical to mechanical ones) but with this difference, that I do not believe in 'matter' and hold Boscovich to be one of the great turning-points, like Copernicus.[41]

It is significant that this comparison between Boscovich and Copernicus is made in terms of their common repudiation of the immediate evidence of the senses. Just as Copernicus overcame the commonsense belief in the stability of the earth, Boscovich overcame a prejudice equally based on familiar experience: the notion of substance.[42] Just as important, however, is the economic aspect of the dynamic approach. Not only does it eliminate matter as a category separate from that of force, but it also abolishes the distinction between matter and space. Matter is nothing but the field of force which occupies the whole of space. There is no longer any empty space, but this is not because space is occupied throughout by matter, for there is no 'filled' space either: the contrast has been abolished.

Born in Ragusa, in the Venetian territory of Dalmatia (now Dubrovnik, in Croatia), Boscovich entered the Jesuit order and completed his education in Rome, where he became a teacher of astronomy, mathematics and physics, and an early European champion of the Newtonian system. His most notable work is the treatise *A Theory of Natural Philosophy*, published in 1758. Here his ideas are developed from consideration of a particular problem in mechanics. When one moving body collides with another, a sudden change in their velocities must occur. But this violates the law of continuity which, for both inductive and metaphysical reasons, Boscovich takes to be valid for all natural phenomena. In order to avoid inconsistency, he argues, we must suppose that bodies having different velocities cannot come into immediate contact. This in turn can only be due to a mutual force of repulsion which increases indefinitely as their distance becomes indefinitely small.[43] There follows a striking conclusion about the constitution of material things. The tendency of force towards infinite magnitude at distances approaching zero implies that no part of matter can be contiguous to any other part. That is, the primary elements must be simple and unextended points of matter, which move in space but never come into contact with one another. What we think of as extended bodies are just finite collections of such points of matter. Our senses deceive us into belief in continuous extension, yet we can overcome this uncritical belief, Boscovich explains, through philosophical reasoning. We have done that in a similar case: it was once believed, on the evidence of the senses, that the earth is at rest, but 'among philosophers it is now universally accepted that such a question has to be answered in a far different manner from that by means of the senses'.[44]

In Boscovich's theory, particles are related by a single 'law of force' which varies in a complicated way according to distance. At very small distances, the force will be repulsive. At greater distances, it may be attractive; in fact, at very great distances it will approximate to the inverse square law of attraction.[45] At intermediate distances, there may be alternations of attraction and repulsion. It is convenient for us to analyse this curve into several components, and to treat each as a separate force in its own right – for instance, the Newtonian forces of gravitation, cohesion and chemical 'fermentation' – so that the curve as a whole is seen as a product of these various factors in combination. But this is an artificial procedure: in reality there is only one law of force.[46]

Boscovich does not speak of 'centres of force', and for a good reason. Points of matter may be unextended, but they still possess another traditional attribute of materiality – namely, mutual impenetrability. A further step was taken in the nineteenth century, when Michael Faraday developed a genuine concept of centres of force in order to deal with a problem arising from the new science of electricity. The question was posed by the differing conductivities of various substances, a puzzling fact on the assumption that they all consist mainly of the same empty space, as the standard version of atomism suggests. An answer, Faraday concluded, could only be found by 'the assumption of atoms consisting merely of centres of force, like those of Boscovich'.[47] The awkward assumption is thus eliminated: there is no empty space as a common factor, because fields of force are present throughout space. Faraday went on to specify that, in his view, 'the atoms of matter would be mutually penetrable'.[48] They might, he considered, pass through one another, or combine and separate in the manner of ocean waves, which intersect and then become distinct again. One suspects that this idea would have appealed to Nietzsche as a decisive departure from the traditional conception of material substance: after all, in one note he criticizes the 'dynamic atom' as not yet far enough removed from the solid atom of traditional thinking.[49]

Closely related to the rejection of material atoms is a rejection of 'laws of nature', for the two concepts seem to go together: the notion of atoms as agents distinct from their activities requires a further account of why those activities take one course rather than another. The notion of 'law' used to express that idea is, Nietzsche insists, a metaphor based on legal or political authority. Commanding and obeying are relations between agents, and if the category of the individual subject is eliminated, these concepts lose their application. A 'law of nature' cannot have any influence unless it acts as a constraint on the activities on things which are agents in their own right. Nietzsche seems to think that such a law would be a kind of persistent interference with a course of events which would otherwise go its own way. To these arguments we might add his general objection to any kind of existence over and above that of natural phenomena. A 'law' of nature would amount to some such higher power, though a rather abstract and impersonal one. Nietzsche concludes: 'Let us beware of saying that there are laws in nature. There are only necessities: there is nobody who commends, nobody who obeys, nobody who trespasses.'[50] The regularities and patterns which we find in nature are not due to a necessity which controls the course of events, but to a necessity present within every process, which he seems to think can be reduced to the logical principle of identity: 'the rule proves only that one and the same event is not another event as well.'[51]

In these arguments, the concepts of substance, causality and law are criticized in two different ways. In the first place, they have no real validity, because their origin lies in misunderstandings about the evidence of mental acts. But in addition, they are simply superfluous. Eliminating them does not reduce the ability of scientific theory to account for a wide range of natural processes, and it adds to the economy with which science carries out that task. So, in all these cases, the fault of mechanism as it stands is its failure to pursue its own programme in a wholehearted manner. The problem is that it has not been reductionist *enough*; it has stopped short in an operation which could be carried much further.

The Challenge of the Final State

One of Nietzsche's more telling objections to mechanism is different, though. It arises from his emphasis on the necessity of continual change in the world of force. Forces can never stand still; they must always be interacting and forming new combinations at every moment. We can *imagine* a state of affairs in which all forces would balance one another – that is, a state of complete equilibrium. However, Nietzsche says that this is impossible. In fact, its impossibility is not just one item of knowledge among many; rather, it is 'the only thing that has been proved'.[52] It has a certainty which goes beyond all other scientific knowledge of the world, and that makes it the premise for a decisive argument against mechanism. Nietzsche writes: 'If the motion of the world had a final state, that state would have been reached. The sole fundamental fact, however, is that it does not have a final state; and every philosophy or scientific hypothesis (e.g. mechanism) which necessitates such a state is refuted by this single fact.'[53] In another entry which deals with the question of a final state, the same point is made: 'If e.g. mechanism cannot avoid the consequence of a final state which Thomson has drawn for it, then mechanism is refuted.'[54]

These are strong expressions which reflect Nietzsche's confidence in an argument against the possibility of a standstill of force which takes the following form. If such a state were possible, it would have occurred at some moment in the past. If it had occurred, it would not have been followed by any further changes. But it is evident that the present moment is one of development. Thus, not only has no state of rest ever occurred, but no such state is at all possible. Nietzsche takes this conclusion to rule out two common ideas about the world as a whole, for it implies that the course of becoming can have neither a beginning nor an ending. The first conclusion rules out the idea of an act of creation. Nietzsche thinks, in any case, that there is no coherent concept here to merit serious consideration and criticizes other writers for conceding even that much.[55] He suggests that any idea that the world may have a beginning in time arises out of an ulterior motive, the desire to make room for old doctrines of religion.[56] If it is certain that there can be no first moment of becoming, we can disallow any such manoeuvre in advance. A further step in the argument leads us to the conclusion that a standstill of force is impossible. In other words, not only is it certain that no such state has ever existed, but we can also be sure that it will never come about at any future time. It is this last point that supplies Nietzsche with his refutation of mechanism in its existing version.

Although Nietzsche refers to 'the consequence drawn by William Thomson', it seems certain that he not only never read Thomson, but had very little idea of how Thomson reached this conclusion. His understanding of physical theory came almost entirely from German writers who were out of sympathy with the British school of physical science for both philosophical and political reasons. To take one example, Otto Caspari's *Die Thomson'sche Hypothese von der endlichen Temperaturausgleichung im Weltall* barely mentions Thomson, despite its title. Caspari writes as a wholehearted partisan of Leibniz, in opposition to the Newtonian tradition of mechanism. He remarks: 'It is highly characteristic for an Englishman to carry the mechanical theory of steam engines over into the universe.'[57] Caspari's alternative is what he calls 'macrocosmic organicism'. He rather fancifully suggests that the universe might reach an apparent standstill and then become active again without any external cause – in much the same way as an animal undergoing hibernation.[58]

Another German author on physical science showed more appreciation of the contribution made by British researchers like Thomson. In his 1854 lecture 'On the Interaction of Natural Forces', Hermann von Helmholtz drew attention to the paper which Thomson had published only two years earlier on the subject. He referred to 'the inferences drawn by William Thomson from the law of Carnot'.[59] Thomson had shown that if heat can perform work only by passing from a warmer to a colder body, there must be a general tendency for the store of force available for such work to be used up. It follows

> ... that if the universe be delivered over to the undisturbed action of its physical processes, all force will finally pass into the form of heat, and all heat come into a state of equilibrium. Then all possibility of a further change would be at an end, and the complete cessation of all natural processes must set in ... In short, the universe from that time forward would be condemned to a state of eternal rest.[60]

Thomson himself had been more cautious in the formulation of his conclusion. He mentioned only that from a general application of Carnot's theorem it followed that within a finite period of time, the earth would become unfit for the habitation of human beings 'as at present constituted'.[61] But it was Helmholtz's version that gained currency. And it was this general conclusion that Nietzsche encountered in his studies of natural science, not the particular calculation derived from Carnot which appears in Thomson's account.

Nietzsche knew that the development of mechanism had given rise to the conclusion that the laws governing the evolution of the physical world implied a cessation of activity at some future time. This theory had been widely discussed by German writers, and various attempts had been made to offer a solution to the problem. Whether Nietzsche knew *why* mechanism led to this consequence is another matter. We can only look into his further remarks on the themes of force and finality to provide a clue. Of central importance are the differences between what Nietzsche sees as the mechanistic approach and what he puts forward as his own approach to the philosophy of nature. In the notebook entry that mentions Thomson, Nietzsche goes on to describe the world as consisting of 'a certain definite number of centres of force' and argues that these are capable of forming only a calculable number of combinations, so that in an infinite time the same sequence of combinations must occur again and again. This is his doctrine of eternal recurrence, which we will examine in some detail in the following chapters. Nietzsche writes: 'This conception is not by itself a mechanistic conception; for if it were that, it would not condition an infinite recurrence of identical cases, but a final state.'[62] He is aware of how close his own view is to a mechanistic one and is concerned to point out the main differences. In fact, he often presents it as something like an improved version of mechanism, which in its present form has failed to avoid the consequence of a final state.

When Nietzsche says that his own approach is not 'by itself' (*ohne weiteres*) a mechanistic conception, this suggests that the important difference is not mentioned in the text of his description, but lies in the presence or absence of some further element. We saw in Chapter 4 that he had been impressed by Zöllner's proposal for a conception of space as finite but unbounded. On that interpretation, it is because mechanism makes a certain assumption about 'the shape of space' – presumably that it is infinite – that it leads to the prediction of a final state. Nietzsche wrote to Köselitz:

> I have already told you in conversation my view: that 'finite' space – that is, space having a determinate shape – is inevitable in the context of the mechanistic world-view, and that the impossibility of a state of equilibrium seems to me to hang together with the question of *how* total space is shaped – it is certainly not spherical![63]

This last point is fairly obscure, but clearly the finitude of space is one important factor in the theory that provides an alternative to a final state.

This alternative, it seems, is the theory of eternal recurrence. Nietzsche says of the doctrine: 'I found it in thinking to the end the mechanistic view of the world.'[64] This remark is worth thinking about. What does the expression 'to the end' imply? That eternal recurrence is arrived at by thinking mechanism through to its end again highlights its analogy with the notion of a final state. For this is, as Nietzsche observes, the consequence drawn by William Thomson from mechanism in its *present* form. In general, the real character of any idea emerges only when it is taken to its final consequence. Thus Nietzsche writes: 'For why has the advent of nihilism become necessary? Because the values we have had hitherto draw their final consequence in it; because nihilism is the logic of our greatest values and ideals, thought to the end.'[65] He considers that our values may be said to have devalued themselves, in so far as they have encouraged the will to truth which leads to just this conclusion. He gives a similar account of the metaphysical concept of a 'true world': thought through to its end, this has lost all content, and as such it is 'an idea which has become useless and superfluous – consequently a refuted idea: let us abolish it!'.[66]

An idea which is thought through to the end is no longer provisional, no longer anticipatory; reality has caught up to it. This means that it has lost the character of untimeliness that Nietzsche regards highly. Hence, it seems, the time has come to abandon that idea and move on to some other idea. Does this hold true for mechanism, as Nietzsche understands it? If so, then the status of the doctrine of eternal recurrence is quite ambiguous. Is it the end of one mode of thinking or the beginning of another? Is it a nihilistic thought or a step beyond nihilism? Nietzsche is well aware of these ambiguities, but does not provide a solution which allows us to say that one answer is right and the other wrong. Perhaps this is in part because eternal recurrence is not a concept which can find any direct confirmation by way of observation. It may be a consequence of mechanism, but it is not one which we can ourselves encounter. It stands outside the bounds of possible experience, although it has nothing to do with any 'world' transcending the world of appearance. At the same time, Nietzsche thinks that the idea can be supported by argumentation. In the next chapter, I turn to that line of thought and examine it in some detail.

Notes

1. Friedrich Nietzsche, *Thus Spake Zarathustra*, 'On Science'.
2. See Friedrich Nietzsche, *Historische-Kritische Gesamtausgabe: Werke*, ed. H.J. Mette and K. Schlechta, Band 4 (München: C.H. Beck'sche Verlagsbuchhandlung, 1937), 36–49, 53–64 and 74–104.
3. Friedrich Nietzsche, *Beyond Good and Evil*, sect. 14.
4. Ibid., sect. 21.
5. Friedrich Nietzsche, *Human, All-Too-Human*, sect. 635.
6. Nietzsche, *Beyond Good and Evil*, sect. 13.
7. KGW VII/3, 158.
8. Ernst Mach, *Popular Scientific Lectures*, trans. T.J. McCormack (La Salle, IL: Open Court, 1894), 193.
9. KGW VII/1, 690–91 (*The Will to Power*, sect. 626). The title is perhaps alluded to in section 14 of *Beyond Good and Evil*. Avenarius was professor of philosophy in Zürich from 1877 onward, so he and Nietzsche may have had some acquaintance. Nietzsche was later in correspondence with his brother Ferdinand Avenarius, editor of the periodical *Der Kunstwart* and a favourable reviewer of *The Wagner Case*. See, for example, KGB III/5, 516–19 and 544 (letters of 10 and 22 December 1888).
10. KGW VIII/2, 201 (*The Will to Power*, sect. 639).
11. Nietzsche, *Beyond Good and Evil*, sect. 36.
12. Nietzsche writes: 'Our drives are reducible (*reduzirbar*) to the will to power': KGW VII/3, 393.
13. It had earlier been used by the alchemists, for whom sublimation was closely associated with spiritual purification; see, for example, Paracelsus, *The Hermetic and Alchemical Writings of Paracelsus*, ed. A.E. Waite (London: James Elliot, 1894), Vol. 1, 152.
14. Nietzsche, *Human, All-Too-Human*, sect. 107. Compare a remark of Freud: 'Our highest virtues have grown up, as reaction formations and sublimations, out of our worst dispositions': *The Standard Edition of the Complete Psychological Works of Sigmund Freud*, ed. James Strachey and A. Freud (London: Hogarth Press, 1953–1975), Vol. 13, 190.
15. KGW VIII/3, 168 (*The Will to Power*, sect. 1066).
16. KGW VII/1, 686.
17. KGW VII/2, 129.
18. KGW VII/3, 385.

19 KGW VIII/1, 86. Cf. KGW VII/2, 259.
20 KGW VII/2, 258–59.
21 KGW VII/3, 158.
22 Friedrich Nietzsche, *The Gay Science*, sect. 112.
23 Nietzsche, *Beyond Good and Evil*, sect. 14.
24 Ibid., sect. 16.
25 Ibid., sect. 18.
26 Richard Avenarius, *Philosophie als Denken der Welt gemäss dem Princip des kleinsten Kraftmasses. Prolegomena zu einer Kritik der reinen Erfahrung* (Leipzig: Fues's Verlag, 1876), sect. 81. Nietzsche copied this and other passages into his notebook: KGW VII/1, 690.
27 Nietzsche, *Historische-Kritische Gesamtausgabe: Werke*, Band IV, 83.
28 Otto Caspari, *Der Zusammenhang der Dinge: Gesammelte philosophische Aufsätze* (Breslau: Verlag von Eduard Trewendt, 1881), 51.
29 Adolf Fick, *Ursache und Wirkung. Ein erkenntnis-theoretische Versuch*, 2nd edn (Kassel: G. H. Wigand, 1882). Reprinted in *Gesammelte Schriften von Adolf Fick, in vier Bänden* (Würzburg: Stahel'sche Verlags-Anstalt, 1903), Band I, 99–131.
30 For a similar view taken by a twentieth-century philosopher, see Richard Taylor, 'Causation', *The Monist*, 47 (1962–63), 287–313.
31 Fick, *Gesammelte Schriften* I, 102. This counterexample was first raised by Thomas Reid as an objection to Hume's account of causality: see his *Essays on the Intellectual Powers of Man*, Essay VI, chapter VI, sect. 2, in Thomas Reid, *Philosophical Works*, 8th edn (Edinburgh: James Thin, 1895). It is also discussed in detail by J.S. Mill in *A System of Logic*, 7th edn (London, Longmans, Green, Reader and Dyer, 1868), Book III, chapter V, sect. 5.
32 Ibid., 103. See Arthur Schopenhauer, *On the Fourfold Root of the Principle of Sufficient Reason*, trans. E.F.J. Payne (La Salle, IL: Open Court, 1974), 76–78.
33 Fick, *Gesammelte Schriften* I, 105.
34 Ibid., 118.
35 Ibid., 109.
36 Ibid., 112.
37 KGW VIII/3, 67 (*The Will to Power*, sect. 551).
38 Ibid., 92–93 (*The Will to Power*, sect. 688).
39 Ibid., 65 (*The Will to Power*, sect. 633).
40 Nietzsche, *Beyond Good and Evil*, sect. 12.
41 KGW VII/2, 264.
42 Nietzsche, *Beyond Good and Evil*, sect. 12.
43 R.J. Boscovich, *A Theory of Natural Philosophy*, trans. J.M. Child (Cambridge, MA: MIT Press, 1966), 42 (art. 77).
44 Ibid., 65 (art. 159). According to some sources, it was Boscovich who persuaded Pope Benedict XIV to rescind the Catholic Church's official ban on the writings of Copernicus in 1757.
45 Boscovich, *A Theory of Natural Philosophy*, 43 (art. 78).
46 Ibid., 54 (art. 119–20).
47 Michael Faraday, *Experimental Researches in Electricity* (New York: Dover Publications, 1965), Vol. 2, 291.
48 Ibid., 292.
49 KGW VIII/3, 50 (*The Will to Power*, sect. 634).
50 Nietzsche, *The Gay Science*, sect. 109; see also *Mixed Opinions and Maxims*, sect. 9.
51 KGW VIII/2, 47 (*The Will to Power*, sect. 552). See also KGW VIII/1, 134 (*The Will to Power*, sect. 631).
52 KGW VIII/2, 201 (*The Will to Power*, sect. 639).
53 Ibid., 276 (*The Will to Power*, sect. 708).
54 KGW VIII/3, 167 (*The Will to Power*, sect. 1066).
55 KGW VII/1, 706.
56 KGW VIII/2, 166 (*The Will to Power*, sect. 1066).

57 Otto Caspari, *Die Thomson'sche Hypothese von der endlichen Temperaturausgleichung im Weltall, beleuchtet vom philosophischen Gesichtspunkte* (Stuttgart: Verlagsbuchhanduung von August Horster, 1874), 57. Thomson was in fact from Belfast, but such subtleties tended to be overlooked by German writers of the period.
58 Ibid., 48.
59 Hermann von Helmholtz, *Popular Scientific Lectures* (New York: Dover Publications, 1962), 73.
60 Ibid, 74.
61 William Thomson, 'On a Universal Tendency in Nature to the Dissipation of Mechanical Energy', in William Thomson, *Mathematical and Physical Papers* (Cambridge: Cambridge University Press, 1882), Vol. 1, 514.
62 KGW VIII/3, 168 (*The Will to Power*, sect. 1066).
63 KGB II/3, 69.
64 KGW VII/3, 210. Similarly Schopenhauer wrote, referring to Kant, 'my philosophy is only his thought out to the end': Arthur Schopenhauer, *Parerga and Paralipomena*, trans. E.F.J. Payne (Oxford, Clarendon Press, 1974), Vol. 1, 132.
65 KGW VII/2, 432 (*The Will to Power*, Preface).
66 Friedrich Nietzsche, *Twilight of the Idols*, 'How the 'True World' Became a Fable'.

Chapter 6

Possibility, Probability and Finality

The concepts of possibility and necessity are crucial to arguments about the final state and eternal recurrence. The doctrine of eternal recurrence teaches 'the absolute necessity' of an endless repetition of the same course of events.[1] In fact, it claims the eternal recurrence not just of every actual state of affair but of every possible state – a much stronger statement. And as we have seen, Nietzsche's rejection of mechanism as a theory is based on his conviction that it leads to the idea of a 'final state' which is impossible. These are not arbitrary pronouncements; Nietzsche attempted on various occasions to set out arguments which would justify such conclusions. The aim of this chapter is to examine and criticize some of the ways in which these lines of thought can be understood, in the first instance by focusing on their structure and the key concepts they depend on.

We will see that the argument which rules out the possibility of a final state requires the use of more than one concept of possibility. However, it is important to consider which concepts of possibility are relevant to the discussion, since use of the wrong ones leads only to confusion. Crucial to this argument is a principle which links the possible and the actual with reference to time: it states that in the course of an infinite time, whatever is possible must also be actual. How is that claim to be justified? Much of the following analysis will consist in an attempt to answer this question. When the same principle appears as part of the argument for eternal recurrence, we find an interpretation suggested which changes the emphasis from possibility to probability. On this view, the argument for eternal recurrence begins with the way in which the probability of a given event increases over a long period of time, and goes on to claim that, in an infinite time, every state of affairs which has a certain probability must occur again and again. I will show that this interpretation is plausible but mistaken, not because (as is sometimes thought) there is an inconsistency between the concept of probability and the principle of determinism, but rather because there is a more rigorous argument present here – one which does *not* involve the concept of probability in reaching the same conclusion.

Possibility and Finality

Let us turn first to Nietzsche's ideas concerning the absence of a final state in the process of becoming. Comments on his arguments about this theme have generally been unsympathetic. Nietzsche, we are told, is inconsistent in using the word 'possible' in several different senses. His talk of possibility is confused in that it fails to observe the important distinction between logical possibility and empirical possibility.[2] Now, I think that each of these claims is partly correct. It is true that Nietzsche uses several different concepts of possibility, and also that he does not make the distinction between logical and empirical possibility. Yet it does not follow that he is either inconsistent or confused. Why does he hold that a final state is not possible, and what kind of possibility is in question? His basic argument is contained in a number of notebook entries dating from 1881 onwards.

> If the world had a goal, it must have been reached: if there were some (unintended) end state for it, this must also have been reached. If it were in any way capable of a pausing and becoming fixed, if there were in its course just one moment of 'being' in the strict sense, there could be no more becoming, and therefore no more thinking of or observing a becoming either.[3]

Nietzsche argues in passages like this that our present ability to think of, and observe, a process of becoming demonstrates that there has never been a state of rest, that the forces whose interactions constitute the world of becoming have never come to a standstill. For if there had ever been such a standstill, it would have continued until the present moment. Now this argument clearly relies on a number of premises. One is the assumption that the present moment is one of change. This is an immediate certainty which Nietzsche seems to think could not be denied without absurdity.[4] Another is the assumption that a state of rest could never be followed by a process of change. This is a premise which appeals to a general principle of sufficient reason. But the premise of interest to our present discussion is the claim that if a final state were possible, it would at some time have been attained.[5] It is this that enables the further conclusion to be reached: 'that a state of equilibrium is never reached proves that it is not possible.'[6]

How are we to understand the concept of possibility contained here? This question is made more difficult by the presence in one note of a statement which seems to contradict what has just been said. Nietzsche writes: 'The standstill of forces, their equilibrium is a thinkable case: but it has never taken place, hence the number of possibilities is greater than the number of actual cases.'[7] Perhaps it is this text more than any other that has given rise to the idea that Nietzsche is seriously confused in his use of the concept of possibility. How, after all, can he first say that whatever is possible must also occur at some time or other, and then allow that the number of possibilities is greater than the number of actual cases?

We need to look at the context of the latter remark to understand it properly. It occurs within a long notebook entry, which is quite unusual for Nietzsche in that it puts forward not a single thought but several contrasting ones. In fact, it is something like a dialogue, in which Nietzsche raises an objection to his own ideas and then attempts to answer it. The remark just cited is located within this objection. For this reason it is too hasty to cite it as an expression of Nietzsche's own opinion. But to see this point we have to look at the whole text in question. It begins as follows:

> If an equilibrium of force had at any time at all been attained, it would still be lasting; thus it has never come about. The present state of affairs contradicts this assumption. If one assumes that there has at some time been a state of affairs absolutely the same as the present one, this assumption is not contradicted by the present state of affairs. Amongst the infinite possibilities however there must have been this case, since an infinity has already passed away up until now. If equilibrium were possible, it must have come about.[8]

Here we have an argument which is simultaneously concerned with two very different cases. The first is the past occurrence of a state of equilibrium, and the second the past occurrence of a state which is the *same* as the present one. Nietzsche begins by pointing out that a certain argument which rules out the first case does not rule out the second one. This is the argument we have already noted: if the present moment is a process of change, and if a state of rest could never be followed by a process of change, then no state of rest has ever occurred. But this argument says nothing about any past occurrence of the present state. In other words, we can be sure that a state of equilibrium has never come about, but we cannot be sure that the present state has not come about in the past. Nietzsche then argues that, on the contrary, we can show that it must have done so. This is where the notion of possibility begins to enter into the discussion. The full argument about a final state contains a further premise: that if a standstill were possible, it would have taken place at some time in the past. This is just one application of a general principle which can also be applied to the other case under discussion. Since we know that the present state is a possible one, we can argue that, in an infinite time, it must have come about.

The next section of the text simply extends this conclusion concerning the present state to cover others as well, using a principle of determination: if the present state has been there before, so has the one before it, and its predecessors in turn. Similarly, the same consequences must have followed in the same order. Thus the conclusion is reached that the total process of becoming consists of a certain limited number of states which occur again and again in the same order. Now this may seem to be the end of the argument: Nietzsche has arrived at a formulation of his doctrine of eternal recurrence. But he goes on to raise a further question about the notion of possibility used in his argument.

> Certainly it cannot be left up to the human head to decide what is possible and what is not: but in any circumstance the present situation is a possible one, quite apart from our capacity or incapacity to judge concerning the possible – for it is an actual one. So could we say that all actual situations must already have had one the same as themselves, assuming that the number of cases is not infinite, and in the course of infinite time only a finite number must take place? If counted back from every moment an infinity has already elapsed? The standstill of forces, their equilibrium is a thinkable case: but it has never taken place, hence the number of possibilities is greater than the number of actual cases.

This last sentence is the one that has seemed to show an obvious inconsistency on Nietzsche's part. But we can now see how it expresses recognition of an objection to the argument so far. Instead of arguing that a standstill is impossible because it has never occurred, Nietzsche is willing to consider a different suggestion: that we should rather abandon the principle that whatever is possible must, in the course of infinite time, also be actual. Since that would invalidate the argument which depends on the same principle to support the theory of eternal recurrence, the challenge is quite an important one. The choice between these lines of thinking raises the question: what do we mean by 'possible' here? Are we to say that a state of equilibrium is possible in so far as it is thinkable? Or should we attach some other sense to the concept of possibility? The final part of the note reads:

> That nothing the same recurs could not be explained by chance, but only by some intentionality present within the essence of force: for assuming an enormous mass of cases, the chance attainment of the same throw is more probable than absolute never-the sameness.[9]

This is rather puzzling, in that it does not directly answer the important question just raised. But it is part of Nietzsche's answer to the objection he has set out. To understand how, we need to fill in the missing argument. Here he asks: if it were the case that nothing the same recurs, how could we explain this fact? There is clearly another question which is the counterpart to this one: how do we explain the fact that a state of equilibrium has never occurred? The answer to that question will throw light on our conception of possibility. Here, however, only the first question is asked and answered. Nietzsche does so by calling on the idea of chance, and uses the word 'throw' to recall the dice game analogy which he uses elsewhere.[10] On this model, he argues, we can show that the same cases always recur, assuming that time is infinite. Therefore, if they do not recur, the explanation must be looked for elsewhere, in terms of some factor not so far considered in assessing them as possible. That is, there must be something that *prevents* them from recurring.

Nietzsche mentions two possible reasons for the absence of any repetition in the course of becoming, but he mentions one only to dismiss it. For the model just mentioned rules out an explanation in terms of chance in this way: given a great number of opportunities, it is more probable that chance will bring about a repetition sooner or later. This leaves only the notion that there is something 'within' the essence of force which prevents it from repeating its states. But what is this something, and why does Nietzsche consider it to be an unacceptable hypothesis? He calls it an 'intentionality' (*Absichtlichkeit*), implying some kind of purpose or intention. This is not the only way that something might belong to the essence of force, so why does Nietzsche insist on such an expression? To answer this we must consider what it is that is supposed to be prevented from occurring. The term 'recurrence' is not the name of a state or a set of states. What makes a state a recurrence is something outside itself – namely, a previous occurrence of the same state. Therefore, if we ask which states would count as instances of recurrence, the answer must be *all* those states which have already occurred. In so far as there is only *one* state which could be called a standstill of force, the task of explaining why that does not happen would seem to be much easier. It is what is required for the prevention of repetition that leads Nietzsche to speak of 'intention', for that includes the need to keep in mind (so to speak) which states have already been there, to foresee those which are to come, and to take measures to prevent certain of these from taking place. All of this amounts to a set of assumptions which he considers quite extravagant:

> The world, even if it is no longer a god, is still supposed to be capable of the divine power of creation, the power of infinite transformation; it is supposed to prevent itself consciously from returning to any of its old forms: it is supposed to possess not only the intention but the *means* of avoiding any repetition; to that end, it is supposed to control every one of its movements at every moment so as to escape goals, final states, repetitions – and whatever else may follow from such an unforgivably insane way of thinking and desiring.[11]

We ought to be clear about just what Nietzsche objects to in this conception. It is not simply that it explains the course of becoming in terms of the 'essence' of force, but rather that it has to think of this essence in terms which resemble a traditional conception of God. Here too, however, we must identify which aspects of the idea he rejects. It is not the notion of power, but rather the notions of knowledge and intention contained in this concept of God that lead him to disallow it as an explanation, for they imply not only a 'total consciousness of becoming' but also the kind of total purpose expressed in the old notion of providence.[12] Because he considers these assumptions to be absurd, Nietzsche rejects any such use of the idea of intentionality.

Two Kinds of Possibility

If recurrence is not ruled out by anything in the essence of force, can we conclude that it is possible? No, for we can think of one circumstance which would make it impossible: the occurrence of a final state, which would prevent any further change from occurring. This brings us back to the other question raised earlier: how do we explain the fact that a state of equilibrium has never occurred? In one notebook passage Nietzsche provides an answer to this question. He writes: 'Complete equilibrium must either be an impossibility in itself, or the alterations of force enter into a circular course before the occurrence of that equilibrium, which is possible in itself.'[13] Here Nietzsche offers a choice between two different ways of accounting for the absence of an equilibrium of force. Let us look at each of these alternatives in turn.

The first is that equilibrium may be seen as impossible 'in itself'. This expression suggests that there might be something about the nature of force that rules out the possibility of any equilibrium. In another note Nietzsche asserts that constant change belongs to the 'essence' of force, and that "force" and "rest", "remaining the same", contradict one another'.[14] These are surely expressions of the same idea. How plausible is it? We can hardly avoid noticing that, when Nietzsche condemns the notion of an intentionality within the essence of force, he describes it as an intention 'to escape goals, final states, repetitions'. It looks as if the two cases were being put on the same footing. But I think this is misleading. We *might* account for the impossibility 'in itself' of a final state in terms of some intentionality, but we *need* not do so. For the avoidance of this particular state does not depend on any reference to past states, nor on any foresight in the usual sense; it requires only that alteration must be a continual process. Thus, when Nietzsche says that change belongs to the essence of force, he is not implying an intentionality of the kind he has rejected elsewhere, but only specifying that force is something whose ontological status is defined by the category of becoming, not of being.

So much, then, for the first alternative. Let us now look at the other one. A state of equilibrium would be ruled out if 'the alterations of force enter into a circular course before the occurrence of that equilibrium, which is possible in itself'. What Nietzsche has in mind here has been well expressed by Arnold Zuboff, who writes:

> I believe it important to note that there must be, in such a universe, many events which are in other respects that we would call possible but which will never have been realized simply because they had been locked out of this ring of recurrence, i.e., those events that do not happen to fall within the recurring cycle which has monopolized reality, which can lead only ever again around itself, never outside.[15]

This is precisely how Nietzsche's second alternative accounts for the absence of a final state. It is important to note that, on this interpretation, we would still have to say that a final state is impossible. For such an account not only explains the non-occurrence of an equilibrium in the past, but also ensures its non-occurrence in the future. The doctrine of eternal recurrence implies that only certain events can occur in the future – namely, those which happen to belong to a cycle of events which has *already* taken place. It has done so not just once but many times, but once is enough: the rule that future events must belong to a certain set of past events makes those states which fall outside this set impossible. As far as we know, on this argument at least, no event is either necessary or impossible in itself. But every event is nevertheless either necessary or impossible. Nietzsche simply assumes in his description of this alternative that the state of equilibrium does not belong to the privileged set of states. This follows from the fact that an equilibrium has never occurred, and that has to be established by the argument mentioned earlier. Once it is established, however, the doctrine of eternal recurrence leads to the further conclusion that the state of equilibrium is impossible.

Our purpose in this analysis was to find out what concepts of possibility were put to use in Nietzsche's treatment of the eternal recurrence and the standstill of forces. We have found that his discussion involves two different kinds of impossibility. Any state of force which is ruled out by something within the essence of force will be impossible 'in itself'. But many states of affairs which are not ruled out in this way are impossible for a different reason. One might express it in general terms by saying that they are rendered impossible by circumstances. In a way, this is a very familiar notion. It seems evident that everything that happens imposes restrictions on the further course of events. That is, it makes some things impossible which would otherwise have been possible (and, we might add, which are still possible 'in themselves').

Here we seem, at first, to have a notion of impossibility which is related to time in this way: something is impossible in this sense only if it was possible before a certain time and impossible after that time. On the other hand, whatever is impossible in itself is impossible at every time. But this interpretation of the distinction is not adequate for the cases we have been considering. The doctrine of eternal recurrence implies that some states are impossible because they do not happen to belong to the set of states which recur eternally. The difference between these states and those which are impossible in themselves cannot be defined in terms of temporality, for the states which are excluded by the cycle of recurrence were never possible at any time. If eternal recurrence has neither a beginning nor an end, whatever it makes impossible is impossible at every time in just the same way as whatever is impossible in itself.

Yet there is something right about the idea that some circumstances render various states of affairs impossible. It has been noted that a process of eternal recurrence makes impossible all those states which have not already taken place. A final state is even more effective: in bringing all change to an end, it makes every state other than itself impossible for the future. Now it may be asked whether there is any other case that satisfies the requirement. Apart from reference to one or other of these special situations, can we ever be sure that a state of affairs which is possible in itself will not come about at some future time, assuming that no appeal to providence is admitted? The problem again concerns the prevention of certain occurrences. Any claim that some event prevents various other events from occurring needs justification: it must rest on assumptions which provide some kind of explanation for such an outcome. Let us look briefly at one line of thought which Nietzsche presents with relevance to this problem.

The concept of eternal recurrence presupposes that the same state may take place at different times. It may appear just as reasonable to assume that any number of variants of the same state – that is, states which share some but not all of its features – may take place. After all, less seems to be required for that to happen. Nietzsche denies that such variation is possible: for him, two total states of the world must either be the same in every feature or have nothing at all in common. He writes: 'It appears that the total state creates properties anew down to the smallest detail.'[16] The point depends on a certain view of properties: 'The state in which men are situated, in relation to nature and men, makes their properties – it is the same with atoms.'[17] We understand a thing only in terms of its properties. But these properties, according to Nietzsche, are constituted by its relations with every other thing. His conclusion is a doctrine of total interdependence: every element within a given total state is conditioned by every other element.[18] It follows that no alteration can take place in isolation; the smallest change in any detail will bring about a general transformation in which nothing remains the same. We may well disagree with the relational conception of properties on which Nietzsche bases this claim, or with his assumption that things are nothing more than their properties. We may not welcome the Heraclitean doctrine which seems to be the only conclusion for this argument. But we can see how anyone adopting his view can hold that every state of affairs does make many other states of affairs impossible. It implies that the occurrence of any state will rule out the occurrence of all those states which share any of its features. On Nietzsche's view, therefore, the notion of prevention has a very wide application: quite apart from questions about eternal recurrence or a final state, many events are impossible because – and only because – they are prevented from occurring by other events.

This is as far as we can go in considering what is meant by possibility and impossibility in the arguments looked at so far. The time has come to answer some of the questions posed at the beginning of this chapter. Does Nietzsche rely on more than one concept of possibility? He uses two concepts of possibility – one expressed in the use of the term 'possible' without qualification, the other indicated by the expression 'possible in itself'. Nietzsche does not seem to confuse the two different senses. On the contrary, his remarks about the impossibility of a final state indicate that he makes a clear use of the distinction. Now, one question arising from these remarks has not been answered. If a final state is impossible, is it impossible in itself or impossible because of a process of eternal recurrence? Although either answer would lead to the result that Nietzsche wants, I think that he would come down on the side of the first one. His remarks on the 'essence' of force indicate this preference, but they do not state the grounds on which it could be justified. Here, I think that the answer lies in another concept which provides Nietzsche with reasons for supposing that constant change belongs to the 'essence' of force. Nietzsche holds that the concept of force needs to be 'completed' by attributing to it an 'inner' aspect usually described as the *will to power*.[19] Setting aside, for the time being, questions about this concept of power, one might ask whether such an inner will amounts to much the same as 'an intentionality present within the essence of force'. It seems to me that it does not. The will to power is a drive, not an intention. This means that the object towards which it is directed need not be an object of consciousness. Of course, we often think and plan out courses of action whose motive is supplied in the beginning by some drive. But the drive itself, in these cases, need not be identified with the *conscious intention*. Nietzsche emphasizes again and again what he sees as the superficial and accidental nature of consciousness.[20] It appears only as the end-product of more fundamental processes within the self. The impulses and drives that constitute this underlying reality are, he believes, all forms of the will to power, a constant striving which may express itself in some form of consciousness only on rare occasions. And it is this that Nietzsche holds to be present within the essence of force. Although the doctrine has many implications, it is only the most immediate one that concerns us here. The will to power can never stand still. It thus provides the ultimate guarantee for a world of becoming in which final goals are absolutely lacking. In such a world, a state of equilibrium is indeed impossible in itself.

What about logical impossibility and empirical possibility? Does Nietzsche use these concepts? If he holds that a final state is possible in one sense but not in another, it would be reasonable to suggest that he thinks it is logically possible but empirically impossible. The only text that could support the first part of this interpretation is the one which suggests that equilibrium must be possible in so far as it is 'a thinkable case'. This does sound like what we would call logical possibility. But the passage is intended by Nietzsche to stand as an objection to this own argument. As I said, Nietzsche does not reply to the objection directly. But he does so indirectly, in that his further argument shows which concepts of possibility are relevant to his discussion. These do not include the notion of logical possibility. There is no *need*, then, for Nietzsche to allow that what is 'thinkable' is for that reason alone possible. Nor does he suggest it in using the expression elsewhere.[21] Similarly, he does not say that what is not 'thinkable' is impossible, but rather that it is a meaningless or vacuous expression.[22] Only when something is 'thinkable' can the question about its possibility be raised in the first place.[23] For this reason, it seems that the idea of logical possibility has no place in this discussion: the fact that a final state is thinkable does not imply that it is possible in any sense that is relevant to the argument. The notion of empirical possibility is also out of place, but for a different reason. It is unclear which of the two kinds of possibility mentioned in our discussion corresponds to this expression; so there remains an ambiguity in the statement that Nietzsche denies the empirical possibility of a final state. It leaves open the choice between two quite different ways of accounting for the impossibility of such a state. To approach that problem we need a different vocabulary concerning possibility.

Probability and Recurrence

We can now return to our main argument. Nietzsche holds that whatever is possible must also be actual, given one condition: that time is infinite. He argues that the present state is a possible one, and that we can be quite certain of this, whatever our inability to make reliable judgements about other possibilities might be. This statement is just an application of the old rule that whatever is actual is also possible. Next, he argues that, since this state is a possible one, it must have occurred within the infinite time which has elapsed up until this moment. Conversely, he argues that since a standstill of forces has never occurred within this infinite time, such a state is impossible. But in the first case another premise is also mentioned: 'assuming that the number of cases which are possible is not infinite.' We need this premise as a counterpart to the assertion of the infinity of time, in this and in the other case as well. The question is: how do these assumptions lead to the conclusion of this argument?

One answer is that Nietzsche is thinking in terms of *probability*. He does, after all, speak of a 'dice game' and of 'chance', and even says that recurrence is 'more probable' than non-recurrence. This suggests that his argument can be restated by using the notion of probability in place of the notion of possibility. In that case, it would rest on a principle taken from the theory of probability – that anything having a probability greater than zero must occur within an infinite sequence of trials. For however small the probability may be to begin with, it will increase over time and eventually come infinitely close to unity. So if we wait long enough, we can be quite sure that the state of affairs in question will come about. As I have noted, this is a familiar consequence of the theory of probability. Furthermore, we can hardly say that Nietzsche would have been unfamiliar with this line of thought, since he must have encountered it in his reading of Boscovich's *A Theory of Natural Philosophy*, where he would have found the following passage.

> The combinations of a finite number of terms are finite in number; but the combinations throughout the whole of infinite eternity must have been infinite in number, even if we assume that what is understood by the name of combinations is the whole series pertaining to so many thousands of years. Hence, in a fortuitous agitation of the atoms, if all cases happen equally, as is always the case in a long series of fortuitous things, one of them is bound to recur an infinite number of times in turn.[24]

One objection raised by some commentators against this line of thought is that Nietzsche's commitment to determinism is inconsistent with any use of the theory of probability.[25] The argument seems to be that the idea of probability makes sense only where events follow one another in an unpredictable or random order. On the other hand, determinism implies that the course of events is governed by some set of laws which would, in principle, allow the prediction of any state of affairs whatever. Hence follows the conclusion that we must discount either Nietzsche's use of the 'dice game' model or else his talk of universal determinism. This is a difficult decision to make, given that we are ourselves accustomed to using both idioms on various occasions. If common sense is not sufficient to guarantee the compatibility of chance and determination, we must look more closely.

Why does Nietzsche compare the world to a dice game? I think the answer lies in his scepticism about the scope of human knowledge. He argues that the regularities we find in nature are really due to a selection and simplification carried out by our mental apparatus. When we speak of a causal relation, for example, we isolate two fragments of a very complex set of processes and call them cause and effect, ignoring or overlooking all the rest.[26] This is so even for the cases that seem most evident to us because they are located within ourselves, such as the link between motive and action. Here too the real process eludes us.[27] Willing is not a single act which might serve as the model for a general understanding of causality.[28] All we can rely on, then, in finding regularities in nature is our ability to recognize occurrences of what we take to be the same sequence of events on different occasions. But now a more radical attack is available to Nietzsche on the basis of his critique of 'sameness'. He has concluded that total states must be different in every respect if they are to be distinct at all. That is, either everything in them is the same or nothing is the same. The first case is one in which knowledge is impossible for us as a matter of course, precisely because everything is the same: the inclusion within one state of any recognition of its identity with another would constitute a difference between the two states. Hence Nietzsche is forced into holding that the only true identity is one which can never be known. As for our recognition of recurring patterns of events, in every case this must be an illusion, one which occurs where we suppose that things are the *same* when they are really only *similar*. In early writings Nietzsche argues that all human knowledge is based on this operation, for which he uses a literary label: 'metaphor'.[29] Later he calls it a 'basic fiction'.[30] Whatever the terminology, he remains sceptical about the validity of our knowledge of causality.

All this is implied in Nietzsche's talk of 'the great dice game of existence'.[31] One obvious feature of our attitude towards dice games is that we admit our inability to predict the next throw of the dice. In fact, we regard this as a desirable situation and look with disfavour on dice games which do not satisfy the requirement. By taking this as the model for the course of becoming as a whole, Nietzsche is demanding that a similar admission be made for every event without exception. As far as the practical business of life is concerned, it is no doubt necessary for us to go on as if we were in possession of genuine knowledge; perhaps a 'will to error' is essential to our survival. But there is also a will to truth which, for some individuals on some occasions, can assert itself in the insight expressed in the 'dice game' metaphor.

As it happens, in one way this analogy is too favourable to human knowledge. It suggests that if we cannot make predictions in categorical terms, we can nevertheless determine the probability of various states of affairs. In that case, the contrast it highlights is not between knowledge and ignorance, but rather between one kind of knowledge and a different kind of knowledge. The fact that the theory of probability deals with uncertainties does not imply that its assertions are themselves uncertain. Now, the 'dice game' analogy may suggest that scientific knowledge about the world is of this kind. But that is not what Nietzsche has in mind when he uses it, because he is just as sceptical about this kind of human knowledge. He remarks that, for all we know, 'a comet might suddenly annihilate the sun, or some electrical force might melt away the stars. What are 'statistics' in these things! In the case of earth and sun we have perhaps a couple of million years in which no such thing has happened: that proves nothing.'[32] Such an acknowledgement of the role of chance in the world rules out claims to statistical knowledge just as much as claims to causal knowledge; this is the point not brought out by the dice game analogy.

The question is whether this talk of chance is inconsistent with a commitment to determinism. On the account given, there seems to be no contradiction. Nietzsche's talk of chance refers to the scope of human knowledge, not to the nature of reality. His determinism asserts the necessity of all becoming, but not our ability to predict its course. The argument which supports the theory of eternal recurrence assumes that every total state is conditioned by the previous state and in turn conditions the succeeding state, but it contains no information that would enable any causal prediction concerning the events of the future. It does not assume that we are in possession of any knowledge of that kind. Conversely, the example of a dice game used in the first part of the argument does not constitute a repudiation of universal determinism. That point is brought out by Nietzsche in a related example. When we look at a waterfall, he observes, we think that its constant play of change is arbitrary and undetermined by anything but itself. Even here, though, there is no contingency, let alone freedom: 'But everything is necessary, and every movement mathematically calculable.'[33] These events are unpredictable because their complexity goes far beyond our powers of observation. The same is true of a dice game. It differs from the case of the waterfall in providing a ready basis for the theory of probability; but this is not due to any difference in respect to determinism. For this reason, it is wrong to suppose that anyone who uses the idea of probability gives up the right to use the principle of determinism as well. After all, Laplace's classic statement of the principle of determinism is to be found in the second chapter of his *Philosophical Essay on Probabilities*, where it is followed by an account of probability in which dice games figure as an example more than once.[34] In so far as this is raised as an objection to Nietzsche's argument, it is simply a mistake.

Recurrence without Probability

I turn now to another objection to the argument in terms of probability. It may be argued that, while a consideration of probability is not mistaken, it is at any rate superfluous. For there is an argument for eternal recurrence which does not involve any consideration of probability. Using Nietzsche's example, if we suppose that we have two ordinary dice, each with six faces, then there are thirty-six possible combinations for any given throw. This implies that if the dice are thrown thirty-seven times, at least one combination *must* occur at least twice. That inference has nothing whatever to do with probabilities. It is a direct consequence of the fact that the number of throws is greater than the number of possible combinations. Taking the argument further, if these dice are thrown an infinite number of times, then some combination must recur an infinite number of times. Again, probability is not a consideration. There is no need to assume that the probabilities of the various combinations are all equal: the conclusion would follow even if that were not the case. It is the same with Nietzsche's argument concerning the world as a whole. The assumption that only a finite number of total states are possible needs no further interpretation in terms of probability in order for a corresponding conclusion to be drawn.

We might even query whether Nietzsche himself uses the word 'probable' in this discussion – that is, whether the word *wahrscheinlich* does mean 'probable' in the sense that would link it with the theory of probability. Consider another use of the same word in a nearby note, where Nietzsche writes: 'Even if the circle of recurrence is only a probability or possibility, even the thought of a possibility can disturb and transform us, not just feelings or particular expectations: What effect has the possibility of eternal damnation had!'[35] Here probability and possibility are mentioned together. Yet it is clear that the term 'probability' refers to the credibility or plausibility of some belief, not to the likelihood of the events in question. This note is concerned with the effects which certain thoughts have when they 'gain power' over us.[36] Its theme is psychological rather than physical reality. In another passage Nietzsche writes: 'In place of fundamental truths I put fundamental probabilities – provisionally assumed guides by which one lives and thinks.'[37] Here, too, the emphasis is on the *attitude* of the individual person – in this case, our willingness to live and think according to assumptions which can never be more than conjectures. Could not one argue that Nietzsche's other use of the word 'probable' has much the same force?

Such considerations throw some doubt on the interpretation of Nietzsche's argument which interprets 'possible' as 'having a certain probability'. However, there are further aspects to the question. The argument I have mentioned may show that at least one state of affairs must recur eternally, but it does not show that the *present* state must do so. Yet this is the one state mentioned in Nietzsche's argument, and he explicitly concludes that 'there must have been this case' in the course of infinite time. Moreover, he adds that the same holds true for every possible state. In the case of the dice game this would be like arguing that, in the course of infinite time, every one of the possible combinations must recur an infinite number of times. And it is hard to see how that could be supported without an argument in terms of probability. Thus whether or not Nietzsche actually uses the notion of probability, the problem he faces seems to demand that we consider such an approach.

Yet in doing so we immediately encounter difficulties. Can we ascribe a definite probability to the present state of affairs? The argument that deduces the possibility of something from its actuality does not carry over into the vocabulary of probability. Nor does an appeal to immediate certainty work here, as it did in the argument against any past occurrences of a state of rest, which depended on identifying the present moment as a process of change. All we have to go on is the assumption that only a finite number of states are possible. This is a standard beginning in applications of the theory of probability, and it is usually uncontroversial, as in the case of the dice game.

When we are considering the states which make up reality as a whole, however, it might be more debatable than for such particular situations. Nietzsche does put forward an argument about the elements of reality and their modes of forming combinations which leads to the conclusion that the number of such combinations must be finite. Or, rather, he endorses what Dühring presented as a 'law of definite number': the world must be thought of 'as a certain definite quantity of force and as a certain definite number of centres of force' and must therefore have 'a calculable number of combinations'.[38]

For our present discussion, the problem is that this thesis is not enough by itself to set in motion the argument in terms of probability. The concept of probability is not explicable only in terms of possibility. It is true that it depends on the notion of possibility, since to use it we begin with assumptions about what is possible. But something more than these is needed. What this is has been the subject of debate and controversy. The classical form of the theory of probability involves providing an analysis of the range of possible states which enables one to assign an *equal* probability to each of them. This was clearly present in Boscovich's presentation of the argument. Later writers, however, criticized the 'principle of indifference' in various ways and offered different accounts of probability. So applying the theory of probability to Nietzsche's argument would involve several difficult tasks; we would not only have to fix upon some one interpretation of the theory itself, but also have to justify its application to this case. In order to use the classical interpretation, for example, we would presumably have to assign an equal probability to each total state of the world. How that could be justified is far from clear.

Yet all this can be avoided. We saw that an argument making no use of the category of probability could be found for eternal recurrence. The problem was that this argument seemed limited in scope: it proved that, in an infinite time, some state would recur an infinite number of times, but it said nothing about *what* state this would be. It did not prove that the present state would recur, or that every possible state would recur an infinite number of times. However, we can construct such a further argument without reference to premises other than those already mentioned. It is assumed now that some one state does recur eternally. If it is also assumed (as it was in the argument concerning a state of equilibrium) that a principle of determinism governs the course of becoming, then the present state is conditioned by the past occurrence of this state. But that means that the future occurrence of this state will condition the future occurrence of the present state. And the same argument holds true for every other state. We can therefore conclude that the recurrence of any one state must bring with it the recurrence of the whole sequence of states. Now this argument is hardly peculiar to Nietzsche. It is a standard one for all supporters of the principle of determinism: John Stuart Mill, for instance, uses it in just the same way. He writes: 'The state of the whole universe at any instant we believe to be the consequence of its state at the previous instant.'[39] From this premise he draws the conclusion: 'And if any particular state of the entire universe could ever recur a second time, all subsequent states would recur too, and history would, like a circulating decimal of many figures, periodically repeat itself.' One might compare this with a typical remark of Nietzsche: 'If only one moment of the world were to return – said the lightning – then everything would have to return.'[40] It need not be assumed that Nietzsche is showing the influence of Mill here. Rather, each is drawing a fairly obvious inference from the basic principle of universal determinism.

If we did not see this earlier, it might have been because the analogy of the dice game, useful in explaining the first part of the argument, becomes misleading at this later stage. Without appealing to a concept of probability, it cannot be proved that, in an infinite number of throws, every possible combination of dice must occur an infinite number of times. In fact, it cannot be proved that every possible combination must occur even once. The crucial point is that here we are dealing only with one part of reality, in which the course of events is influenced by various external circumstances. One combination of the dice does not by itself determine the next combination, and so it cannot be assumed that the recurrence of the same combination will lead to the recurrence of the combination which succeeded it, or of the whole subsequent sequence. On the other hand, it is just when we are considering 'the state of the whole universe' that we are entitled to make this inference, provided we assume the principle of universal determinism which asserts that every such total state is determined by the previous total state. Hence, in this case, the eternal recurrence of every actual state follows from the eternal recurrence of any one state, whereas for the dice game no such conclusion could be drawn.

There remains only the move from asserting the recurrence of every *actual* state to the recurrence of every *possible* state. The argument to be used here has already been indicated. It is that a cycle of events which recurs without variation in the same sequence makes all other events impossible, because it prevents them from occurring. Thus, although some event may be possible in itself, it is nevertheless impossible if it happens not to fall within the privileged set of events which has 'monopolized' reality. Thus, only those events are possible which do in fact occur, and all of these occur again and again in the same order without end. This is precisely the doctrine of eternal recurrence.

Whether our reconstruction of the argument can be attributed to Nietzsche is another matter. On the whole, it seems doubtful. Most of his attempts to formulate a proof of the doctrine make reference to determinism only *after* reaching the conclusion that every possible event must take place again and again, and only in order to prove that the *order* in which these events succeed one another must always be the same.[41] If this restriction is taken seriously, it means that some other justification must be given for the earlier thesis – and so it might be necessary after all to make use of the theory of probability. But all this shows is that philosophers do not always make the most economical and effective use of their assumptions. Nietzsche's presentations of his own argument are misleading in just this way, and so one can hardly blame later writers for errors of a similar kind.

Notes

1. KGW VIII/2, 201 (*The Will to Power*, sect. 639).
2. See, for example, Bernd Magnus, *Nietzsche's Existential Imperative* (Bloomington and London: Indiana University Press, 1978), 95.
3. KGW V/2, 451. See also KGW VII/3, 280 (*The Will to Power*, sect. 1062).
4. As we noted in Chapter 1, this point is found in African Spir's *Denken und Wirklichkeit. Versuch einer Erneuerung der kritischen Philosophie*, 2 vols (Leipzig: J.G. Findel, 1873).
5. See also KGW V/2, 414.
6. KGW VII/3, 258 (*The Will to Power*, sect. 1064).
7. KGW V/2, 432.
8. Ibid., 432.
9. Ibid., 432–33.
10. See, for example, KGW VIII/3, 168 (*The Will to Power*, sect. 1066).
11. KGW VII/3, 280 (*The Will to Power*, sect. 1062). Cf. KGW V/2, 420 and 451.
12. KGW VIII/2, 277 (*The Will to Power*, sect. 708). See also 173–43 (*The Will to Power*, sect. 1037).
13. KGW V/2, 441.
14. KGW VII/3, 258–59 (*The Will to Power*, sect. 1064).
15. Arnold Zuboff, 'Nietzsche and Eternal Recurrence', in Robert Solomon (ed.), *Nietzsche: A Collection of Critical Essays* (New York: Doubleday Anchor, 1973), 350.
16. KGW V/2, 421.
17. Ibid., 422.
18. See KGW VIII/1, 135 (*The Will to Power*, sect. 638).
19. KGW VII/3, 287 (*The Will to Power*, sect. 619). See also KGW VIII/3, 52–54 (*The Will to Power*, sect. 693 and 689).
20. See especially, Friedrich Nietzsche, *The Gay Science*, sect. 354 and 357; and KGW VIII/2, 281–82, 286–87 and 309–10 (*The Will to Power*, sect. 676, 678 and 524).
21. For another use of the word, see KGW VIII/3, 50 (*The Will to Power*, sect. 634): 'The adiaphorous state is missing, though it is thinkable.'
22. See, for example, his remarks on the idea of an indeterminate force: KGW V/2, 452; or on the concept of 'creation': KGW VIII/3, 166 (*The Will to Power*, sect. 1066).
23. Friedrich Nietzsche, *Thus Spake Zarathustra*, 'On the Blessed Isles'.
24. R.J. Boscovich, *A Theory of Natural Philosophy*, trans. J.M. Child (Cambridge, MA: MIT Press, 1966), sect. 540, 191.
25. See, for example, Richard Schacht, *Nietzsche* (London: Routledge and Kegan Paul, 1983), 264.
26. See, for example, Nietzsche, *The Gay Science*, sect. 112.
27. KGW VIII/3, 66–68 (*The Will to Power*, sect. 551).
28. Friedrich Nietzsche, *Beyond Good and Evil*, sect. 19.
29. KGW III/4, 86.
30. KGW VII/3, 259.
31. KGW VIII/3, 168 (*The Will to Power*, sect. 1066).
32. KGW V/2, 427.
33. Friedrich Nietzsche, *Human, All-Too-Human*, sect. 106.
34. Pierre-Simon Laplace, *A Philosophical Essay on Probabilities*, trans. F.W. Truscott and F.L. Emory (New York: Dover, 1952), 3: 'Present events are connected with previous ones by a tie based upon the evident principle that a thing cannot occur without a cause which produced it.'
35. KGW V/2, 421–22.
36. Nietzsche, *The Gay Science*, sect. 341.
37. KGW VII/1, 686.
38. KGW VII/3, 168 (*The Will to Power*, sect. 1066). Cf. Proclus, *The Elements of Theology*, trans. E. R. Dodds, 2nd edn (Oxford: Clarendon Press, 1963), Prop. 197, 173:

The sum of things is finite both in number and in magnitude; and the sum being finite, it is not possible that change should proceed in an infinite straight line, neither can anything perpetually in motion pass through a finite number of changes. Therefore what moves perpetually will return to its starting-point, so as to constitute a period.

39 J.S. Mill, *A System of Logic*, 7th edn (London: Longmans, Green, Reader and Dyer, 1868), Book III, chapter V, sect. 7.
40 KGW VII/1, 503.
41 KGW VIII/3, 168 (*The Will to Power*, sect. 1066).

Chapter 7

The Mathematics of Eternal Recurrence

We noted that Boscovich describes a theory which is very similar to the one defended by Nietzsche. However, he also offers what is intended to be a refutation of it, giving two reasons for judging the argument to be invalid. The first is an objection to any argument which relies on the concept of chance. Since everything has a cause, he claims, those who use such arguments 'err in the fact that they consider that there is anything that is in itself truly fortuitous'.[1] For we use the word 'chance' only when we are ignorant of the cause of something, and so it is an empty expression. The same objection is sometimes raised against Nietzsche, on an assumption that his argument depends on both probability and determinism in reaching its conclusion. As we saw in the last chapter, however, the objection is mistaken in two ways: Nietzsche's argument does not rely on any use of probability and, in any case, would not be chargeable with inconsistency if it did. These points need not be repeated now.

Having made this objection, Boscovich moves on to a different one which is more complex: 'But, leaving that out of account, it is quite false to say that the number of combinations from a finite number of terms is finite, if all things that are necessary to the constitution of the universe are considered.' Boscovich sees clearly that the crucial question concerns the way in which combinations of these elements are formed. If we imagine them as arranged along a single line and consider only their order to be significant, the argument will not be open to this objection.

> I readily acknowledge this much; that, if all the letters that go to form a poem of Virgil are shaken haphazard in a bag, and then taken out of it, and all the letters are set in order, one after the other, and this operation is carried on indefinitely, that combination which formed the poem of Virgil will return after a number of times, if this number is greater than some definite number.

However, the 'constitution of the universe' involves more than this. For one thing, it involves the arrangements of the points of matter within a space which has three dimensions, and moreover is infinitely divisible in each of them. Thus, even if we do imagine these terms to be located along a single line, there will be an infinite number of locations for this line with respect to each of the three dimensions of space. Furthermore, when we take into account not only the order of the points of matter on this line, but also their distances from one another, we find that each of them can be arranged in an infinite number of possible ways with respect to the others. Considering their possible speeds and directions of motion adds still more opportunities for an infinite number of differences. Boscovich concludes:

Hence, the number of combinations is infinite of an order that is immensely higher than the order of the infinity of instants of time; and thus, not only does it follow that not all the combinations are not bound to return an infinite number of times, but the ratio even of those that do not return is infinite, of a very high order.

Now, this objection is valid in relation to an argument which makes no mention of probability, but simply relies on the contrast between a finite number of possible states and an infinite time during which they continue to occur. We need not enter into Boscovich's claim that the number of possible combinations is, so to speak, even *more* infinite than the number of moments. In terms of a modern theory of infinite cardinalities, this is incorrect. However, that does not remove the force of his objection. If there are infinitely many possibilities, then the argument set out in the last chapter is invalid. Many of the assumptions of that argument are in fact accepted by Boscovich. He agrees that the number of points of matter is finite,[2] and this indeed provides him with an argument for the existence of God. How else, he asks, can we account for the fact that there is this number of points rather than some other? He also accepts that the totality of matter occupies only a finite space. Yet he does not accept that the combinations of a finite number of terms are finite in number.

Even though these arguments of Boscovich are not strong ones, they do raise the important issues surrounding the finite and the infinite in the argument concerning eternal recurrence. In this chapter I will follow that lead, and consider some mathematical arguments which take up the theme of infinity and apply it to the case of eternal recurrence, with various results. Since mathematics was not Nietzsche's strong point, most of these debates concern writers either before or after him – in the second instance, including his commentators and critics. Nevertheless, their relevance to his thinking, especially about the 'sameness' of recurrence, will become clear as we proceed.

The Incommensurability Argument: from Oresme to Simmel

A well-known argument directed against Nietzsche's theory of eternal recurrence is found in Georg Simmel's lecture series *Schopenhauer and Nietzsche*, first published in 1907. In discussing Nietzsche's attempts to construct a proof of the doctrine of eternal recurrence, Simmel raises an objection which takes the form of a particular counterexample.[3] He describes a system of three wheels which move with incommensurable speeds, in such a way that their initial position will never again be reached, even if their motions continue for an infinite time. Simmel's argument has given rise to much discussion, yet none of its commentators has remarked on its longer history. In fact, the counterexample goes back to the middle of the fourteenth century. Its real originator was Nicole Oresme (c. 1325–1382). In a treatise intended primarily as a rebuttal of the doctrine of eternal recurrence, Oresme constructs an example which consists of three objects moving in circular courses with incommensurable speeds, and draws a conclusion which is the same as Simmel's: the initial position of the three objects can never recur, no matter how long they continue to move in the way described.

I begin by discussing some features of the argument common to Oresme and Simmel. After this, I will look at the applicability of the notion of *approximation* to the theme of recurrence. The idea enters into an argument raised against the inference Oresme and Simmel draw from their example. This objection charges that their conclusion is reached by an excessively strict interpretation of the concept of recurrence. It suggests that an approximation to identical positions is acceptable in practice as a criterion for applying a concept of recurrence, and that the construction described by Oresme and Simmel is quite consistent with its use in this sense, so that it does not provide an exception to eternal recurrence. In discussing this dispute, we will see that more than one idea of approximation is in question. However, we will also see that the scope of the counterargument just described is very limited.

We begin, then, with Nicole Oresme and his treatise *On the Commensurability or Incommensurability of the Celestial Motions*.[4] It is there that the archetype of the example used by Simmel is to be found. Oresme did treat the theme of incommensurability in earlier writings, but in this treatise he puts it to work in an extended critique of the assumptions which underlie the doctrine of eternal recurrence. At the same time, his target is the pretended science of astrology, because he regards the idea of the 'Great Year' as one of its leading doctrines. According to this conception, there is a periodic return of the celestial bodies to any initial configuration and, when this occurs, it follows that the corresponding events which occurred before on the earth will occur again in precisely the same fashion. The expression 'Great Year' comes from the Stoics, although they owed the idea to their Pythagorean predecessors. Estimates of the length of the Great Year varied widely: the theory most current in the Middle Ages, and explicitly condemned by the bishop of Paris in 1277, took it to be 36000 years.[5] Oresme, however, regards this as the Great Year only of the sun and the eighth sphere – that is, the sphere of the fixed stars.[6] He remarks that an extension of this to include all the planets would make the Great Year much longer. His own view, however, is that neither case has any validity.

Oresme's strategy is to attack the doctrine on purely mathematical grounds, avoiding the sort of collision between assertion and counterassertion which is so common in controversies over astrology. The question is reduced to one concerning the commensurability or incommensurability of the motions of celestial bodies. In the two main parts of his treatise on the subject, Oresme explores the consequences of these alternatives in turn. In the third and final part, he discusses various arguments for or against commensurability and incommensurability. Although no final decision is reached, it is clear that Oresme considers the balance of probability to fall on the side of incommensurability. He has shown that it has a plausibility which entitles us, in the absence of empirical evidence sufficiently precise to decide the issue, to be sceptical about the assumption of commensurability.

The proposition in which our example occurs is found in Part Two of the treatise; but it also relies on results established in Part One. Here Oresme is assuming, for the sake of argument, that the motions under discussion are mutually commensurable. He shows that under this circumstance, two bodies which are in conjunction at one time will also be in conjunction at many other times in the same place, and will have been so at many other times in the past.[7] In further propositions, he shows how to find other places, if there are any, where the same objects will be in conjunction. Such places will always be separated from the present place of conjunction by a distance which is commensurable with the whole circle.[8] In each case, the same conclusion follows: the objects must conjunct in that place at other times in the future, and must have done so in the past. In further propositions, Oresme considers more complex examples involving three or more bodies, and dealing with aspects other than conjunction. In proposition 22 he draws a general conclusion: if the motions of the celestial bodies are mutually commensurable, there will be a period in which they return to a given configuration – that is, a 'Great Year'.[9]

Part Two of the treatise develops the consequences of the assumption that the motions of the celestial bodies are mutually incommensurable, in a way that displays the differences between these consequences and the conclusions of Part One. Again Oresme begins with a consideration of the simple case of two bodies. The first proposition asserts that two bodies now in conjunction but moving with incommensurable speeds will never again be in conjunction in that place.[10] The next proposition states further that, when they do come into conjunction again, it will be at points which are separated from their present point of conjunction by a distance which is incommensurable with the whole circle.[11] In the eighth proposition of Part Two, Oresme considers three moving objects:

> If three or more mobiles are now in conjunction moving with commensurable motions, except for one whose motion is incommensurable to the others, they will never conjunct elsewhere [in the future], nor have they conjuncted in another place [in the past].[12]

This proposition is a consequence of the propositions already established in Part One and earlier in Part Two: it combines Oresme's findings about the cases of commensurability and incommensurability. It is particularly relevant to an application of these mathematical concepts to the motions of the celestial bodies, since their ratios may well be of both kinds. As an example, Oresme considers three objects A, B and C, which are at the present moment in the same place d. A and B move with commensurable speeds, and therefore they will conjunct again in the same place, and in other places which are separated from the same place by a distance which is commensurable with the whole circle. However, B and C move with incommensurable speeds, and so they will never conjunct in any of these places. It follows that there will never be another conjunction of all three objects, however long they continue to move.

> For example, if it is assumed that A moves twice as quickly as B, then, by the eleventh proposition of the first part, A and B will never conjunct except in point d. And since, by assumption, B and C have incommensurable speeds, it follows, by the first proposition of this part, that they will never conjunct in point d. Hence A, B, and C will never again be in conjunction at the same time; and the same argument is applicable to the past and to more [than three] mobiles.[13]

Oresme goes on to make the general observation that three or more objects will either never conjunct, conjunct only once, or conjunct an infinite number of times. These are the only possibilities, whether their motions are commensurable or incommensurable. Oresme is particularly interested in the case whose possibility he has just established. He suggests elsewhere that a conjunction which occurs only once may be the natural cause of the appearance of some new species, or of some unique event, such as the Great Flood.[14] But the general importance of such conjunctions is that their occurrence constitutes a refutation of the doctrine of the Great Year.

Part Three of Oresme's thesis is different in style from the previous Parts. It begins with an admission that human observation of the celestial motions is not accurate enough to decide the question of their commensurability or incommensurability. There follows a survey of various arguments designed to make one or the other alternative appear more plausible. This survey takes the form of a debate between the personified figures of Arithmetic and Geometry, who argue respectively for commensurability and for incommensurability. Most of the points raised appeal to considerations of an aesthetic or moral kind, but one made by Geometry is different. She states that 'where any two unknown magnitudes have been designated, it is more probable that they are incommensurable than commensurable, just as it is more probable that any unknown [number] proposed from a multitude of numbers would be non-perfect rather than perfect'.[15] So, in the absence of any other consideration, we are entitled to make this assumption in considering any motions whose ratio is unknown to us. The debate in Part Three of the treatise does not end with a definite decision, but it seems that Oresme's own view is in accordance with this mathematical argument. In other words, although a conclusive demonstration is not available, the incommensurability of the celestial motions is far more probable than their commensurability.

Oresme provides no reason here for supposing two unknown magnitudes are more likely to be incommensurable than to be commensurable, apart from his suggestion that the case is similar to that of perfect numbers.[16] One obvious comment to be made about this argument is that it applies only to finite sets of ratios, just as the argument about cube or perfect numbers applies only to finite sets of numbers. Whether Oresme intended the argument to be extended to infinity is unclear, although his assertion that its result holds true 'however many numbers are taken in series' does suggest an infinite series. The problem is that Oresme's propositions are not valid for infinite sets of ratios or numbers. Assuming a definition of equivalence as one-to-one correspondence, there are just as many cube numbers as natural numbers.[17] Similarly, when the series of ratios described by Oresme is taken as infinite, a one-to-one correspondence between commensurable and incommensurable pairs of ratios can be established. His strategy of arguing from the properties of finite sets of ratios is an invalid one, given a conceptual apparatus which enables us to assign arithmetical properties to infinite as well as finite sets.

Despite all this, Oresme's claim that unknown magnitudes are far more likely to be incommensurable than commensurable is one that, at first sight, appears both familiar and plausible to a modern reader who will be disposed to restate it in terms of the relation between the real and the rational numbers. Since the rational numbers are denumerably infinite, whereas the real numbers are non-denumerably infinite, the probability that a number taken at random from the real numbers will be rational is zero. And, in that case, the argument stated by Geometry in the final part of *On the Commensurability or Incommensurability of the Celestial Motions* can proceed in a form which is not merely persuasive, as Oresme may have considered it, but demonstrative.

Simmel's Counterexample

We turn now to Simmel's argument against the line of thought which Nietzsche presents in support of eternal recurrence. Since the world contains only a finite number of elements, it goes, the possible combinations or configurations of these elements must also be finite in number. In the course of infinite time, the same combinations must therefore occur again and again. Furthermore, if each is conditioned by those that preceded it, they must recur in the same order. Simmel's objection is aimed at one step in this argument – the claim that a finite number of elements allows only a finite number of combinations. He suggests that we can readily imagine a combination of elements which will never be repeated in infinite time. The simplest case is one that consists of three elements.

> Imagine three wheels of equal size rotating around the same axle. There is one point marked on each one of them so that the three points are aligned on a straight line at a certain moment, which may be indicated by a thread straightened across the wheels. Now the wheels start to rotate, the second wheel at twice the speed of the first one. The two marked points on the wheels will be aligned under the thread when the first wheel has finished one revolution and the second wheel has completed two revolutions. They will be aligned again after the second revolution of the first wheel and the fourth revolution of the second wheel, and so on. In short, both wheels return to their starting positions after n revolutions of the first one and 2n revolutions of the second. Now let us suppose that the speed of revolution of the third wheel is $1/\pi$ of that of the first wheel. Then the 1, 2, 3, ..., n rotations of the first wheel are expressed by $1/\pi$, $2/\pi$, $3/\pi$, ..., n/π rotations of the third wheel. According to the nature of the number π,

none of these fractions can be a whole number. This means that the third wheel will never have finished a whole number of rotations when the first wheel has completed a whole number of rotations. But because the instantaneous position of alignment, under the thread, of the points marked on the first and the second wheels will occur only after the first wheel has made a whole rotation, the marked point on the third wheel never can pass under the thread at the same moment that the marked points of the two other wheels pass under it. In consequence, the starting position of the three wheels cannot be repeated through eternity.[18]

Simmel goes on to say that if the world does contain any motions related to one another in this fashion, then a given state of affairs will never be repeated. The mere possibility of such a case is enough to disallow the argument used by Nietzsche in support of his doctrine of eternal recurrence, for it establishes that the finitude of the elements does not imply the finitude of their combinations.

One can see that this argument is valid by following a *reductio ad absurdum* procedure. Let us suppose that, at some time, the three points do return to their original line-up. We can tell when the first wheel returns to its initial position because, whenever this happens, and only when it happens, the points on the first and second wheels are aligned. Having noted this fact we can forget the second wheel, whose function is to enable us to identify complete revolutions of the first wheel without reference to outside objects. (Simmel adds that a thread is held in place across the wheels in order to mark the starting position; if this remains it seems to me that the second wheel is superfluous.) Now suppose that the third wheel also returns to its original position. Clearly the first and third wheels will each have revolved an integral number of times. If we call these numbers a and b respectively, then, given our information about the relative speeds of the wheels, it follows that $b = a/\pi$. But π is an irrational number, which means that there are *no* two integers a and b for which the formula $\pi = a/b$ holds true. Thus our hypothesis that the original position can again be reached must be abandoned because it has led to a contradiction.

It is evident that Simmel's counterexample is essentially the same as that given by Oresme in proposition 8 of Part Two of his treatise. This is strong circumstantial evidence for the influence of Oresme on Simmel, but the exact source used by Simmel remains to be identified. Each example consists of three objects moving uniformly in circular paths of equal size, but with different speeds. In each example, the speeds of the first two objects are mutually commensurable, but the speed of the third is incommensurable with those of the first two. The conclusion drawn is exactly the same: the initial position of the three objects will never recur, however long their motions continue.

Oresme and Simmel make their examples more concrete in slightly different ways. If we refer to Simmel's three wheels as A, B and C respectively, then he is saying that B moves not half as fast as A, but twice as fast as A. Furthermore, he defines the speed of C in terms of the speed of A, whereas Oresme defines it in terms of the speed of B. All these differences amount to, however, is a transposition of A and B. More significant is the fact that Simmel specifies the speed of C as being $1/\pi$ times the speed of A, whereas Oresme says only that the speed of C is incommensurable with that of B. If Oresme had mentioned a particular ratio of speeds, it is unlikely to have been this one. His mode of thinking is geometrical, and in giving an example, he usually has in mind some possible construction. But if our methods of construction are restricted to the traditional ones, it is not possible to produce the model described by Simmel. The problem is akin to that of constructing a line which is π times the length of a given line. Anyone capable of doing this would also be capable of squaring the circle.[19] Simmel is going the other way, as it were, since his ratio is $1/\pi$ rather than π, but the construction is no less impossible. It is clear that Simmel – typical in this respect of a modern – is thinking from an arithmetical rather than geometrical point of view, for which one irrational number is as good as any other in this example. Oresme, on the other hand, associates arithmetic with a strong hostility toward incommensurability. In those examples of incommensurability for which he does specify a particular ratio, it is generally that of the diagonal of a square to its side. Hence the number in question tends to be $\sqrt{2}$ or $\sqrt{8}$ – that is, the diagonal of a square whose side is 1 or 2 units. Presumably he would have used one of these in the present instance.[20] We might also note, while discussing the choice of ratio, that the irrationality of π was not demonstrated until the eighteenth century.[21] The standard proof of the irrationality of $\sqrt{2}$ is much older, going back to ancient times.[22] So, again, it can be seen that Simmel's model has in this detail a specifically modern character. Despite that, it remains the same example and rests on the same assumptions.

The Question of Approximation

One assumption concerns the concept of recurrence itself. An objection raised against both Oresme and Simmel picks out this aspect of their argument and subjects it to criticism. Writing in 1451, John de Fundis attacked Oresme for supposing that a conjunction of celestial bodies required their presence in the same point. He wrote: 'It suffices here, indeed, that they be conjuncted in a degree, minute, second, or third, and not in an infinite division as Oresme subtilized ....'[23] De Fundis had in mind the practice of astrologers and astronomers, both of whom work within the limits which their senses and instruments impose on their observations. His assertion is that, in this context, an appropriately close approximation is accepted as a criterion for making judgements about the positions of the celestial bodies. Once it is acknowledged that differences in position falling within certain limits can reasonably be overlooked, Oresme's conclusions no longer hold true.

Much the same criticism of Oresme has been made in the twentieth century. In the eighth volume of *Le Système du monde*, Pierre Duhem argues that, since the periods of the celestial bodies are determined only by observation, we can never be certain whether they are commensurable or incommensurable with one another. For any incommensurable proportion, there will be a commensurable proportion which comes as close to it as one wants.[24] The standpoints of the empirical scientist and the pure mathematician are put in sharp contrast by Duhem, who sums up: 'For a mathematician, every relation is commensurable or incommensurable; for the physicist, one can assert indifferently, of the relation between two observed magnitudes, that it is commensurable or incommensurable.'[25] He makes the same point, in a slightly different way, with reference to the effects of the celestial motions on the earth.

> Does it matter, anyway, to the astrologer, whether the periods of celestial revolution are commensurable or incommensurable? If they are mutually incommensurable, then it is clear that the stars will never regain exactly the configuration they had a first time; but at the end of a sufficient time they will form a constellation which will differ as little as one likes from the constellation previously formed. Without being, on the second occasion, strictly identical with what they were on the first, the effects produced by these stars here below will resemble them as closely as one could want, so closely that no observer could tell them apart. Is not this, for the astrologer, just as if they were reproduced exactly?[26]

What Duhem says here coincides with a proposition stated by Oresme, who writes: 'If three or more mobiles are moved with incommensurable velocities, they could never be so close that at some other time, they could not be even closer; and so into infinity.'[27] This approximation will, Oresme explains, occur everywhere in the circle. So, while the bodies will never again be in conjunction, they will eventually be separated from the point at which their conjunction occurred by a distance which is smaller than any one cares to mention.

> I say, then, that these planets would, at some time, arrive in the same minute, and at some time in the same second, and at some time in the same third, or fourth, and so on, approaching closer and closer into infinity, and yet they will never conjunct exactly.[28]

Now, this statement has nothing to do with the limits of empirical observation; it is as purely mathematical as any of the other propositions advanced by Oresme in the treatise. Yet it is presumably on a similar basis that Duhem makes his criticism of Oresme's position. Duhem, then, is not pointing out anything that one could say was overlooked by Oresme. Rather, his claim is that the appropriate standpoint for approaching the question of the Great Year is that of the scientist rather than the mathematician.

Before considering this question of approximation in more detail, let us note a corresponding argument raised in relation to Simmel's counterexample to Nietzsche's theory. Arnold Zuboff has suggested that Simmel has failed to take into account the limits of human experience. He writes: 'How many different phenomenal possibilities are there in Simmel's line-up of wheels?

I would say that there can be only finite phenomenally discernible line-ups.'[29] This assertion may be supported by an appeal to human physiology, Zuboff argues: if our nervous system allows only a finite number of neural processes, the experiences available to us must also be finite in number, so that the same experience may correspond to somewhat different states of the external world. His conclusion is that if the world were similar to Simmel's example, the improbability of repetition in a strict sense would not rule out a 'phenomenal' repetition.

> Phenomenal repetition, which would be overwhelmingly likely, would represent indifferently any one of the infinite varying sub-phenomenal states which could be responsible for it below the level of phenomenal discernibility. But, again, such phenomenal repetition would not entail that there had been a sub-phenomenal – and effective – repetition and so would not signify a ring of recurrence.[30]

The similarity with Duhem's argument about the effects of closely similar configurations of the celestial bodies is plain enough. Once again, the underlying point is a mathematical one. Although Simmel's wheels will never return to their initial configuration, there will be a time when they are closer to it than any particular distance, however small. One can proceed from the figures given by Simmel to estimate when these approaches will occur. All that is needed is to recall the best-known fractional approximations for π, such as 22/7 or 355/113. Using the latter of these ratios, we may say that when A has undergone exactly 355 revolutions, B has undergone exactly 710 revolutions, and C has undergone almost exactly 113 revolutions. In fact, the figure is slightly less than 113.00001 revolutions.[31] The position of the wheels at this time might well qualify as one which could be mistaken for the original alignment. In case it does not, there remains an infinite number of later occasions on which the separation of the points marked on the three wheels will be even less. One can well imagine that at such a time, the wheels would appear to an observer to be in their original position. For some of us, of course, that occasion might arrive relatively soon.

However, there is a serious problem in taking this argument as a successful defence of the doctrine of eternal recurrence. The appeal to approximation, either in its mathematical or in its observational version, does not lend itself to the kind of indefinite extension that such a defence requires. The proposition stated by Oresme, and repeated by his critics, has nothing to do with a constant period of recurrence throughout an infinite time. On the contrary, given any instance of an approximation to the original conjunction of elements such that their separation is less than a given distance, a continued repetition of the intervening process will increase the separation to one that is greater than the given distance. After 355 revolutions of Simmel's wheel A, the three points would be separated by only 0.00001 of a circle, but after 355 000 revolutions of wheel A, the separation would increase to 0.01 of the circle and so on. Clearly, any arbitrarily chosen distance would in due course be exceeded. Similarly, with approximations which are closer than observation can detect, repetition of the process will bring about a difference which is observable, as accumulated 'sub-phenomenal' differences turn into phenomenal differences. Oresme pointed this out in commenting on the practice of astronomers, when he remarked that 'a minute, undetectable error would produce a perceptible discrepancy when multiplied over a long [period of] time'.[32]

In either version, then, the prospect of a regular recurrence of the same state of affairs is ruled out. The recurrence implied by these models is a very irregular one, with varying periods of time between one approximation and the next, according to the phenomenal or numerical limit taken as a standard. One could say that this recurrence is still an eternal one, in that the approximations will continue to go on throughout an infinite time. Nevertheless, it is not an 'eternal recurrence' in the Nietzschean sense. This is not just because of the absence of a constant 'Great Year', because that is not of great importance by itself. What matters to Nietzsche is the recurrence not of single states of affairs, but of whole sequences of them, such as those constituting a particular human life. He is not alone in this: the astrologers Oresme is arguing against would have understood the doctrine in the same way. Its deterministic or fatalistic implications depend on assumptions about the identities of particular persons, and these in turn refer to certain sequences of states of affairs which establish patterns of experience or behaviour. If such sequences undergo disruption, the patterns in question change, and the basis for asserting the identity of anything more than a momentary state is lost. These versions of recurrence, therefore, leave out what is of most importance in the doctrine of eternal recurrence: they eliminate its personal significance. Being confronted with the prospect of reliving every part of one's life an infinite number of times is something that, as Nietzsche suggests, could decisively affect one's attitude towards that life. In contrast, the sporadic reappearance of various isolated states is, and must remain, a possibility of only theoretical interest.

The other problem facing these arguments concerns the use of approximation as a substitute for identity. This is particularly important for Nietzsche's thought of eternal recurrence. He stresses that what he means is a recurrence of the *same* states of affairs, and not ones that are *similar*, however great the degree of similarity may be. In *Thus Spake Zarathustra* the doctrine is announced in these terms: 'I come again, with this sun, with this earth, with this eagle, with this serpent – *not* to a new life or a better life or a similar life: I come again eternally to this same and self-same life, in what is greatest as in what is smallest.'[33] In general, Nietzsche wants to keep the concepts 'same' and 'similar' quite apart from each other. He writes: 'The similar is not a degree of the same: rather something totally different from the same.'[34] This suggests that he would not be inclined to take an approximation, however close, as equivalent to an identity. Further, he denies that *any* of the things we take to be the same are really the same. This is one of the basic illusions of our experience – that in order to organize it into a pattern which will allow us to cope with our environment, we identify things as the same when they are merely similar. Nietzsche asserts, however, that reality is a process of absolute becoming: 'The tree is something new in every moment: the form is asserted by us because we cannot perceive the finest absolute movement.'[35]

Now it is quite striking that Nietzsche's insistences on this point are to be found in much the same places as his sketches of the doctrine of eternal recurrence. That is because the two are complementary: Nietzsche places great importance on the 'sameness' of eternal recurrence precisely because he denies the sameness of anything else. He even offers an argument designed to prove that this is impossible: two things the same as each other and existing at the same time would have to have the same causes, and that in turn would imply an endless regress: 'Thus we would have to assume that something the same had been present back into all eternity, despite every alteration of the general state and creation of new properties – an impossible assumption!'[36] I take it that Nietzsche's reason for ruling out this assumption as impossible lies in his view that everything in reality is related to everything else or, in other words, that there is only one world. If we accept this assumption, we must reject the notion of any series of causes which would stand apart from the general course of the world. Thus in turn we must reject the claim that within one state of the world there can exist two things the same as each other.

What is wrong with the argument from approximation which relies on the limits of human observation is not just that this is out of place in a thought experiment, but that it is out of place in considering a concept which can be approached *only* in terms of a thought experiment. The eternal recurrence of the same is not an event for which evidence of the empirical kind can be provided. Nor can familiar kinds of experience be cited in its support. If for instance I could *remember* the occurrence in a previous cycle of the experience I have at this moment, it would not be the same experience after all, because it would contain this added element. In just the same way, I cannot *foresee* the future recurrence of this same experience. Nor therefore can I (as some writers seem to think) have any of the kinds of feeling about this recurrence which would presuppose such a cognition. Another interesting consequence is that commonsense questions about the criterion of personal identity, for instance, simply make no sense in this context. Such questions arise only for concepts which can be applied to experience in the way that has specifically been ruled out by Nietzsche for the concept of sameness. In this respect, Simmel's argument is noticeably faithful to the doctrine which it attacks, and all the more effective as a result.

Poincaré's Recurrence Theorem

It has been argued that Nietzsche was mistaken in supposing eternal recurrence to be inconsistent with the mechanistic standpoint, since Henri Poincaré's 'recurrence theorem' is a major contribution to modern science which is based on mechanistic assumptions.[37] Poincaré showed that a mechanical system must always return to a state which is infinitely close to any initial position.[38] His theorem was used by Ernst Zermelo as an argument against the second law of thermodynamics. Zermelo concluded: 'In such a system all processes are *periodic* from a mathematical viewpoint, hence *not irreversible* in the strict sense, so that one may not assert that there is an actual progressive increase of entropy as the second law, in its usual meaning, would require.'[39] Given the importance of this question for modern science, it is not surprising that comparisons should be made with Nietzsche's treatment of eternal recurrence, especially given his concern with the avoidance of a 'final state'.[40] In this concluding section, I intend to widen the discussion to explore some of the similarities and differences between this theorem and the ideas looked at so far.

Poincaré first stated his theorem in his prize paper of 1890 entitled 'On the Three-Body Problem and the Equations of Dynamics'.[41] He restated it several years later in the third volume of *Les méthodes nouvelles de la mécanique céleste*.[42] The theorem demonstrates that an isolated mechanical system will return at a future time to a state which is closer to its initial state than any given amount. The context is, of course, a very different one from that of the Oresme/Simmel example. The problem that concerns Poincaré is one of dynamics, not kinematics. It is the three-body problem which has challenged physicists since the time of Newton. The task is to establish the stability of a system of three bodies whose behaviour is governed by the laws of Newtonian mechanics, including its law of gravitation. The practical aim, however, is to establish the stability of the solar system – if it is stable.

Poincaré is mainly concerned with the problem in what he terms its 'restricted' form – that is, in which one of the three bodies is considered to have a mass which is small enough to be neglected in any calculation. Sometimes he mentions an even more restricted version of the problem, in which two of the three bodies are regarded as having no significant mass. In that case, there is no interaction between those two bodies, barring collisions, and the solution is a long-established one: the two small bodies move around the large body in elliptical paths, in accordance with Kepler's laws. Poincaré adds one comment which sounds like an echo of Oresme: 'It is clear, then, that if the average motions of these two small masses are commensurable with each other, the whole system will return to its initial situation at the end of a certain time, and consequently the solution will be periodic.'[43]

Unfortunately, solutions for cases other than this special one are hard to come by. The 'restricted' case mentioned above is important because of its application to the solar system – for instance, to the motions of the sun, the planet Jupiter and one of its moons. The aim is to establish the 'stability' of such a system, but this term has a number of senses. Poincaré stipulates that a 'complete stability' would involve three conditions, which we can state as follows.[44]

1 The distances between the bodies do not increase indefinitely.
2 The bodies do not collide or come indefinitely close to one another.
3 The system returns an infinite number of times indefinitely close to its initial position.

The first condition is satisfied by the 'restricted' case just mentioned, and the second is one that Poincaré says he cannot comment on. It is the third kind of stability that concerns him in his 'recurrence' theorem. He adopts a mode of representation in which the whole system is represented by a single point P, located within a space whose dimensions are determined by the degrees of freedom in the system.[45] Changes in the system are represented by the movement of this point through its space, and so the question of the stability of the system is just the question whether the trajectory of the point is a *closed* one. As Poincaré puts it, 'For there to be stability, the point P must return at the end of a sufficient time to its initial position, or at least to a position as close as one wishes to this initial position.'[46] His 'recurrence theorem' demonstrates that there are an infinite number of initial positions which satisfy this description – that is, such that a point which is located within a small region at a certain time will pass through this region an infinite number of times in the course of an infinite time.

Poincaré's demonstration is highly technical, and so only a very general indication of its strategy can be given here.[47] If one asks whether it resembles either of the arguments considered in the last chapter, the answer is that there are certain resemblances with both. Its main argument does not involve probability.[48] Rather, it relies on the concept of finite regions within an overall space which is itself finite. If we begin with a small region within which many points exist and trace their later movement, then, assuming their volume to remain constant, they will eventually occupy a space which overlaps with the original region. The area of overlap will correspond to a certain area within that region in which those points were at first located. That is, the points that were earlier within that area will have returned to their original region. But when we consider the further movement of these points, then it follows from the same reasoning that some of them will return to a certain part of that smaller area. Again, the key principle is just that continual addition of a finite quantity will eventually exceed any given finite quantity.[49] By repeating this procedure indefinitely, Poincaré is able to identify a region whose points will necessarily return to their original location an infinite number of times.

One further feature of Poincaré's theorem, however, is the use of the concept of probability in a corollary which determines the scope of its applicability. Poincaré allows that there are an infinite number of 'exceptional' positions for which the theorem does not hold, but shows that it is infinitely improbable that a point will occupy one of these positions. He compares this with the infinite improbability that a number taken at random from the real numbers will be a rational number. These cases, Poincaré says, 'are exceptional by the same title that commensurable numbers are only an exception in the series of numbers, whereas incommensurable numbers are the rule'.[50] We have noted the close relation between this observation and Oresme's reasoning in pointing out that two unknown magnitudes are far more likely to be incommensurable than commensurable. The difference is that, whereas for Poincaré the prevalence of incommensurability confirms the applicability of the recurrence theorem, its significance for Oresme is just the opposite: it implies that there can be no recurrence, in the strict sense, of a given configuration of the celestial bodies.

How does Poincaré's theorem stand in relation to the problems confronting the standard replies to Oresme and Simmel? Is it, like them, an argument for recurrence, but not for eternal recurrence? First of all, the theorem is stated in terms of a concept of approximation which is purely mathematical. Poincaré makes it clear that his results are not reached by considering the limits of possible observation. In one passage, he contrasts two approaches to the idea of convergence.[51] The 'astronomical' approach takes account of the terms in a series only as far as they are relevant to possible observations. The 'geometrical' approach, on the other hand, is guided by an insistence on rigour which is not disturbed by the practical problems of calculation, and so it takes the character of a series as determined by the presence or absence of a final limit. Both rules are legitimate, Poincaré says, but they belong to different domains: the geometrical approach is for theoretical investigations, and the astronomical approach for numerical applications. He states that his own concept of convergence is strictly the geometrical one.

If Poincaré's recurrence is a genuine one in this sense, does it also have those features which are so important in the doctrine of eternal recurrence proposed by Nietzsche and, for that matter, the earlier astrologers? Does it imply a constant period of recurrence, or predict that not only single states of affairs but the whole sequence of such states will recur in the same order? This is really a single question, since the same sequence of states will presumably have the same duration and since, conversely, it is hard to see how the period of recurrence could be constant for any other reason than the sameness of the intervening process. If Poincaré had shown that the trajectory of P must return infinitely many times to the same point, or even to the same finite set of points, then these further conclusions could be drawn, at least on the assumption that the system's behaviour is fully determined. As it is, his theorem says only that P must return infinitely many times to the same region. Although this region may be as small as one likes, it is still finite in extent. In that case, we cannot assume those features of recurrence that belong to the doctrine in its strong form. Even in Oresme's account, acknowledgement was made of the infinitely many close approximations to conjunction of bodies moving with incommensurable speeds. The situation described by Poincaré's theorem is not so different. The theorem is genuinely about recurrence, then, if and only if we regard an indefinitely close approximation as equivalent to a recurrence. Poincaré does not commit himself on the matter. He does use the word *récurrence*, but only in referring to a formal mathematical operation.[52] He does not use the expression to characterize the outcome of the theorem: it seems to have been others who originated the label 'recurrence theorem'. No doubt this is because the further implications of the term, mentioned with reference to Nietzsche, are not Poincaré's concern. The question remains whether his theorem *is* about recurrence, given that it predicts an indefinitely close approach of a system to its former state, rather than an exact coincidence. It is not necessarily a question for which there is a 'right' or 'wrong' answer. Duhem's distinction between the scientist and the mathematician, as well as Poincaré's between the astronomical and the geometrical standpoints, express differences of interest, not disputes over truth and falsity. It is when the same terminology is appropriated by both sides to express their results that misunderstanding or confusion is likely to appear.

Despite its rigorous character, Poincaré's recurrence theorem has not led to a general acceptance by scientists of a doctrine of eternal recurrence. A major controversy arose surrounding the relation of the theorem to the second law of thermodynamics. Although well-established on empirical grounds, this law seemed to be quite inconsistent with the prediction of an infinitely close return of any closed mechanical system to a previous state. For some scientists, it appeared that the law would therefore have to be abandoned. The standard reply to their argument, however, has been that of Boltzmann: the period of recurrence which follows from the theorem for any system of reasonable size is so great that it has no relevance to the phenomena of experience.[53] More recently, models of the universe based on general relativity have replaced those of classical mechanics. But as Frank J. Tipler points out, 'in general relativity, singularities intervene to prevent recurrence. General relativistic universes are thought to begin and end in singularities of infinite curvature, and these singularities force time in general relativity to be linear rather than cyclic.'[54] Such developments, therefore, provide further reasons for a rejection of the idea of eternal recurrence.

Notes

1 Roger Joseph Boscovich, *A Theory of Natural Philosophy*, trans. J.M. Child (Cambridge, MA: MIT Press, 1966), 191 (sect. 540).
2 Ibid., 192 (sect. 546).
3 Georg Simmel, *Schopenhauer and Nietzsche*, trans. Helmut Loiskandl, Deena Weinstein and Michael Weinstein (Amherst, MA: The University of Massachusetts Press, 1986), 172–73.
4 Edward Grant, *Oresme and the Kinematics of Circular Motion* (Madison, WI: University of Wisconsin Press, 1971). See also Edward Grant, 'Nicole Oresme and the Commensurability or Incommensurability of the Celestial Motions', *Archive for History of Exact Sciences*, 1 (1960–62), 420–58.
5 This figure is derived from the assumption that the equinoctial points move in a circle at a rate of one degree in a hundred years – an estimate attributed to Hipparchus. See T.L. Heath, *Aristarchus of Samos* (Oxford: Clarendon Press, 1913), 172–73.
6 Grant, *Oresme and the Kinematics of Circular Motion*, 243.
7 Ibid., 193.
8 Ibid., 205.
9 Ibid., 243.
10 Ibid., 249.
11 Ibid., 251.
12 Ibid., 265.
13 Ibid., 267.
14 Oresme, *De proportionibus proportionum and Ad pauca respicientes*, ed. and trans. E. Grant (Madison: University of Wisconsin Press, 1966), 423–25.
15 Ibid., 249.

16 A detailed analysis of Oresme's definition of incommensurability is given in Robin Small, 'Incommensurability and Recurrence: From Oresme to Simmel', *Journal of the History of Ideas*, 52 (1991), 121–37.
17 It has not been established whether the perfect numbers are infinite or not. If they are, a similar consequence follows. If they are not, then the probability that a number picked at random from the natural numbers will be perfect is zero. For a report on this problem, see Paulo Ribenboim, *The Book of Prime Number Records* (New York: Springer-Verlag, 1988), 81–85.
18 Simmel, *Schopenhauer and Nietzsche*, 172–73.
19 The next step is just to find the geometrical mean of the two lines, using a simple procedure supplied by Euclid in *The Elements of Elucid*, ed. Isaac Todhunter (London: Dent, 1993), pp. 69–70. The square which has this as its side will be equal to the circle whose radius is the original line.
20 This is confirmed by another example of incommensurability given by Oresme, which involves objects moving with equal speeds along the sides of two squares, one of which has as its side the diagonal of the other. See Oresme, *De proportionibus proportionum*, 399.
21 Lambert's proof, published in 1761, is given in A. De Morgan, *A Budget of Paradoxes*, 2nd ed. (1915; reprint ed., Freeport, NY: Books for Libraries Press, 1969), Vol. 2, 367–72.
22 See Kurt von Fritz, 'The Discovery of Incommensurability by Hippasus of Metapontum', *Annals of Mathematics*, 46 (1945), 242–64.
23 Grant, *Oresme and the Kinematics of Circular Motion*, 139.
24 Pierre Duhem, *Le Système du monde* (Paris: Hermann, 1958), Vol. 8, 452.
25 Ibid., 461.
26 Ibid., 452.
27 Grant, *Oresme and the Kinematics of Circular Motion*, 269.
28 Ibid., 271.
29 Arnold Zuboff, 'Nietzsche and Eternal Recurrence', in Robert Solomon (ed.), *Nietzsche: A Collection of Critical Essays* (Garden City, NY: Doubleday Anchor, 1973), 354.
30 Ibid., 354.
31 The points will be even closer to each other when B overtakes C, though further from their original place.
32 Grant, *Oresme and the Kinematics of Circular Motion*, 179.
33 Friedrich Nietzsche, *Thus Spake Zarathustra*, 'The Convalescent'.
34 KGW V/2, 403.
35 Ibid., 452.
36 Ibid., 421. See also ibid., 428.
37 Stephen G. Brush, 'Nietzsche's Recurrence Revisited: The French Connection', *Journal of the History of Philosophy*, 19 (1981), 235–38.
38 Henri Poincaré, 'On the Three-Body Problem and the Equations of Dynamics', in S.G. Brush (ed.), *Kinetic Theory* (Oxford: Pergamon Press, 1966), Vol. 2, 194–202. For an interesting use of Poincaré's theorem in a more restricted area, see Kenneth R. Meyer, 'An Application of Poincaré's Recurrence Theorem to Academic Administration', *The American Mathematical Monthly*, 88 (1981), 32–33.
39 Ernst Zermelo, 'On the Mechanical Explanation of Irreversible Processes', in Stephen G. Brush (ed.), *Kinetic Theory* (Oxford: Pergamon Press, 1966), Vol. 2, 230.
40 See, for example, Stephen G. Brush, *The Temperature of History* (New York: Burt Franklin, 1978), 72–76.
41 Henri Poincaré, *Oeuvres de Henri Poincaré* (Paris: Gauthier-Villars, 1952), Vol. 7, 314–15.
42 Henri Poincaré, *Les méthodes nouvelles de la mécanique céleste*, 3 vols (1892–99; reprint ed., New York: Dover Publications, 1957), Vol. 3, 142–44.
43 Poincaré, *Les méthodes nouvelles de la mécanique céleste*, Vol. 1, 95.
44 Ibid., Vol. 3, 141.
45 Poincaré, *Oeuvres de Henri Poincaré*, Vol. 7, 476.

46 Ibid., 313.
47 Unfortunately, the available English translation contains several errors, noted in Robin Small, 'Incommensurability and Recurrence: From Oresme to Simmel', 136–37. Hence, anyone attempting to understand the theorem would be well advised to refer to one or other of Poincaré's original texts.
48 It is surprising how many writers suppose that it does; see, for example, Milic Capek, *The Philosophical Impact of Contemporary Physics* (New York: Van Nostrand Reinhold Company, 1961), 126.
49 This is known by mathematicians as the 'Archimedean axiom', although it is also attributed to Eudoxus of Cnidos. See T.L. Heath, *The Works of Archimedes* (1897; reprint ed., New York: Dover Publications, 1953), 4 and 234.
50 Poincaré, *Les méthodes nouvelles de la mécanique céleste*, Vol. 3, 154.
51 Ibid., Vol. 2, 1–2.
52 See, for example, ibid., Vol. 1, 361.
53 See Stephen G. Brush (ed.), *Kinetic Theory* (Oxford: Pergamon Press, 1966), Vol. 2, 194–245.
54 Frank J. Tipler, 'General Relativity and the Eternal Return', in Frank J. Tipler (ed.), *Essays in General Relativity* (New York: Academic Press, 1980), 22.

Chapter 8

The Physics of Eternal Recurrence

One way of understanding Nietzsche's thought is through the concept of *force*. It is this more than other ideas that allows him to range over diverse topics, ranging from cosmology to psychology and social theory, and to suggest links or analogies between them. But what is Nietzsche's idea of force, and how is it related to that of other thinkers? Calling it a scientific concept leaves unspecified which scientific account one has in mind. Is it the Newtonian theory, or the dynamic approaches of Boscovich, Kant and Faraday, or a more modern physics? Many of Nietzsche's uses of this concept are bound up with his reading, so that understanding them requires us to ask not just what Nietzsche meant by force, but what he believed science meant by force. In this chapter I will survey the sources of Nietzsche's conception of force, and then look into his use of these theories to construct a model of reality corresponding to his doctrine of eternal recurrence.

As we have seen, Nietzsche was impressed in his earlier years by Boscovich's programme for replacing material atoms with unextended 'points of matter' whose interactions are expressed economically in a single 'law of force'. When he took his reading in natural philosophy further, he was biased towards approaches which seemed to build on the dynamic approach of Boscovich and eager to find evidence that those ideas had become generally accepted in recent science. One contemporary author proved very suitable in this regard. This was Johannes Gustav Vogt, a professor of physics at the University of Leipzig whose book *Die Kraft*, published in 1881, offered a comprehensive account of the natural world, based on a few simple assumptions.[1] Another writer read by Nietzsche at the same time was Otto Caspari, a philosopher who attempted to vindicate a Leibnizian standpoint in opposition to scientific materialism. These authors appealed to him far more than Julius Robert Mayer, a figure of greater importance in the history of natural science. It was Mayer whose principle of the conservation of energy established physics for the first time as the science of energy, in parallel with chemistry as the science of matter. Yet Nietzsche found more of interest in Vogt and Caspari than in Mayer, at least in relation to the problem of understanding the world as a whole and, in particular, of finding a conception of force consistent with the idea of eternal recurrence. Beyond this is a more ambitious demand for some account of the process through which the same course of becoming is repeated endlessly, and even for the kind of explanation which the argument for eternal recurrence, taken by itself, fails altogether to provide.

Nietzsche and J.G. Vogt

Johannes Gustav Vogt (who should not be confused with Karl Vogt, a materialist writer of the previous generation) wrote a number of books on cosmology, from a standpoint which owes little to empirical research. His systematic work, *Die Kraft*, begins with a statement of the basic principles from which a comprehensive physical theory will be developed. It starts with a repudiation of the 'naive realism' that attributes reality to the familiar things of everyday experience. Its error, pointed out by Kant and confirmed by the modern science of physiology, lies in the identification of our sensations with the real objects that give rise to them. People use the word 'matter' to describe this substratum, Vogt observes, but nobody has managed to give a clear account of its meaning. In fact, it is just an empty label, like Kant's 'thing-in-itself'. Not that we can do without some such concept: if the world of experience is more than a mere dream, it must have a basis in some underlying reality. In that case, we are faced with the task of conceptualizing its substratum. The choice must be made on methodological grounds: which concept leads to the most consistent and comprehensive theory? Vogt's answer is: the concept of *force*. He proposes an 'absolute monism' in which it is force, not matter, that occupies space, offers resistance and exhibits other 'material' properties.[2]

The alternative theory, which Vogt takes to be the standpoint of contemporary science, is a kind of dualism, in that it contains both force and matter as distinct realities. Robert Mayer championed this view when he rejected the notion of heat and electricity as immaterial substances, proclaiming: 'Let us speak out the great truth: there are no immaterial matters.'[3] Quoting his statement, Vogt replies: 'Let us speak out the great truth: there are no material forces.'[4] This retort does not simply express a preference for monism as opposed to dualism. Vogt presents several arguments to show that a dualism of matter and force leads to insoluble puzzles. Modern mechanics postulates material atoms existing in empty space, and ascribes several kinds of force to them – not just kinetic energy, but cohesion and weight as well. To this Vogt objects that we cannot imagine how forces which are not just different but antagonistic to one another could be present together within a single body. Yet this is what the kinetic theory must claim for the atoms in which its forces are supposed to be located.[5]

Vogt adds another objection to any plurality of forces, by raising a cosmological problem about the balance or imbalance of these forces as a whole. Taking weight and cohesion together, we can see that they imply a tendency for the formation of more or less enduring, solid bodies out of the matter constituting the world. Kinetic energy, on the other hand, represents the tendency of matter to disperse. Which of these two influences is stronger? Vogt argues that 'The slightest preponderance of one or the other force must lead in the end either to permanent concentration and rigidity or else to permanent dispersion'. Thus, if cohesion and weight were greater than kinetic energy, the world would have reached a final state, with matter collapsing into a rigid, dead mass. If kinetic energy were greater than cohesion and weight, all matter would long since have dispersed – or rather, it would never have formed into solid bodies in the first place. It is evident that the world as we know it cannot be identified with either of these outcomes. Since that is the case, Vogt concludes, the assumed plurality of elementary forces must be rejected.[6] That in turn implies that the kinetic theory as it stands is unacceptable.

One can see a parallel with Nietzsche's argument for the inadequacy of any physical theory which predicts a final state. Vogt claims that mechanism in its existing form leads to such a conclusion because of its belief in solid atoms whose behaviour can be explained only by several different kinds of force. In that case, given an infinite period of time, one or other force would gain the upper hand, and the phenomena for which several forces were postulated could never exist. One way of avoiding this conclusion might be to appeal to an omnipotent being, through whose intervention a seemingly final state of the world could give way to some new course of developments. Vogt replies that a genuinely *mechanical* theory must avoid such suppositions. Instead, it must find a way to postulate a cosmic cycle which has neither a beginning nor an ending, but goes on eternally: 'a cosmic *perpetuum mobile* of a purely mechanical nature.'[7]

Having clarified the task before him, and established to his own satisfaction the absolute monism on which his system is based, Vogt proceeds to construct a cosmological model which will behave in the desired fashion. He takes it that the world is infinite in extent: 'The spatial and temporal infinitude of substance is simply a postulate for us, but one from which we will not retreat, since our whole structure stands or falls with it.'[8] This way of dealing with cosmological questions is very characteristic of Vogt. After all, he points out, everyone has the right to speculate about ultimate things, all the more since everyday experience is unable to establish their nature. Vogt exercises this right with considerable freedom. He builds up a very elaborate model of the universe which includes explanations of electricity, heat, light, chemical properties and other phenomena.

Vogt assumes that force is infinite, and also that it is absolutely continuous in space.[9] That enables him to avoid any debate concerning the reality of space itself, since there will be no empty space in this model. Although this substratum is continuous and homogeneous, it is not uniform. Variations in its density are accounted for by 'centres of force' which bring about contractions or concentrations of force about themselves. 'An atom', Vogt writes, 'consists of numerous, of thousands, hundreds of thousands, even perhaps millions of centres of force.'[10] Each centre has a sphere of influence, which may grow or contrast according to that centre's ability to bring about a concentration of force. Vogt calls concentrated energy 'positive', in contrast with the 'negative' energy which is dispersed in the space between spheres of concentration. We can, he says, regard the continual expansion and contraction of these spheres as a ceaseless struggle between 'positive' and 'negative' energy, in which each in turn takes the predominant role.[11] A contraction may be identified with an increase in potential energy, whereas an expansion represents an increase in actual energy, or *vis viva*. Centres of force undergo both processes alternately in a kind of vibration, at a rate of perhaps a billion times per second.[12]

All this is just the beginning. Vogt proceeds to discuss the interactions between centres of force, as they compete or combine to constitute wider 'spheres of influence', out of which come all the phenomena of nature, from atoms to the cosmos. After developing this model over six hundred pages of detailed elaboration, which we may pass over here, Vogt returns, in his final chapter, to the question concerning a circular course of becoming. Force must have an infinite capacity for work, he argues, for otherwise the world-process would long ago have come to an end.[13] Thus we can foresee the coming of countless worlds, just as countless worlds have appeared and disappeared in the past. If this is an eternal recurrence, it is a recurrence of species, not of numerically individual things.[14] That is, it involves a succession of worlds rather than a repetition of the same world. Our world may come and go forever, but the energies that make it up will be recycled elsewhere in the cosmos: 'An eternal circular course, an eternal coming and going of worlds and, with them, of feeling, thinking and knowing beings.'[15]

Nietzsche's first acquaintance with Vogt's work came from his reading of Otto Caspari's *Der Zusammenhang der Dinge* in the summer of 1881. This collection of articles and reviews on a range of philosophical topics provided him with further reading as he ordered copies of some of the works discussed. One chapter of Caspari's book was primarily a long critical review of *Der Kraft*.[16] Caspari was in full agreement with Vogt's attack on materialism as an epistemologically unsound standpoint. He agreed, too, with a monistic and dynamic philosophy of nature. However, he considered Vogt's account of force to be too close to existing mechanism. The real solution to the problem of avoiding a final standstill of force, in Caspari's opinion, had already been provided: 'Only with Leibnizian basic perceptions are we in a position to fulfil the postulate of an eternal cycle and the justified demand for eternal and infinite change.'[17] That means attributing an 'inner aspect' to the elements of the world: it is because 'centres of force' have the power to feel and perceive their situation that they are capable of avoiding any final state of rest. 'Unfortunately', Caspari writes, 'Herr Vogt has not tried to clarify the perpetuity of motion and change in the universe by an improvement and development of the Leibnizian doctrines.'[18] He adds that Vogt seems unaware of recent literature, and that he presents a picture of the world which is more like the ancient Greek thinkers.[19]

This last criticism may have been read by Nietzsche as a strong point in Vogt's favour. In any case, Vogt's conception of a cosmic cycle of becoming was a timely discovery for Nietzsche, whose first thoughts on eternal recurrence began at this time, during August 1881. Although he did not obtain a copy of *Die Kraft* until the end of that month, he had already read Caspari's detailed review, and so knew about Vogt's basic propositions. Later, his own attempts to provide a physical account of eternal recurrence found their strongest source of ideas in Vogt's work. A series of notebook entries dating from 1881 to 1885 confirms Nietzsche's repeated reading of *Die Kraft*, especially its first and last sections.[20] In *The Gay Science* he calls on Vogt's ideas to contribute to his presentation of a world picture freed from anthropomorphic conceptions of law and order.[21] At the same time, Vogt's speculative style of theorizing, his pictorial presentations and his avoidance of mathematics were all congenial to Nietzsche. Finally, and importantly for our present discussion, Nietzsche's interest in Vogt was to determine his reaction to a very different contemporary figure in physical science, Robert Mayer.

Nietzsche and Mayer

Although overlooked at first by the scientific community, the Heilbronn physician Julius Robert Mayer came to be generally recognized as having given the law of conservation of energy its first definite statement. In a series of publications beginning in 1842, Mayer announced 'an attempt to make the idea of *force* as precise as that of matter and to denote thereby only objects of real inquiry'.[22] His starting-point is an account of causality in which the maxim *causa aequat effectum* is given a new interpretation. Cause and effect, he argues, must be equivalent in quantity and identical in substance. This means that anything capable of acting as a cause can be neither created nor destroyed by natural means, but only altered in its form. The two kinds of cause known to us are matter and force. For each, therefore, the law of conservation must be valid. Once it is based on this fundamental principle, physics, now defined as the science of force, will have the same standing as chemistry, the science of matter.

Mayer summarizes his theory in a series of aphoristic remarks which emphasize the close analogy between force and matter:

> We call force an entity which through its expenditure brings about motion. Force as a cause of motion is an indestructible entity. No effect arises without a cause. No cause disappears without a corresponding effect. *Ex nihilo nil fit. Nil fit ad nihilum.* The effect is equal to the cause. The effect of force is once again force.[23]

He distinguishes five distinct forms of force: motion, heat, potential energy, chemical energy and electricity (together with magnetism). Force in any one of these forms can be turned into force in any other form, yet its magnitude will remain the same throughout all such processes. The relation between motion and heat was of particular interest to Mayer, because his conservation law suggested the possibility of establishing a quantitative equivalence between these two forms of force. Unfortunately, he did not have an opportunity to carry out the required experiment with an adequate degree of precision; that was accomplished in 1843 by James Joule, using a development of heat by friction to find the mechanical equivalent of heat. Since Joule's work was independent of Mayer's, he is recognized as joint discoverer of the law of conservation of energy.

Robert Mayer came to Nietzsche's attention through his friend Heinrich Köselitz, who shared an interest in science and often introduced scientific topics into their correspondence. In a letter of January 1880, Köselitz reported that he had read Eugen Dühring's recently published book *Robert Mayer der Galilei des neunzehnten Jahrhunderts*.[24] He was enthusiastic about both Mayer's ideas and Dühring's presentation of them as the basis for a 'rational' rather than 'empirical' physics.[25] If Nietzsche had known something about this new science, Köselitz suggested, he would have made some alterations to the first part of *Human, All-Too-Human*. In particular, he would have directed his attention towards a physiological, rather than an historical, explanation of moral phenomena. Nietzsche was on the move from Germany to Italy at the time and did not reply to this letter. It is interesting to speculate on his immediate reaction to Köselitz's rather excited report, however. Nietzsche would not have welcomed the idea of taking lessons from Dühring, a writer with whom he was familiar and for whom he had a particular dislike. They shared the same publisher, Ernst Schmeitzner, who wrote to Nietzsche mentioning that Dühring's book on Mayer had not only been widely discussed in the press, but had almost completely sold its first printing of a thousand copies.[26] The sharp contrast with the reception and sales of *Human, All-Too-Human* and its sequels would have been evident.

Nietzsche could have found more defensible reasons to dislike the book. Dühring is always a polemical writer, even on subjects which seem to call for a strictly objective treatment. As the title of the work indicates, he is concerned to champion Mayer's place in the history of scientific discovery. He had already done this in his *Kritische Geschichte der allgemeinen Prinzipien der Mechanik*, criticizing the leading scientists of Germany in a way that led to his formal dismissal from the University of Berlin in 1877. Shortly after that event, Dühring met Mayer himself while staying at the health resort of Wildbad, near Heilbronn. His subsequent book on Mayer gives an entertaining account of their meeting. It was an encounter between two very different people, neither of whom knew quite what to make of the other. Dühring was taken aback by Mayer's provincial accent and manners, his retiring (and, in fact, depressive) personality and his unsympathetic family. His description of Mayer as 'a martyr for science'[27] is largely based on what Mayer told him about the harsh 'water cure' he had undergone in the name of medical treatment following a diagnosis of mental illness some years previously. In Dühring's opinion, the academic leadership of natural science in Germany was to blame for Mayer's personal troubles, since they had discounted his theories as those of an amateur, standing outside their closed professional circle.[28]

To his credit, Köselitz was able to separate the more sensational aspects of Dühring's book from its useful summary of Mayer's contribution to the scientific understanding of force. In the following year, he was assisting Nietzsche by preparing the final manuscript of *Daybreak* for publication, and wrote to him making a suggestion, or rather announcing a *fait accompli*.

> In one aphorism I have written something else instead of 'law of gravity' (*Gesetz der Schwere*): weight (*Schwere*) is only a property and not a force; weight is

only the cause of acceleration in falling, but not of falling itself. The centre of the earth also has weight, although it does not fall.[29]

The place is not specified, but in section 271 of *Daybreak* we find one kind of happiness described as 'a rolling downwards without effort, as if by the blind force of gravity (*wie in blinder Schwerkraft*)'. This is probably the altered passage, since its use of 'force of gravity' accords with Mayer's insistence on a sharp distinction between properties, such as weight, and forces, such as the potential energy due to gravitation.[30] By now, Köselitz had gone on to study Mayer's own presentation of his ideas, instead of relying on Dühring's account of them. He acquired a copy of Mayer's *Mechanik der Wärme*, together with two later essays which were bound together with the book. A few days later, he wrote to Nietzsche: 'I am now reading Robert Mayer's writings, and will forward them to you as soon as I have finished with them.' Dühring's picture of Mayer turned out to be misleading, Köselitz reported: Mayer was not just a victim of the scientific establishment, but 'a quite precise, succinct and thoughtful man, who rejects anything that is not scientific (with the exception of God)'.[31]

The book was sent in April, and received by Nietzsche with immediate enthusiasm: 'In books as splendidly simple and gay as Mayer's, one can hear a harmony of the spheres: a music that is designed only for scientific people.'[32] This is an unlikely description of Mayer's rather stolid scientific prose. Nietzsche may have meant that Mayer's *ideas* were suited to a poetic form, like that provided for atomism by Lucretius. Another possible explanation is that he had merely glanced at the book. He did, however, add in a postscript: '"Über Auslösung" is the most essential and useful thing in the book for me.' His notebooks of the period confirm that he had read that essay, and some other passages as well.[33] A year later, he was reading it again. Now he wrote to Köselitz in a quite different vein: 'I have been reading Robert Mayer: my friend, he is a great specialist – and no more. I am amazed how crude and naive he is in all general statements: he thinks he is being wonderfully logical when he is merely opinionated.' The great failure of Mayer, Nietzsche informed his friend, was retaining the concept of *matter*. Boscovich had long since refuted this prejudice, and on strictly mathematical grounds; in doing so, he had thought the atomistic theory through 'to the end'. Pursuing his critique of Mayer, Nietzsche showed that he had not forgotten being corrected on the distinction between weight and gravity.

Weight is quite certainly not a 'property of matter', simply because there is no matter. The force of gravity is, just like the force of inertia, certainly a phenomenal form of force (simply because there is nothing other than force!): only the logical relation of this phenomenal form to others, e.g. to heat, is still quite obscure. But assuming that one still believes, with Mayer, in matter and in solid atoms, one cannot proclaim: 'There is only one force'. The kinetic theory must attribute to atoms, as well as kinetic energy, at least also the two forces of cohesion and weight. All of the materialist physicists and chemists do this! And even Mayer's best followers. Nobody has given up the force of gravity! Finally,

Mayer also still has a second force in the background, the *primum mobile*, God – alongside motion itself. This is quite necessary to him![34]

Why had Nietzsche's opinion altered so radically since the previous year? If he had read more of Mayer in 1881, would he have made a similar judgement then? A more probable factor is that, in the meantime, he had been reading J.G. Vogt. For the line of criticism which attacks a dualism of matter and force by finding insoluble problems in any plurality of forces is taken directly from *Die Kraft*. Nietzsche does not identify his source in the letter, or even set out the argument in full. Not surprisingly, therefore, Köselitz was puzzled by the unexpected attack. 'Does Mayer speak of atoms?' he asked in his next letter.[35] Köselitz was still prepared to defend Mayer's distinction between weight and gravitational force, and returned to the issue in several further letters, repeating his earlier theme: 'In the centre of the earth a body no longer falls (though as a constituent part of the earth it falls with the earth about the sun) but weight cannot be denied to it.'[36] Nietzsche did not respond to any of these remarks, and the subject lapsed from their correspondence for the time being.[37]

How appropriate was Nietzsche's use of arguments taken from *Die Kraft* against Mayer's theory of energy? Vogt's attack is first and foremost on the recently developed kinetic theory of heat. His point is that, although the theory may succeed in reducing heat to motion, it must still postulate cohesion and weight as other forms of force, with the fatal consequences mentioned earlier. As it happens, Mayer was not a supporter of the kinetic theory. He wrote:

> The relation in which forces stand to each other I have characterised by naming them different forms of one and the same entity. In this connection, however, I have expressly declared myself against the closely associated but in my opinion unwarranted and too far-reaching conclusion that heat phenomena are to be considered after all merely as motion phenomena.[38]

Further, Köselitz was right in querying Nietzsche's reference to atoms in this context, for Mayer regards the atomic question as going beyond experimental evidence and declines to commit himself to its support. He writes: 'We really do not know whether atoms exist.'[39] Nietzsche was jumping to conclusions in taking Vogt's arguments against the kinetic theory to be directly applicable to Mayer's account of force.

His other comments are more revealing, and less easy to pass off as a misunderstanding. Mayer's approach to science was not one with which Nietzsche could sympathize. Despite occasional allusions to Leibniz and uses of scholastic expressions, Mayer is a thinker for whom what cannot be measured is not a proper object of scientific inquiry.[40] He addresses himself to 'friends of a clear, hypothesis-free view of nature'[41] and warns against 'an attempt to construct a universe *a priori*'[42] – which is more or less what Vogt had done in *Die Kraft*. He is far closer in this respect to his British counterparts than to German writers such as Caspari or Vogt. But the empiricist and mechanistic model of physical inquiry was not Nietzsche's favoured model, as we have already seen. Despite their differences, however, all these writers were forced to deal with a question which had arisen from the mechanistic science of thermodynamics – the concept of entropy and its implications for the overall course of the world. I turn now to the ways in which Caspari and Vogt tried to meet that challenge, and to Nietzsche's response to their approaches.

Entropy versus Eternal Recurrence

The cosmological significance of the law of entropy aroused lively discussion amongst German philosophers in the second half of the nineteenth century. The debate was initiated by Hermann von Helmholtz's 1854 lecture 'On the Interaction of Natural Forces', which predicted a future state of thermal equilibrium and 'the end of the history of the universe'.[43] Helmholtz based his argument on a paper of William Thomson, 'On a Universal Tendency in Nature to the Dissipation of Mechanical Energy', which had appeared just two years earlier.[44] Thomson had been more cautious in spelling out his conclusions, referring only to a future state of the earth which would make it uninhabitable by the human race 'as at present constituted'. His aim is stated as being 'to call attention to the remarkable consequences which follow from Carnot's proposition, that there is an absolute waste of mechanical energy available to man when heat is allowed to pass from one body to another at a lower temperature'. Running in turn though the various processes in which heat is created, diffused or absorbed, Thomson shows that each involves a dissipation of mechanical energy which makes any restoration of the preceding state impossible.

This outlines the question as Nietzsche would have understood it. It also poses a problem for the idea of eternal recurrence that he sketched out in the middle of 1881. It is not enough to establish *that* such a recurrence must occur; we also want to know *how* it occurs, and what theory of force might account for such a cyclical process. A year later, we find Nietzsche drawing on his recent reading, and especially his study of Vogt, to add detail to the picture of eternal recurrence. In one 1882 notebook entry he writes:

> The final physical state of force that we deduce must also necessarily be the first. The dispersal of the force in latent force must be the cause of the emergence of the most living force. From the negative state must follow the most positive state.[45]

Here Nietzsche speaks of a final state, as in various other places, but in a quite different sense. Usually he means a state which puts an end to the course of becoming by making any state other than itself impossible. According to conventional mechanism, a state of universal thermal equilibrium would be such a standstill. Here, however, Nietzsche refers to the final state 'that we deduce' – that is, to the state which represents the furthest limit of prediction, according to our scientific knowledge. Whether this is a final state in the stronger sense is another matter. According to Nietzsche, there can be no such state: that fact is 'the sole certainty we have in our hands to serve as a corrective to a great host of world hypotheses possible in themselves.'[46]

> If the motion of the world had a final state, that state would have been reached. The sole fundamental fact, however, is that it does not have a final state; and every philosophy or scientific hypothesis (e.g. mechanism) in which such a state becomes necessary is *refuted* by this fact alone.[47]

Having said that he adds: 'I seek a conception of the world which takes this fact into account.' Clearly it must be a conception which, if based on mechanistic principles, is somehow able to avoid predicting any future state as a 'final' one in the strong sense. In the passage cited above, Nietzsche suggests one way in which that might be done: by identifying this state with the state which is, so to speak, the *first* one that we deduce – that is, the most distant *past* state that can be inferred from our theory. A few pages further on in the same notebook, Nietzsche comes back to this idea, and spells it out in more detail.

> The present world of forces leads back to a simplest state of these forces: and in the same way forward to a simplest state – cannot and must not the two states be identical? From a system of determinate forces, or from a certain measurable force, there cannot result an uncountable number of states. Only on the false assumption of an infinite space, in which force so to speak evaporates, is the final state an unproductive, dead one. The simplest state is at the same time – and + .[48]

In a later notebook he writes: 'Physical problem, to find the state which is + and – .'[49] The vocabulary of these passages is a mixed one: Nietzsche refers to states of force as negative or positive, and also uses the contrast between potential and actual energy, or 'latent force' and 'living force'. Vogt had taken potential energy – in his language, force in a contracted or concentrated form – to be positive, and its counterpart, 'living force', to be negative. The expressions 'positive' and 'negative' appear again in a third entry made by Nietzsche in the same notebook, a few pages later:

> On the re-emergence of the world. Out of two negative things arises something positive, if the negative things are forces. (Darkness arises out of light against light, cold out of heat against heat, etc.)[50]

Presumably he is counting light and heat as 'negative' forms of force, and darkness and cold as 'positive' forms. That is not what one would naturally expect by these terms. We can make some sense of the examples given, however, by recognizing that, when Nietzsche speaks of 'light against light', he is referring to the phenomenon of *interference* which occurs when light waves coming from different directions interact to produce alternating bands of light and darkness. Furthermore, we can identify his source. It is Otto Caspari's book *Die Thomson'sche Hypothese von der endlichen Temperaturausgleichung im Weltall*, in which the concept of interference is invoked to explain the persistence of differences between parts of the world, apparently in defiance of the second law of thermodynamics. As Caspari explains:

> Motion directed against motion does not always therefore give rise to further motion, but in certain particular circumstances, according to the laws of interference, to a neutral equilibrium of motion, and correspondingly, heat directed against heat does not without exception produce further heat, but in particular circumstances, and apart from other sources of heat and heat processes going on in the surrounding environment, gives rise to indifferent static heat, i.e. a lack of temperature compared with the environment, or the creation of cold.[51]

Caspari suggests that there may be dark and cold zones produced by such interference located very close to the hottest zones of the universe.[52] More importantly, this argument is his solution to the problem of a final equilibrium. Differences in temperature between parts of the universe can never be wholly eliminated, because zones of heat and cold will continually arise as interference occurs between different heat sources. One cannot call this a worked-out theory, and in any case the wave theory of heat on which it depends had only a brief prominence in the middle of the nineteenth century. Still, it does appear that Nietzsche thought these ideas worth noting down for his own use.

The 'initial' or 'simplest state' he refers to must be one in which all force is stored up as latent force. The 'final' state would be one in which latent force has been depleted. It would be a state of equilibrium, and so another 'simplest' state. The puzzle is to understand how it could be the *same* as the initial state. In Nietzsche's terminology: how could the most negative state also be the most positive one? This is hard to see, and there is no clear answer in a later note where Nietzsche sketches out the circular model at greater length:

> Regarded mechanistically, the energy of the totality of becoming remains constant; regarded economically, it rises to a high point and sinks down again in an eternal circle. This 'will to power' expresses itself in the interpretation, in the manner in which force is used up; transformation of energy into life, and 'life at its highest potency', thus appears as the goal. The same quantum of energy means different things at different stages of evolution.[53]

Here Nietzsche posits a process which is the opposite of a 'running down' of force. But he is also describing a complete cycle which returns to the state from which it began – a cycle having two phases and therefore two points at which one phase turns into the other, labelled here as a 'high point' and a 'low point'. Not only is it hard to see how these can be one and the same, but there is a more serious problem in this model. An accumulation of energy in one part of a closed system can proceed only at the expense of other parts of the system, in a way that causes an overall loss of energy available for work. This is the 'consequence' drawn for the mechanistic theory by William Thomson. Accordingly, the idea of an increase of power in the system as a whole seems to be ruled out by a fundamental law of physical theory.

What else did Nietzsche find in Caspari's book on Thomson's prediction of a final state? Despite his title, Thomson does not figure prominently in Caspari's discussion: rather, his main point of reference is Hermann von Helmholtz. Caspari reminds his readers of the opposition of Leibniz to the mechanistic picture of the physical world drawn by Descartes. Everything in the world is essentially related to everything else, and our spiritual eye, the soul, is an organic mirror of the whole universe. The work of art is a better symbol of the eternal and infinite organism than any machine of human construction. As for the scientific debate, it is highly characteristic of the English, according to Caspari, to carry the mechanical theory of heat over into the universe. In contrast, Germans have 'the immortal Leibniz' with his 'macrocosmic organicism' on their side.[54] On this view, the universe is an enormous living organism which, like many other organisms, may undergo a period of hibernation before spontaneously returning to an active condition.[55] In addition, Caspari suggests that the law of entropy may be only a local condition. A loss of heat may be due to the interference of heat radiation – a phenomenon similar to the interference of light waves – and, in that case, the eternal motion of force will maintain differences in temperature.

Nietzsche's position in relation to the debate between Leibnizians and mechanists is not always straightforward but, as we saw in Chapter 6, he is explicit in rejecting the notion that force is somehow capable of foreseeing, and taking steps to avoid, any state of equilibrium.[56] Without naming Caspari, Nietzsche ridicules any conception of the universe as an enormous organism. 'This nauseates me,' he writes in *The Gay Science*.[57] A related notebook entry is explicit on the subject of monadism:

> And a disguised polytheism in the monads which together constitute the universal organism! With foresight! Monads which know how to prevent certain possible mechanical outcomes, such as the equilibrium of forces! Fantasising![58]

In rejecting any attribution of consciousness to the 'inner aspect' of force, Nietzsche is placing himself in opposition to all those writers, such as Caspari, who characterize mechanism by using adjectives such as 'dead' or 'blind'. As an opponent of teleology in scientific thinking, he stands on the same side as Vogt and the mainstream of mechanism.

It is true that a cycle of accumulation and discharge of energy can go on in one part of the world, interacting with other parts. According to Nietzsche, this is the typical pattern of living systems: 'In the smallest organism force is steadily built up and must then be discharged, either of its own accord, when fullness is reached, or through a stimulus from outside.'[59] The life process is an interaction between the living organism and its environment, in which force is continually absorbed and discharged. But the universe cannot acquire new force or expel the force it contains: 'Let us beware of thinking that the world is a living being. Where should it expand? On what should it feed? How could it grow and multiply?'[60] The objection appeals to the first, rather than the second, law of thermodynamics: there is by definition no further location for force, and its creation from nothing or destruction without trace would be incompatible with the principle of conservation.

Suppose, however, that more and more of the world comes under the control of a particular organizing system. In this case, Nietzsche wants to make the point that the final outcome would necessarily be unstable. A complete integration could be no more than a momentary state, leading to a disintegration of the accumulated forces. Nietzsche sees such a pattern in many phenomena, such as the histories of particular societies: 'as a consequence of this highest force, which, turning against itself when it no longer has anything left to organise, expends its force on disorganisation – .'[61] It seems that this alternation of accumulation and discharge may not need the intervention of an outside cause, although in the most familiar examples there would be stimulus for the reversal of the process. This idea is found in the cosmology of Vogt's *Die Kraft* but, as a model applicable to very diverse phenomena, it owes far more to Robert Mayer's 'Über Auslösung', one of the essays which were bound in with the copy of *Die Mechanik der Wärme* which Nietzsche borrowed from his friend Köselitz – and apparently never returned, since it is listed in his surviving library.

Force and Power

The short essay 'Über Auslösung' is important for Nietzsche in a number of ways. It provides valuable clues for a connection between the concept of force and that of power, which becomes increasingly prominent in his thinking during this later period. Despite his unfavourable verdict on Mayer, Nietzsche had been genuinely impressed by his discussion of processes in which a cause seems to produce a much greater effect, as when a spark sets off an explosion, or a small nerve impulse releases an outburst of muscular energy. Mayer asks whether such phenomena constitute an exception to the law of conservation of energy. His answer is that they do not, because they involve the release (*Auslösung*) of energy which was already present, but stored up in a 'latent' form. If a small push causes a body to fall and thereby produce a much greater amount of motion, this is only because the same amount of force was already at hand as *potential* energy. The other cases mentioned are accounted for in the same way, by distinguishing between 'latent' and 'living' force.

Why was Nietzsche impressed by this piece, which most readers would not see as one of Mayer's major contributions to science? As he said to Köselitz, its ideas were useful for his own purposes. The concept of *Auslösung* provides a way of describing important relations between forces. If one force can *control* the transformations of other forces from a latent into an active state, or vice versa, then the notion of 'power' as a relation between forces can be given a physical meaning. Mayer's background as a physician gave him a special interest in living systems. His theory of conservation of energy was developed in the first instance to account for biological phenomena, and his presentations often include examples of transformations of energy occurring within a living organism. Nietzsche had encountered the general idea before – for instance, in Friedrich Mohr's *Allgemeine Theorie der Bewegung und Kraft*.[62] Mohr had used familiar examples of controlled and uncontrolled releases of energy, and had also acknowledged cases where the discharge seems to occur of its own accord. However, it was Mayer's treatment that suggested the applications that appear in Nietzsche's subsequent writing.

In his account of the physical world, Mayer's discussion helped Nietzsche elaborate the kinds of relations between centres of force which constitute a particular combination. He calls them 'power-relationships'.[63] It appears that a power-relationship is asymmetrical: what happens in such an interaction is that 'the stronger becomes master of the weaker, in so far as the latter cannot assert its degree of independence'.[64] In other words, the relation is a *control* or *domination* of one force by another. Several features of this concept can be stated readily enough: for instance, that it is a transitive relation, and that whereas a force can control more than one other force, one force cannot be controlled by more than one force. If there are indirect, as well as direct, relations between forces, that might explain how Nietzsche could hold that everything is somehow related to everything else.

Space must play an important role in these relationships. Nietzsche states that every force has a certain spatial *range*. Just as we see things only within a certain horizon, so too all our senses are active only within particular limits.[65] 'In the same way, every force has its sphere; it acts only so far and so strongly and only on this and that, not on anything else, a sphere of limitation.'[66] Similarly he writes: 'Even in the domain of the inorganic an atom of force is concerned only with its neighbourhood.'[67] Without this limitation, he claims, a force would be indeterminate in one respect, and that would be something of an absurdity. Perhaps this is why he thinks that, in an infinite space, a final state would be necessary. In the process that Zöllner called 'evaporation', forces would eventually pass out of range, and so could no longer interact with, or exercise power over, one another.

When Nietzsche describes a power-relationship between forces as one in which 'the stronger becomes master of the weaker', the words 'stronger' and 'weaker' do not refer to the quantities of force contained on each side, for he emphasizes that a small force can 'become master' of a much larger force. To understand this we must recall the distinction between 'latent force' and 'living force'. When a force 'becomes master' of another, it controls whether the second force assumes one or other of these forms. That is, it determines whether a latent force remains as it is or turns into a living force, and whether a living force remains a living force or becomes a *latent* force. In modern terminology, this is the transformation of potential energy into kinetic energy and vice versa. More generally, then, we can say that the strength or power of a force lies in its control over the accumulation or the discharge (*Auslösung*) of other forces.[68] Accordingly, Nietzsche makes the distinction between a 'directing force' and a 'driving force'. He points out that people often mistake one for the other, and so suppose that 'more power' implies 'more force'. On the contrary, it is the economical use of force which is the criterion of power in such interactions. That is, the directing force which expends as little as possible of itself to produce the greatest outcome has the most power. The idea that this kind of cause, taken by itself, has to be 'equal' to its effect is a fallacy, based on the assumption that every cause is a driving force.

In Book Five of *The Gay Science*, this idea is applied to the psychology of motivation. Nietzsche writes: 'I have learned to distinguish the cause of acting from the cause of acting in a particular way, in a particular direction, with a particular goal.'[69] The 'cause of acting' is some sizeable accumulation of energy, while the 'cause of acting in a particular way' is a relatively minor force which exercises control over the manner and timing of the release of that energy. Since this second cause is given impressive titles like 'purpose' and 'vocation' (*Lebensberufe*), it is imagined to be the driving force behind the action. In reality, it is like the helmsman who directs the course of a steamship with the touch of a hand. Having made this point, Nietzsche takes his idea one step further, to the stage at which even that minimal element of control disappears altogether, leaving a spontaneous process: there is no helmsman, and the vessel is simply 'following the current into which it has entered accidentally'.

The idea of power as control is linked with the 'economic' concept discussed earlier: 'That which constitutes growth in life is an ever more healthy and far-seeing economy, which achieves more and more with less and less force – as an ideal, the principle of the smallest expenditure – .'[70] In its highest development, this tendency is sometimes expressed by Nietzsche with a surprising choice of image: 'The sole possibility of maintaining a meaning for the concept "God" would be: God not as a driving force, but God as a *maximal state*, as an *epoch* – a point in the evolution of the will to power by means of which further development just as much as previous development up to him would be explained.'[71] God, he says, is not to be understood as a 'driving force', but rather as the 'highest power', from which everything follows.[72] This is the concept of guidance using minimal force in its most extreme form. It is hard to say how seriously Nietzsche intended this redefinition of God to be taken. He returns to it in a few places, including one passage in *Beyond Good and Evil*,[73] but it plays little or no part in the imagery of *Thus Spake Zarathustra*.

Nevertheless, there are some related concepts in *Thus Spake Zarathustra*, and I give two examples to conclude this chapter. One occurs at the very beginning of the work, in a speech which describes what Zarathustra calls 'three metamorphoses of the spirit'. These are successive stages of personal development which manifest a steady growth in power, in a way which is consistent with the 'economic' conception, although expressed here in metaphor and imagery. The stages are expressed in terms of activities through which the 'spirit' engages with the surrounding world. The first image is that of a camel; here the spirit expresses its strength in seeking responsibilities and bearing heavy burdens. The second stage is symbolized by the lion which rebels against the weight of authority and seeks a new freedom for itself in desert solitude. Finally, the highest metamorphosis involves an innocent and playful childlike activity. Nietzsche borrows from Heraclitus the image of a child playing with counters, gathering and scattering, without any purpose other than the game itself.[74] This corresponds closely to the idea of the 'godlike' being whose power involves no exercise of force, but consists solely in being a 'centre' around whom a 'world' follows of its own accord.[75] Many further passages in *Thus Spake Zarathustra* emphasize the crucial importance of influences whose effects are far greater than those of more conspicuous factors. Zarathustra says: 'The greatest events – they are not our loudest but our stillest hours.'[76] Later, the same thought receives a more poetic expression which is attributed to the 'stillest hour' itself: 'Thoughts that come on doves' feet guide the world.'[77] In these images, the contrast between power and force is clearly a dramatic one.

Another example found in *Thus Spake Zarathustra* is the 'gift-giving virtue' which figures prominently in Part One. This is a version of the theme of accumulation and discharge, turned into a psychological and ethical concept. In his opening soliloquy, Zarathustra compares himself with the sun which overflows with light: 'Behold, I am weary of my wisdom, like a bee that has gathered too much honey; I need hands outstretched to receive it.' Just as the sun must go down to distribute its wealth, he explains, so too Zarathustra must descend to the human world to satisfy this need by becoming a teacher. Such generosity has nothing in common with the moral virtue of charity: it arises not from sympathy, which for Nietzsche is a token of weakness, but instead is a sign of health and an affirmation of life. Hence, it is not an arbitrary choice involving 'free will' but rather an expression of the individual's own nature. As a value, it is not derived from the benefits received by recipients, and so is not an obligation imposed by any outside authority, even that of an abstract moral principle. In all these ways, the 'gift-giving virtue' is quite different from any traditional moral concept.

This revaluation of the familiar moral themes of giving and receiving is just one of many instances in Nietzsche's later writings of a systematic use of a concept of power which is distinct from, and yet related to, the concept of force. That new approach is, in fact, surprisingly similar to the programme that Heinrich Köselitz had proposed as an improvement on the historical approach which Nietzsche, at the time under the strong influence of Paul Rée, had adopted in works such as *Human, All-Too-Human*. In this sense, some of Nietzsche's most fruitful applications of the concept of force were, after all, inspired largely by the scientific ideas of Robert Mayer.

Notes

1. J.G. Vogt, *Die Kraft. Eine real-monistische Weltanschauung* (Leipzig: Verlag von Haupt und Tischler, 1878).
2. Vogt, *Die Kraft*, iv.
3. Robert Mayer, 'The Motions of Organisms and their Relation to Metabolism', in R.B. Lindsay, *Julius Robert Mayer: Prophet of Energy* (Oxford: Pergamon Press, 1973), 99; see also 203.
4. Vogt, *Die Kraft*, 3.
5. Ibid., 7.
6. Ibid., 7–8 and 11–12.
7. Ibid., 14.
8. Ibid., 10.
9. Ibid., 18.
10. Ibid., 426.
11. Ibid., 27.
12. Ibid., 36.
13. Ibid., 645.
14. The distinction is made by Aristotle in *De generatione et corruptione*, II.11, 338b in *The Basic Works of Aristotle*, ed. R. McKeon (New York: Random House, 1941), p. 531.
15. Vogt, *Die Kraft*, 655; see also 642.
16. Otto Caspari, *Der Zusammenhang der Dinge: Gesammelte philosophische Aufsätze* (Breslau: Verlag von Eduard Trewendt, 1881), 25–68.
17. Ibid., 38.
18. Ibid., 43.
19. Ibid., 50.
20. See KGW V/2, 428 and 457–59; VII/1, 705–06 and VII/3, 439–40.
21. Friedrich Nietzsche, *The Gay Science*, sect. 109. See Martin Bauer, 'Zur Genealogie von Nietzsches Kraftbegriff. Nietzsches Auseinandersetzung mit J.G. Vogt', *Nietzsche-Studien*, 13 (1984), 211–27 for a perceptive discussion of this passage.
22. Lindsay, *Julius Robert Mayer*, 68.
23. Ibid., 78.
24. Eugen Dühring, *Robert Mayer der Galilei des neunzehnten Jahrhunderts* (Chemnitz: Ernst Schmeitzner, 1880).
25. KGB III/2, 19.
26. Ibid., 12. Dühring claimed that the real number printed was greater; see KGB II/6/2, 1229.
27. Dühring, *Robert Mayer der Galilei des neunzehnten Jahrhunderts*, 179.
28. Not much troubled by consistency, Dühring attacks James Joule for being 'not a professor, but one of those dilettantes who hide behind the academic professionals and flatter them': ibid., 55.
29. KGB III/2, 136–37.
30. See Lindsay, *Julius Robert Mayer*, 69 and 217–19.
31. KGB III/2, 138. For Mayer's references to God, see, for example, Lindsay, *Julius Robert Mayer*, 95, 170 and 219.
32. KGB III/1, 84. Cf. Nietzsche's praise of 'simplicity of style' in Nietzsche, *The Gay Science*, sect. 226.
33. See, for example, KGW V/2, 349–51, 390–91 and 439–40.
34. KGB III/1, 183–84.
35. KGB III/2, 243.
36. Ibid., 246.
37. When Köselitz (now calling himself Peter Gast) edited this correspondence for publication in 1908, he took the opportunity to deplore Nietzsche's rejection of Mayer's ideas in favour of 'the purely mathematical, pre-Daltonian standpoint of Boscovich': *Nietzsches Briefe an Peter Gast*, ed. P. Gast (Leipzig: Insel-Verlag, 1924), 334.
38. Lindsay, *Julius Robert Mayer*, 223.

39 Ibid., 224.
40 Ibid., 200.
41 Ibid., 68.
42 Ibid., 76.
43 Hermann von Helmholtz, *Popular Scientific Lectures* (New York: Dover Publications, 1962), 90.
44 William Thomson, *Mathematical and Physical Papers* (Cambridge: Cambridge University Press, 1882), Vol. 1, 511–14.
45 KGW VII/1, 5. The note goes on to deny the reality of empty space, though not of time.
46 KGW VIII/3, 167 (*The Will to Power*, sect. 1066).
47 KGW VIII/2, 276 (*The Will to Power*, sect. 708).
48 KGW VII/1, 11.
49 KGW VII/2, 66.
50 KGW VII/1, 15.
51 Otto Caspari, *Die Thomson'sche Hypothese von der endlichen Temperaturausgleichung im Weltall, beleuchtet vom philosophischen Gesichtspunkte* (Stuttgart: Verlagsbuchhandlung von August Horster, 1874), 39.
52 Ibid., 41. Cf. Nietzsche's statement: 'Countless dark bodies are to be inferred near to the sun – and we shall never see them', Friedrich Nietzsche, *Beyond Good and Evil*, sect. 196.
53 KGW VIII/2, 201 (*The Will to Power*, sect. 639).
54 Ibid., 57.
55 Caspari, *Die Thomson'sche Hypothese*, 40 and 48.
56 KGW V/2, 420.
57 Nietzsche, *The Gay Science*, sect. 109.
58 KGW V/2, 420. Cf. ibid., 423 and 451. The last of these 1881 entries reappears in KGW VII/3, 280–81 (*The Will to Power*, sect. 1062).
59 KGW V/2, 391. See also Nietzsche, *Beyond Good and Evil*, sect. 13; and KGW VIII/1, 87 (*The Will to Power*, sect. 650).
60 Nietzsche, *The Gay Science*, sect. 109. See also KGW V/2, 420 and 423.
61 KGW VIII/2, 7 (*The Will to Power*, sect. 712).
62 Mohr, *Allgemeine Theorie der Bewegung und Kraft, als Grundlage der Physik und Chemie* (Braunschweig: Druck und Verlag von Friedrich Vieweg und Sohn, 1869), 115–17. Nietzsche borrowed this book from the Basel University library in 1873.
63 KGW V/2, 224 and 259, VII/3, 387 and VIII/1, 133 (*The Will to Power*, sect. 631).
64 KGW VII/3, 283 (*The Will to Power*, Sect. 630).
65 Friedrich Nietzsche, *Daybreak*, Sect. 117.
66 KGW V/1, 642.
67 KGW VII/3, 284 (*The Will to Power*, sect. 637).
68 KGW V/2, 349–51, 390–91 and 439–40.
69 Nietzsche, *The Gay Science*, sect. 360.
70 KGW VIII/2, 201 (*The Will to Power*, sect. 639). See also VIII/3, 53 (*The Will to Power*, sect. 689).
71 Ibid. Note the link with the immediately preceding note, included in *The Will to Power* as sect. 707.
72 Ibid., 173–74 (*The Will to Power*, sect. 1037). A detailed discussion of this concept is found in Robin Small, 'Nietzsche's God', *Philosophy Today*, 26 (1982), 41–53.
73 Nietzsche, *Beyond Good and Evil*, sect. 150.
74 See KGW VII/1, 127 (*The Will to Power*, sect. 797). The source of this fragment is Lucian, trans. A.M. Harmon, Loeb Classical Library (London: Heinemann, 1960), Vol. 2, 476.
75 Nietzsche, *Beyond Good and Evil*, sect. 150.
76 Friedrich Nietzsche, *Thus Spake Zarathustra*, 'On Great Events'.
77 Ibid., 'The Stillest Hour'.

Chapter 9
Sensualism and Knowledge

Previous chapters have explored Nietzsche's thinking on the themes of metaphysics and cosmology. Now I turn to some issues of epistemology and ethics with the same purpose – that is, to locate the development of Nietzsche's ideas within a context provided by other writers of his own time. Their theories about the impulses and feelings out of which both claims to knowledge about the world and moral judgements arise are the background against which some of his most original ideas were formed. This chapter will substantiate the first of these claims by examining themes in his epistemology, leaving the corresponding discussion of moral values for the following chapter.

'Today we are all sensualists,' Nietzsche writes in Book Five of *The Gay Science*.[1] This striking assertion provides a signal for a set of problems concerning knowledge or, more particularly, the relation between knowledge and life. Nietzsche had been concerned with these questions for a long time, but only after *Thus Spake Zarathustra* did he define them in the ways that provide the theme of this discussion. As his thinking increasingly found its own path, Nietzsche moved decisively away from the pessimism and romanticism which had earlier influenced him, and gained a new appreciation of the philosophers of the French Enlightenment, even describing their sensualism and hedonism as the 'best inheritance' available to his own century.[2] Hence, for example, his suggestion that the credit for Stendhal – in his opinion the greatest French writer of the nineteenth century – must go to 'the best, most rigorous philosophical school in Europe, that of Condillac and Destutt de Tracy'.[3] The term 'sensualist', as used here, refers in the first instance to these thinkers who, proceeding from the empiricism of Locke, attempted to derive all ideas from elementary sensations. (Hence the alternative expression, 'sensationalism'.) It does not imply a preoccupation with sensual pleasure, although the English word may be used most often in that sense.[4] On the other hand, it can hardly be denied that any moral philosophy which finds its basic evidence in sensation will be naturally inclined towards hedonism, or at least utilitarianism. Less evident, but equally seen in these French writers, is the affinity between sensualism and a materialist interpretation of human nature.

Nietzsche is aware of these points, but his own concern with sensualism is prompted by its relevance to the problem of knowledge; he considers it as a respect for the worth of the evidence of the senses. Quite apart from his announcement that 'we' are all sensualists, it might be assumed that Nietzsche is clearly a supporter of this view. Even at an earlier stage, he described his thinking as an 'inverted Platonism',[5] for it not only refuses to devalue appearance in favour of some reality which is accessible to thought alone, but asserts that the further we depart from 'being', the more we encounter what is beautiful and valuable. Is this what his endorsement of sensualism in the passage just cited means? The main concern of the section is to draw a contrast between certain 'new' philosophers of today – the 'fearless ones' of Book Five's title – and the thinkers of the past, in terms of their relation to the senses. Nietzsche writes: 'Formerly philosophers were afraid of the senses. Have we perhaps unlearned this fear too much? Today we are all sensualists, we philosophers of the present and future, *not* in theory but in *praxis*, in practice.' The older philosophers, he explains, were afraid of the senses, likening them to music of the sirens which lured travellers to their death. Now we recognize the danger of an abstract thinking which removes the life from the world. Such idealism is like a disease, although in Plato's case idealism was perhaps just the opposite – 'the caution of an over-rich and dangerous health, the fear of *over-powerful* senses'. On that assumption, he concludes, our own untroubled acceptance of sensualism may testify to the weakness of our senses rather than to the strength of our character.

Some of the complexities in this theme are signalled by the distinction that Nietzsche wants to make between theoretical and practical versions of sensualism. How can one be a sensualist in practice, but not in theory? If this were said of sensualism in the common sense, it would be something like a charge of hypocrisy. Even with the different meaning Nietzsche intends, there is a suspicion of inconsistency in his position, assuming that one expects theory and practice to correspond to each other. Taking this puzzle as a starting-point for our discussion, I shall explore three particular issues raised by the theme of sensualism. The first is about the association of sensualism with materialism, recognized by Nietzsche as a dominating influence in modern science. There, again, an ambiguity in his attitude is already apparent, and it will be seen that the two cases throw light on each other. The second problem concerns the relation between the vocabulary of the senses and the categories of objective knowledge, understood as defined by the demands of scientific method. Whether the two can be made consistent with each other, or even connected in useful ways, is one puzzle addressed by Nietzsche which remains in philosophical debate today. Finally, I shall look at Nietzsche's approach to the special cases of pleasure and pain, and the place of these feelings within a general theory of the senses. The further question is whether sensualism and hedonism do go together, as has often been supposed, or whether, as Nietzsche seems to think, such an assumption reveals a misunderstanding of the nature of pleasure and pain.

Sensualism and Materialism

Running through Nietzsche's published and unpublished writings is a dialogue with scientific materialism which cannot be resolved into either straightforward sympathy or straightforward hostility. Previous chapters have discussed several aspects of that tension; here my concern is to look more closely at a further theme concerning the role of the senses. One place where Nietzsche raises this question while expressing himself as a seeming opponent of mechanism is in *The Gay Science*, where he writes:

> A 'scientific' interpretation of the world, as you understand it, might even be one of the *most stupid*, that is, poorest in meaning [*sinn-ärmsten*], of all possible interpretations of the world. This thought is intended for the ears and consciences of our mechanists who nowadays like to pass as philosophers and insist that mechanics is a doctrine of the first and last laws on which all existence must be based as on a ground floor. But an essentially mechanistic world would be an essentially *meaningless* [*sinnlose*] world. Assuming that one estimated the *value* of a piece of music according to how much of it could be counted, calculated and expressed in formulas: how absurd would such a 'scientific' estimation of music be! What would one have comprehended, understood, known of it? Nothing, really nothing of what is 'music' in it![6]

In the immediately preceding section, cited earlier, Nietzsche had emphasized the power of the senses, comparing their attraction to the seductive music of the sirens. Here he makes the same link, but in the other direction: the qualities of music which determine its meaning and value are accessible only through the senses. In other words, music is essentially sensual, a reality that lies in appearance. Nietzsche does not say this, however: he chooses to express himself in terms of cognition, referring to 'understanding' and its object, 'meaning'. This agrees with the earlier part of the section, which criticizes natural science for eliminating the 'ambiguous character' of reality; yet the example given seems rather to be directed against a subordination of the senses to the understanding.

Turning to a typical expression of sympathy with materialism, one finds Nietzsche declaring his agreement with the mechanistic movement of the present day, 'tracing back all moral and aesthetic questions to physiological ones, all physiological questions to chemical ones, all chemical questions to mechanical ones' – but with an important reservation, 'that I do not believe in "matter"'.[7] This difference is closely bound up with the issue of sensualism. The physical theory of Boscovich, which replaces substantial extended atoms with unextended 'points of matter' is, Nietzsche says, 'the greatest triumph over the senses that has been gained so far', comparable only with that of Copernicus who overcame the apparent certainty of sense experience in proving that the earth does not stand fast.[8] Nietzsche's reading in natural science had convinced him that the dynamic physics of Boscovich, recently renewed in Faraday's development of the new science of electricity, would replace materialism in its older form. Neither Boscovich's 'points of matter' nor Faraday's 'centres of force' could be identified with the solid particles of Boyle's atomism, but, more importantly, neither could be pictured by analogy with the familiar objects of everyday experience, known through the senses.

For Nietzsche, the question about sensualism as a theory of knowledge is also a question about materialism, as these examples demonstrate. For materialism is the world interpretation which gives these concepts a systematic form and asserts their sole validity in explaining phenomena. We may note two main sources for his interest in materialism. The first is its oldest and, for him, purest version in the thought of Democritus. Possibly this arose from his work on Diogenes Laertius, but some aspects of the thought and personality of Democritus, as Nietzsche reconstructed or imagined them to be, appealed to him at an early stage of his career. And that sympathy continued: in *Daybreak*, Nietzsche nominates Democritus as the high point of natural philosophy in the classical age, corresponding to Sophocles in poetry, Pericles in politics, Thucydides in history and Hippocrates in medicine.[9] Democritus represents an advance beyond his nearest predecessors, in that he achieves for the first time an account of natural phenomena which makes no use of mythology. Empedocles and Anaxagoras had come close to this, but in each case had retained a certain element of teleology within their systems, in the *nous* of Anaxagoras and the 'love' and 'hate' of Empedocles. Democritus alone is fully consistent in that he admits only concepts that refer to what is visible and tangible. These ideas were revived by modern atomism, to such an extent that Nietzsche could describe Democritus as 'the only philosopher that is still alive'.[10]

The other main source for Nietzsche's preoccupation with materialism is F.A. Lange's *History of Materialism*, which he read shortly after its first publication in 1866 and at many later times. A sympathetic critic, Lange gives full credit to the contributions of the materialist standpoint in both philosophy and science, while ultimately rejecting it in favour of a Kantian idealism. According to Lange, the great appeal of materialism lies in its use of the vocabulary of the senses:

> Materialism trusts the senses. Even its metaphysics is formed by analogy with the world of experience. Its atoms are small corpuscles. Certainly one cannot represent them as small as they are, because that goes beyond human perception, but one can represent them by analogy, as if one were seeing and feeling them.[11]

Although materialism, from Democritus onwards, denies that qualities such as colour, taste and sound are objective features of the world, its conception of reality is nevertheless formulated in the categories of two senses – vision and touch. It postulates atoms which move and interact, combine and separate, exerting force upon one another by pressure and impact (*Druck und Stoss*).[12] This is the Democritean model of nature which, although modified and supplemented in various ways, has been the most durable of all scientific theories.

Lange's influence can be seen in *Beyond Good and Evil*, written at the same time as Book Five of *The Gay Science*. Here Nietzsche seems, at first sight, quite unsympathetic to sensualism. He follows Lange in suggesting that the success of mechanism in gaining public acceptance is, to a large extent, due to its affinity with sensualism. He speculates on the growing support for a new conception of physical science as an interpretation or exegesis of the world, determined by practical interests rather than by the authority of objective truth. The fact remains that mechanistic science is commonly regarded as providing an explanation of the natural world, and this is because it is 'based on belief in the senses'.

> It has eyes and fingers in its favour, it has visual evidence and palpableness in its favour; this strikes an age with fundamentally plebeian tastes as fascinating, persuasive and *convincing* – after all, it follows instinctively the canon of truth of eternally popular sensualism. What is clear, what can be 'explained'? Only what can be seen and felt – every problem has to be pursued to that point.[13]

For this reason, Nietzsche concludes, mechanism may be an appropriate philosophy for crude and unrefined personalities. In contrast, the charm of the Platonic way of thinking consisted precisely in its *resistance* to immediate sense-evidence, and this asceticism suited it for a period of noble natures.

In the next section of *Beyond Good and Evil*, Nietzsche continues to discuss sensualism, but in a completely different way – this time in refutation of an argument which uses the evidence of the senses to prove the inadequacy of philosophical materialism. Nietzsche's target here, although unnamed, is clearly Lange, for the position addressed is one adopted by Lange in the course of his critique of materialism. We may summarize his main line of thought, rather briefly, along the following lines. Lange gives full credit to the materialist contribution: the many successes of modern science arise from a research programme whose aims and methods are inspired by the Democritean doctrine that 'Nothing exists but atoms and empty space: everything else is mere opinion'. Yet this reductionist orientation reveals both the strength and the weakness of atomism. For, despite all its advances, natural science has never explained the occurrence of even the simplest sensation. There seems to be an unbridgeable gap between material motion and consciousness, and this failure to account for an entire domain of reality makes philosophical materialism an untenable doctrine.

Even if this problem were somehow solved, Lange argues, there would be another fatal objection to materialism. When natural science turns its attention to the human subject and its capacity for gaining knowledge, a surprising outcome is seen. The science of physiology points to idealism by demonstrating that the senses cannot be regarded as providing an accurate picture of the real character of the world. Lange endorses Helmholtz's theory that all perception involves a hidden process of inference from what is given to the senses.[14] Hence, scientific theory confirms the Kantian claim that the world, as we perceive and understand it, is a product of our own organization. Even our own bodies and their organs, Lange concludes, are pictures of something that transcends our knowledge and must remain unknown to us.

> Just as it was once amazingly difficult for people to think of this fixed earth on which we stand, the prototype of rest and stability, as moving, so it will be even harder for them to recognise their own body, the prototype of all reality for them, as a mere scheme of representation, a product of our optical apparatus,

which must be distinguished from the object that occasions it as much as any other representational picture.[15]

Thus, the bodily senses too are only representations, like the objects of the outside world: 'The eye, with which we believe we see, is only a product of our ideas.'[16]

It is this line of thought that inspires the admiration expressed in *Beyond Good and Evil* for those contemporary thinkers who are bold enough to deny the reality of the whole world of appearance. Nietzsche says that they 'rank the credibility of their own bodies about as low as the credibility of the visual evidence that "the earth stands still," and thus, apparently in good humour, let their securest possession go (for in what does one at present believe more firmly than in one's body?'.[17] But this praise is soon followed by a firm rebuttal of any scepticism concerning the body:

> To study physiology with a clear conscience, one must insist that the sense organs are *not* appearances in the sense of idealistic philosophy; as such they could not be causes! Sensualism, therefore, at least as a regulative hypothesis, not to say as a heuristic principle.[18]

Nietzsche goes on to state a *reductio ad absurdum* objection to the proposition that the external world is the work of our organs: since our bodily organs are themselves part of this external world, they would have to be their own causes – an apparent philosophical absurdity.

In the previous section, sensualism was identified with 'belief in the senses'. Now it is characterized as a regulative or heuristic principle – a very different matter. This is clearly another version of the distinction between sensualism as a theory and as a practice. In the first case, there is a dogmatic commitment to the truth of the doctrine; in the second, it is used as a guideline which directs the course of inquiry without anticipating its outcomes. What this might mean in practice is indicated in *Twilight of the Idols*: 'Today we possess science precisely to the extent to which we have decided to *accept* the testimony of the senses – to the extent to which we sharpen them further, arm them, and have learned to think them through to the end.'[19] Spelt out in this way, an affirmation of the importance of the senses is turned into a vigorous research programme, one that improves its techniques of observation and makes the best theoretical use of their findings.

What, then, is the outlook of the practical sensualists? Their intention is to achieve a better, more detailed and accurate *description* of natural processes, 'perfecting the image of becoming' rather than pretending to grasp its underlying causes.[20] They treat the senses not as an authority for conviction, but as a source of provisional hypotheses. For the senses themselves do not contain the interpretations we impose upon them, as Nietzsche explains in commenting on the philosophical tradition which postulates a 'true' world separate from that of appearance. These idealists, he says, repudiated the world of the senses because they could not endure the facts of growth and decay, of birth and death. Heraclitus was right in opposing this prejudice with a reaffirmation of becoming, but he fell into a similar error concerning the senses.

> Heraclitus too did the senses an injustice. They lie neither in the way the Eleatics believed, nor as he believed – they do not lie at all. What we *make* of their testimony, that alone introduces lies; for example, the lie of unity, the lie of thinghood, of substance, of permanence. 'Reason' is the cause of our falsification of the testimony of the senses.[21]

Thus, rather unexpectedly, Nietzsche seems to be saying that most people are sensualists in theory but not in practice. For while they trust the evidence of the senses, they are not committed to developing this approach to knowledge as far as it can go. In that case, they are unlikely to encounter the problem to be addressed in the next part of our discussion. The distinction between primary and secondary properties, already present in early Greek thought, has been a prominent theme in modern philosophy from Locke onwards. Empirical knowledge encourages us to make this distinction, in order to establish a single scheme of categories which will cover the greatest possible range of phenomena. If this does not lead to the general scepticism inferred by Lange, it does pose the problem of relating a scientific description of reality to the evidence of the senses. Nietzsche's reflections on this issue are scattered and incomplete, but they also bear on some important themes in his thought.

Quantity and Quality

Sharp differences between the various presentations of Nietzsche's thought of eternal return have always puzzled commentators. One principal form of the doctrine uses a vocabulary taken from natural science. It portrays the world as a configuration of basic elements, and so understands recurrence as a reappearance of the same configuration of elements. The other version uses the ordinary language of human experience. In one notebook he writes, 'Everything has returned: Sirius and the spider and your thoughts in this hour and this thought of yours that everything returns.'[22] This passage is cited by Martin Heidegger as evidence that a quasi-scientific reading of Nietzsche is of little value. He comments, 'Since when are "thoughts" and "hours" objects of physics or biology?'[23] This is not a request for information, I take it, but a dismissive statement. Heidegger thinks that scientific thinking is irrelevant to the doctrine of recurrence, at least with regard to its philosophical importance. Nietzsche's interest in scientific theories, a feature of his thinking at every stage, finds little or no response in Heidegger. The text quoted occurs in the same notebook as an extensive series of notes on the scientific significance of eternal return. That suggests that the incongruity which Heidegger is assuming was not so evident to Nietzsche himself. For the ancient Greek thinkers he admired over later philosophers, divisions such as that between 'ethical' and 'cosmological' ideas – a commonplace in Nietzsche interpretation since Simmel's lectures – did not exist.

Oddly enough, the problem we are concerned with here is hinted at in what seems to be Nietzsche's first reference to the notion of eternal return, in his 'untimely meditation' on history. There he writes:

> That which was once possible could present itself as a possibility for a second time only if the Pythagoreans were right in believing that when the constellation of the heavenly bodies is repeated the same things, down to the smallest detail, must also be repeated on earth: so that whenever the stars stand in a certain relation to one another a Stoic again joins with an Epicurean to murder Caesar, and when they stand in another relation Columbus will again discover America.[24]

It is clear enough that Nietzsche does not accept the picture he attributes to the Pythagoreans. He does not seem to doubt that the same constellation of the heavenly bodies might occur again, although this assumption had been questioned by critics of astrology such as Nicole Oresme, as we saw in Chapter 7. Rather, what Nietzsche doubts is whether such an event would lead to a return of the corresponding events of human history. But this raises the same issue that faces his own later doctrine. Even the terminology is very similar: the question is whether the same 'constellation' of points of force would condition a return of the same things and their properties 'down to the smallest detail'.[25] Again, it is the relation between these two sets of concepts that constitutes the problem. How does the language of scientific knowledge translate into a discourse which we can recognize as an expression of our own experience?

On looking more closely at Nietzsche's own vocabulary, we see that he speaks of properties (*Eigenschaften*) and of qualities (*Qualitäten*) in quite different ways. In discussing the world as a collection of elements, Nietzsche asserts that their *properties* are to be identified with their *relations* to other things. The sum of a thing's relation to other things he calls its 'state' (*Lage*): 'The *state* in which people find themselves, in relation to nature and other people, makes their properties – it is the same as with atoms.'[26] The world as a whole has a 'general state' (*Gesammtlage*) which is just the totality of the relations between its elements. This idea figures prominently in some discussions of eternal recurrence. When Nietzsche speaks of the world as consisting of 'centres of force' rather than the solid atoms of mechanistic materialism, he uses the word 'constellation' – as in the earlier reference to the stars and planets – to designate the overall configuration of these centres at any given time.

Properties are closely linked with the project of a systematic formulation of knowledge and, on that basis, a scientific understanding of the world. Quantity is prominent in this conception, because measurement and calculation are powerful procedures for organizing knowledge. Quality, on the other hand, seems to be an idea not driven by any theoretical need, but expressing directly what we experience through our various senses. Nietzsche sometimes characterizes qualities as the *effects* that things have on us – a familiar claim made by empiricist theories of knowledge. This means that the same things may have different qualities for different perceivers, according to their constitutions. In addition, some beings are aware of aspects of the world that others fail to perceive – for instance, those animals that hear sounds or see colours outside the human range of experience. Nietzsche concludes that our human experience of the world is an idiosyncratic perspective which should not be generalized: 'It is obvious that every creature different from us senses different qualities and consequently lives in a different world from that in which we live.'[27]

How can these different worlds be reconciled with the single world of objective knowledge? This is just the task of finding some relation between quality and quantity. One answer is already found in Nietzsche's early lectures on pre-Platonic philosophy, where it is attributed to Democritus: 'All qualities are conventions, things vary only quantitatively. Thus all qualities are to be traced back to variations in quantity.'[28] The idea here is that quality arises from quantity by way of *difference*. In a later notebook, Nietzsche writes:

> Our 'knowing' limits itself to establishing quantities; but we cannot help sensing these differences in quantity as qualities. Quality is a *perspectival* truth for *us*; not an 'in-itself'. Our senses have a definite quantum as a mean within which they function; i.e., we sense bigness and smallness in relation to the conditions of our existence. If we sharpened or blunted our senses tenfold, we should perish; i.e., with regard to making possible our existence we sense even relations between magnitudes as qualities.[29]

A nearby entry describes qualities as 'insurmountable barriers for us'.[30] We know that the colours we see correspond to different wavelengths of light, but we still experience them as various qualities which cannot be reduced to one another. If this substitution is an illusion, it is one of the most necessary illusions that living things undergo. For the transformation of differences in degree into differences of kind – firstly between qualities and then between things themselves – has valuable advantages in the task of survival. Since failure to recognize beneficial and harmful features of the environment is very dangerous for any creature, any factor that guards against such errors will be favoured by natural selection. A further advantage comes from the association of sensations with pleasure and pain, owing to the influence those feelings have on behaviour. This important point will be discussed in detail later.

This emphasis on the differences between quantities, rather than simply on quantities, seems quite hard to understand. Any attempt to make better sense of the idea will require some interpretation. At this point I make a suggestion which draws on the distinction between two kinds of quantities – those that involve extension and those that involve intensity. My suggestion is that the quantities figuring in Nietzsche's approach to quantity and quality should be interpreted as *intensive* quantities. The difference is rather hard to define in a non-circular way, and one finds little helpful discussion in the literature of philosophy. One writer who does raise this issue is Kant: he explains the distinction by saying that, with an extensive magnitude, the representation of the parts precedes that of the whole, whereas, with an intensive magnitude, the representation of the whole precedes any representation of the parts.[31] Some familiar examples may be more instructive. Length, duration and mass are all extensive quantities, while temperature, pressure and brightness are intensive quantities. Kant's definition makes some sense when we reflect that these latter phenomena are apprehended all at once. This explains the ability of perceived qualities to evoke immediate reactions – an important consideration in their usefulness for sentient beings, for whom making quick decisions may be a vital factor in self-preservation.

We may still want to say, as Kant does, that intensive magnitudes do have parts, for otherwise it is difficult to see how any numerical value could be assigned to them. So, how do their parts differ from those of extensive magnitudes? Instead of following Kant's emphasis on the relation between parts and whole, we may simply note that intensive magnitudes involve succession: their parts are essentially *ordered* in a way that those of extensive magnitudes are not. This is why we cannot add them together in the same way. It makes sense to add one length to another length, but not one temperature to another temperature. From this point about addition follows one about subtraction: the difference between two intensive quantities is not itself an intensive quantity. For instance, the difference between one temperature and another is not a third temperature. What is the difference between 20 degrees Celsius and 40 degrees Celsius? The correct answer is not 20 degrees Celsius, but 20 Celsius degrees. Now there is a further puzzle, for although two intensive magnitudes cannot be added, an intensive magnitude can be multiplied or divided – for instance, doubled or halved. We must be careful, however, in carrying out these operations. It would be quite meaningless to say that a temperature of 40 degrees Celsius is 'twice' a temperature of 20 degrees Celsius. That is because this scale does not start from a genuine zero point, but arbitrarily designates a finite magnitude as having that numerical value. Further, since intensity has to do with *order*, it is represented by ordinal rather than cardinal numbers: in our example, it is not a question of forty degrees, but of the fortieth degree. The fortieth degree does not *include* the twentieth degree, any more than Henry VIII includes Henry V.

The proposition that intensive magnitudes cannot be added together has been put to ingenious use by C.S. Lewis. He begins by observing that if two people are each suffering a toothache of intensity x, it does not follow that anyone is suffering a toothache of intensity 2x. He continues:

> There is no such thing as a sum of suffering, for no one suffers it. When we have reached the maximum that a single person can suffer, we have, no doubt, reached something very horrible, but we have reached all the suffering there can ever be in the universe. The addition of a million fellow-sufferers adds no more pain.[32]

A reply is that sensations have not only intensive but also extensive magnitude, in the multiplicity of subjects who experience them and, within a single person, in their bodily extent and temporal duration. Accordingly, we can say that there is more or less pain in so far as any of these magnitudes increases or decreases. Someone who overlooks that consideration might attempt to prove that eternal punishment is no more severe than the most brief or even momentary punishment, since the intensities of the successive states of pain cannot be added together. Anyone arguing in that way, though, would be forced to concede that eternal bliss is no more rewarding than a very fleeting pleasure.

In Kant's treatment, intensive magnitude is closely linked with the element of *sensation* in knowledge. It is because our sensations are more or less intense that we can perceive intensive magnitudes, and it is because all empirical perception involves sensation that Kant can formulate the principle of the 'anticipations of perception', which states that 'In all appearances, the real that is an object of sensation has intensive magnitude, that is, a degree'.[33] Sensations are of various kinds, as are the corresponding qualities of the things that cause them. For Kant, that is enough to justify a rejection of the atomism which banishes qualities from the external world, allowing only extension and solidity. If there are intensive magnitudes in reality, there must be qualities which are capable of varying in intensity. What these may be is left open. Kant seems to be acknowledging that, depending on the nature of their sense organs, different sentient beings will experience different sensations and thus perceive different qualities. All we can say of these in advance is that they must have some degree of intensity. As for the relation between the intensities of sensations and those of their external causes, that too is a subject for research by empirical psychology.[34]

Now one might ask: if the difference between two such quantities is not a quantity, what is it? Given his earlier statement, Nietzsche's answer seems to be: a quality. One might object that quality has already been assumed, in that every intensive magnitude is associated with some quality – temperature with heat, brightness with colour and so on. But the point at issue concerns the circumstances under which qualities are perceived by us, and this may involve conditions of a narrower kind. Sometimes Nietzsche suggests that qualities are our awareness of *changes* in quantity, rather than just differences: 'N.B. Given particular alterations of quantities, what we sense as a distinct quality arises.'[35] This is not surprising, if one reflects that a difference in quantity will usually not just be present, but have some consequence – that is, give rise to some change. An example will make this clearer. What do we mean by describing things as 'hot' and 'cold'? As used in everyday language, these terms are relative to one's own body; any object whose temperature is noticeably above that will be judged as 'hot', and below it as 'cold'. We sense these differences because they *affect* our own body, since heat passes into or out of it as a result. That process of change, not the difference by itself, is what produces the sensation that we experience. In other words, something is hot or cold because it makes us hot or cold. This conclusion coincides with the earlier notion of a quality, understood as the effect of a stimulus on our bodily organization.

All this is still a long way from 'thoughts' and 'hours', no doubt, but it suggests that a dismissal of the problem posed by the differences between Nietzsche's vocabularies may be premature. Despite their dissimilarity, the life-world and that of objective knowledge have a common ground. Nietzsche writes: 'Belief in the "senses" is the basis of all science, as of all life.'[36] Should we take the word 'belief' at face value here? He has already insisted that sensualism need not be a dogmatic claim, amounting to one of those convictions which he says 'are more dangerous enemies of truth than lies'.[37] Rather, it may serve as a regulative hypothesis or a heuristic principle, both in science and in life. In that case, the relation between scientific concepts and the ideas of sense experience is still an open question, for which a closer analysis of the nature of sensation is an appropriate procedure.

Pleasure and Pain

As well as bodily sensations, there are what Nietzsche refers to in *Human, All-Too-Human* as 'the moral sensations'. The term is borrowed from his friend Paul Rée, whose book *The Origin of the Moral Sensations* had offered a speculative account of feelings such as sympathy, gratitude, justice and self-regard, along the lines suggested by Darwin's theory of evolution by means of natural selection.[38] In his later writings, Nietzsche suggests that *all* sensations are valuations: he notes that 'all our value sensations (i.e., simply our sensations) adhere precisely to qualities'.[39] Our senses have evolved in accordance with our conditions of life, and so the qualities we attribute to things are determined by what has been beneficial or harmful in the past.[40] Every sensation thus involves assumptions about benefit or harm; and this is especially evident with pleasure and pain.

I shall approach Nietzsche's ideas on the subject of pleasure and pain by way of a contemporary writer whose 'scientific theory of sensibility' links pleasure and pain with sensation in general. Léon Dumont (1837–1877) was a French author on philosophical psychology and aesthetics. He was not an academic philosopher but the sort of marginal figure that appealed to Nietzsche.[41] His principal work, published in 1875, is an attempt to formulate a scientific theory of pleasure and pain.[42] As Dumont observes, this has never been done before; and he expresses the hope that his theory will make possible a science of aesthetics, as part of a more general science of feeling.[43] The term 'science' may suggest consistency with a reductionist and materialist programme in psychology, but does not imply a reliance on empirical evidence; indeed, Dumont argues that a science of pleasure and pain is like dynamics or mathematics, in being concerned not with facts, but with more general and abstract objects. The background for that approach is a scientific reductionism which, it is argued, modern psychology has substantiated by explaining all facts of consciousness as combinations of elementary sensations, eliminating both a separate self and any notion of free will.

With this in mind, one may at first suppose that pleasure and pain are simply elementary sensations, which are irreducible and hence indefinable. The association of these sensations with others will vary greatly, since we know that the same perception may give pleasure on one occasion and displeasure on another. In that case, Dumont points out, there could hardly be general laws, and a science of pleasure (and hence of aesthetics) would be impossible. His own opinion is that, while pleasure and pain arise from sensations, they are not themselves sensations. Rather, they correspond to certain relations between successive mental states:

> What we have said is sufficient to show that pleasure and pain are not *real* phenomena, like sensations, ideas, perceptions, concepts; that they are, rather, strictly speaking, the transition from one phenomenon to another, that they correspond to a change and not to a state.[44]

This theory explains why we cannot identify pleasure and pain with qualities of the object, as we do with sensations: such feelings express what is happening within the subject itself, and are related to objects only indirectly. Again, since pleasure and pain are not particular states, they have no place in the causally connected sequence of our experiences and actions. They accompany these phenomena, but are not their antecedent conditions – in other words, pleasure and pain do not act as motives for the will. But, one may object, is not there such a thing as a love of pleasure, which may readily be a cause of action? Dumont agrees, but says that it is found only in higher animals, who are capable of memory and foresight in judging the consequences of their actions.[45] As a motive, then, this is not reducible to a mode of feeling, taken by itself.

Dumont has a further theory about the sorts of change involved in feelings of pleasure and pain – that they are symptoms of the union and dispersal of forces. Pleasure arises when the sum of force that constitutes the self undergoes an increase (provided this is not sufficient to disrupt its organization) and pain when a corresponding decrease in force occurs.[46] So although pleasure and pain have a relative character – they do not arise from a single sensation or set of sensations, and are not caused by a single kind of external object – they nevertheless occur according to a general principle, which in turn points to a more detailed theory. Later, Dumont goes on to discuss kinds of pleasure and pain which differ from one another not just because they are located in different locations or activities but, more significantly, because force increases or decreases in them in different ways. For example, the sum of force may decrease owing to an increased output (as in fatigue and related states) or to a decreased input (as in boredom, doubt, impatience, grief, pity and fear or, more generally, the frustration of our desires). The rest of his discussion outlines a classification of pains and pleasures which will provide the plan for a general science of feeling.

Sensations themselves, in so far as we are conscious of them, are identical with brain states; they are the 'subjective side' of these observable phenomena. Similarly, pleasure and pain are the subjective side of the causal relations between successive states. Dumont considers that pleasure and pain – and feeling in general – extend beyond consciousness to processes located within the human organism but outside the system that constitutes the self. Local anaesthesia, he thinks, confirms this idea: sensations continue to occur in the organs concerned, but are not communicated to the brain.[47] Further, if feeling is just one aspect of motion, it may even occur in the inorganic world, despite the absence of organization there; for the nerve system does not create sensations, but only carries and combines them. It may be, Dumont speculates, that pleasure and pain are found throughout nature, wherever force is gathered or dispersed. The metaphysical character of his theory is evident here: its ultimate aim is to provide knowledge of the absolute being which, he believes, underlies and expresses itself in all phenomena.

An equally surprising result of his theory emerges when the principle of the conservation of energy is taken into account. This law implies that any increase of energy in one location must correspond to a decrease of energy elsewhere. According to Dumont's theory, these processes are identical with pleasure and pain respectively.[48] Hence, the amount of pleasure in the world must always be exactly equal to the amount of pain. This invalidates any claim that existence as a whole contains more pain than pleasure, or vice versa – in other words, it disposes of both pessimism and optimism, so understood. It has an even more startling implication – that for every subject experiencing pleasure, another must experience pain. Dumont acknowledges this only by referring to the successes of the human race at the expense of other species in the struggle for existence. He forbears to mention that a similar conclusion must also apply to individuals. Accordingly, he does not address the novel ethical problems that would arise from an assumption that one person's pleasure necessitates another's pain.

Nietzsche owned a copy of Dumont's treatise, which had been translated into German and published in 1876 as *Vergnügen und Schmerz*. That he was reading Dumont in early 1883 is clear from a notebook which contains several quotations from that work.[49] Only later does Nietzsche go into the subject of pleasure and pain on his own account, and then he endorses several of Dumont's leading propositions. He agrees that pleasure and pain are not primary facts of consciousness but only epiphenomena.[50] Hence the absurdity of those philosophies, such as hedonism and utilitarianism, which take pleasure and pain as their standard for evaluating the world. He repeats Dumont's claim that these feelings are not part of the causal process:

> Upon reflection, however, we should concede that everything would have taken the same course, according to exactly the same sequence of causes and effects, if these states 'pleasure and displeasure' had been absent, and that one is simply deceiving oneself if one thinks they cause anything at all.[51]

And because they are only epiphenomena, Nietzsche concludes that pleasure and pain are not motives for action: ' – there is no striving for pleasure: but pleasure occurs when what is being striven for is attained: pleasure is an accompaniment, pleasure is not a motive ....'[52]

One aspect of Dumont's theory is of particular importance for Nietzsche – his identification of pleasure with an increase of force, which is readily assimilable to Nietzsche's own theory of the will to power. Hence he can refer to 'that general feeling of overabundant, overflowing power that constitutes the essence of pleasure'.[53] This description is part of a much broader picture. Nietzsche postulates an economy of force which entails a cyclical process of accumulation and release of force (or rather energy, in modern terms) in all living things, and includes a conception of power as a relation of control and submission between such forces. In a speculative mode, he suggests that the instinct which drives the development of organic beings is a drive to discharge their strength, rather than the imperative of self-preservation which he supposes to be the leading principle of a Darwinian approach in biology.[54] Even more speculatively, he sometimes hints at a cosmic cycle with a similar pattern, resembling that of pre-Socratic thinkers like Heraclitus. But these are wider areas, which will not be entered here.

Despite these overlaps, Nietzsche advances other ideas which make his account of pleasure and pain quite distinct from Dumont's. One is an emphasis on the role of interpretation, especially in the case of pain. In *The Gay Science*, Nietzsche had written:

> Second, when a strong stimulus is experienced as pleasure or displeasure, this depends on the *interpretation* of the intellect which, to be sure, generally does this work without rising to our consciousness: one and the same stimulus can be experienced as pleasure or displeasure.[55]

The interpretation Nietzsche has in mind is a judgement about the benefit or harm expected to follow from the phenomenon – a more or less complex calculation which is condensed into an immediate reaction, presumably as a result of the past history of the individual or species. In contrast, Dumont explains the variability of pleasure and pain in terms of the varying context within which the stimulus occurs, and excludes a process of thinking, even unconscious, from his account.[56]

Further, Nietzsche's ideas often resemble a theory of pleasure and pain which Dumont has considered and rejected. The 'Epicurean' view, as he labels it, is that pain arises from obstacles to the satisfaction of our wishes, and that pleasure is the overcoming of such obstacles. Hence, pleasure is always bound up with pain. Pessimistic thinkers such as Schopenhauer and Hartmann, who argue that pain must always outweigh pleasure, recommend a policy of renunciation as the only solution for the predicament. The conclusion usually drawn from the 'Epicurean' theory, according to Dumont, is that avoiding pain is more important than achieving pleasure. However, he notes, Jerome Cardan suggested that we must seek out what causes pain, in order to gain greater pleasure by overcoming it. It is significant that this is a reference noted down by Nietzsche for his own use.[57] While Dumont may have reported Cardan's idea only as a curiosity, or as a *reductio ad absurdum* of the theory, Nietzsche takes it seriously. He is prepared not only to admit the interdependence of pleasure and pain, but to go further, questioning whether they are really distinct, let alone opposites. Pleasure may be a series of small pains, he suggests, a 'game of resistance and victory'.[58]

While it is hard to identify a single account of pleasure and pain with Nietzsche, the question remains: how do his ideas on the subject fit in with the 'sensualism' which is prominent in his thought after *Thus Spake Zarathustra*? If a distinction is made in epistemology between sensualism as a theory and as a practice, is there a corresponding distinction for morality? If all of us are sensualists these days, are we also hedonists in some sense or other? Nietzsche's dismissive remarks on utilitarianism suggest otherwise: 'Man does not strive for pleasure; only the Englishman does.'[59] Yet he does not want to abandon a material element in value judgement, in favour of an formalistic ethic of abstract principle such as Kantianism. Hence his interest in a subtler account of pleasure and pain, which denies them the authority they would have in a hedonistic system, but gives them a certain role as indicators or clues, and perhaps even as heuristic principles. Rather as sensations were earlier seen as functions of differences in force, pleasure and pain are interpreted as symptoms of differences in power.[60]

If we ask why the theme of sensualism becomes so important for Nietzsche in his later development, the answer seems to be that it brings together concerns which, until then, he could deal with only one at a time. It is true that the relation between knowledge and life was a central issue in, for example, the 'untimely meditation' on history, and in writing of the same time on higher education and scholarship. But these are largely programmes for a project which could not be fulfilled at that stage. The contribution of the concept of sensualism is made possible by the emergence in Nietzsche's thinking of a radical denial of distinctions between sense and spirit or, in the language of *Zarathustra*, between passions and virtues. His new account is both an explanation and a revaluation. The higher authority traditionally attached to reason disappears when we recognize that it 'evolved on a sensualistic basis'.[61] Similarly, our picture of the virtues is transformed when their origin is disclosed as a sublimation of the passions, rather than an insight into some higher realm. In either case, the activity of 'thinking to the end' corresponds to the adoption of sensualism, understood as a method rather than a doctrine.

Some other issues might be linked with sensualism in a fuller treatment, although they have not been touched on here. For instance, the idea of 'order of rank' is evoked when Nietzsche writes: 'The most spiritual men feel the stimulus and charm of sensuous things in a way that other men – those with "fleshly hearts" – cannot possibly imagine and ought not to imagine.'[62] No example is given, but an artist such as Goethe comes to mind readily and would, indeed, probably be Nietzsche's own nomination. Those representatives of the highest culture who can be said to attach a more fundamental value to the senses than to 'spirit' may, he suggests, be called 'sensualists in the best faith'. So, if 'today we are all sensualists', it is to the extent that we can recognize the achievement of such figures and use it as a model – one which points the way, not only in scientific knowledge, but in life itself.

Notes

1. Friedrich Nietzsche, *The Gay Science*, sect. 372.
2. KGW VII/2, 234.
3. KGW VIII/3, 455.
4. Not trusting his readers on this point, Kaufmann translates *Sensualisten* as 'believers in the senses', a rather misleading phrase in view of the qualification Nietzsche goes on to make in this passage.
5. KGW III/3, 207.
6. Nietzsche, *The Gay Science*, sect. 373.
7. KGW VII/2, 264.
8. Friedrich Nietzsche, *Beyond Good and Evil*, sect. 12. One may here recall the admiring words of Galileo when referring to the heliocentric theories of Aristarchus and Copernicus: 'Nor can I ever sufficiently admire the outstanding acumen of those who have taken hold of this opinion and accepted it as true; they have through sheer force of intellect done such violence to their senses as to prefer what reason told them over that which sensible experience plainly showed them to the contrary.' Galileo, *Dialogues Concerning the Two Chief World Systems*, trans. Stillman Drake, 2nd edn (Berkeley, CA: University of California Press, 1967), 328.
9. Friedrich Nietzsche, *Daybreak*, sect. 168. See also KGW VII/3, 278 (*The Will to Power*, sect. 443).
10. Friedrich Nietzsche, *Historische-Kritische Gesamtausgabe: Werke*, ed. H.J. Mette and K. Schlechta (München: C.H. Beck'sche Verlagsbuchhandlung, 1937), Band 4, 84.
11. F.A. Lange, *Geschichte des Materialismus und Kritik seiner Bedeutung in der Gegenwart* (Iserlohn: Verlag von J. Baedecker, 1866), 345.
12. See, for example, ibid., 405, for this phrase which is often used by Nietzsche: *Beyond Good and Evil*, sect. 21; also KGW VII/3, 224 and 288 (*The Will to Power*, sect. 618), KGW VII/3, 439 and KGW VIII/1, 90 and 110 (*The Will to Power*, sect. 622).
13. Nietzsche, *Beyond Good and Evil*, sect. 14.
14. Lange, *Geschichte des Materialismus*, 500.
15. Ibid., 485.
16. Ibid., 496.
17. Nietzsche, *Beyond Good and Evil*, sect. 10.
18. Ibid., sect. 15. See also KGW VII/1, 88 and 230.
19. Friedrich Nietzsche, *Twilight of the Idols*, '"Reason" in Philosophy', sect. 3. Similarly, Zarathustra says, 'You should think your own senses through to the end': Friedrich Nietzsche, *Thus Spake Zarathustra*, 'Upon the Blessed Isles'. Cf. KGW VII/2, 124 (*The Will to Power*, sect. 1046).
20. Nietzsche, *The Gay Science*, sect. 112.
21. Nietzsche, *Twilight of the Idols*, '"Reason" in Philosophy', sect. 2.
22. KGW V/2, 422.
23. Martin Heidegger, *Nietzsche*, trans. D.F. Krell (San Francisco: Harper and Row, 1980), Vol. 2, 114.
24. Friedrich Nietzsche, *On the Uses and Disadvantages of History for Life*, sect. 2. A somewhat similar passage occurs in the book which was the occasion of Nietzsche's first 'untimely meditation', David Friedrich Strauss's *Der alte und der neue Glaube*. Strauss writes: 'When the great year of the world has thus elapsed, the formation of a new world begins, in which – according to the Stoic fancy – the earlier one repeats itself precisely, down to particular events and persons (Socrates and Xanthippe).' Strauss, *Der alte und der neue Glaube* (Leipzig: Verlag von S. Hirzel, 1872), 155.
25. For 'constellation' see KGW VIII/3, 68 and 165 (*The Will to Power*, sect. 551 and 636); and for 'smallest detail', KGW V/2, 421.
26. KGW V/2, 421.
27. KGW VIII/1, 244 (*The Will to Power*, sect. 565).
28. KGW II/4, 333.
29. KGW VIII/1, 201 (*The Will to Power*, sect. 563).

30 Ibid., 244 (*The Will to Power*, sect. 565).
31 Immanuel Kant, *Critique of Pure Reason*, trans. Norman Kemp Smith (London: Macmillan, 1929), A162/B203 and A168/B210.
32 C.S. Lewis, *The Problem of Pain* (London: Geoffrey Bles, 1940), 103–104.
33 Kant, *Critique of Pure Reason*, B207.
34 The pioneers in this area were E.H. Weber and G.T. Fechner, who developed a model for estimating the intensities of sensations, and on that basis postulated a formula in which the magnitudes of sensation and stimulus are related in a logarithmic function.
35 He goes on: 'It is the same with morality. Here accompanying feelings of beneficence or utility arise in someone who perceives a human characteristic in a certain quantum; doubled or tripled, he is afraid of it ....' KGW VII/2, 238.
36 KGW VII/2, 234; reading *'die Sinne'* for *'das Sein'*, as indicated by KGW VII/4/2, 654.
37 Friedrich Nietzsche, *Human, All-Too-Human*, sect. 483.
38 Paul Rée, *Der Ursprung der moralischen Empfindungen* (Chemnitz: Verlag von Ernst Schmeitzner, 1877).
39 KGW VIII/1, 244 (*The Will to Power*, sect. 565).
40 KGW VII/2, 183.
41 For an outline of Dumont's life and work, see Alexander Buechner, *Un philosophe amateur. Essai biographique sur Léon Dumont (1837–1877) avec des extraits de sa correspondance* (Paris: Librairie Félix Alcan, 1884).
42 Léon Dumont, *Vergnügen und Schmerz. Zur Lehre den Gefühlen* (Leipzig: F.A. Brockhaus, 1876). This volume is a translation of Dumont's *Théorie scientifique de la sensibilité. Le plaisir et la peine* (Paris: Librairie Germer Baillière, 1875).
43 Dumont, *Vergnügen und Schmerz*, 100.
44 Ibid., 98.
45 Ibid., 307.
46 Ibid., 82.
47 Ibid., 129.
48 Ibid., 136.
49 KGW VII/1, 308 and 322.
50 Nietzsche, *Beyond Good and Evil*, sect. 225. See also KGW VIII/1, 338; VIII/2, 272 and 275; VIII/3, 127 and 152 (*The Will to Power*, sect. 579, 701, 669, 478 and 702).
51 KGW VIII/3, 127 (*The Will to Power*, sect. 478).
52 Ibid., 92 (*The Will to Power*, sect. 688).
53 Ibid., 150 (*The Will to Power*, sect. 699).
54 Nietzsche, *Beyond Good and Evil*, sect. 13.
55 Nietzsche, *The Gay Science*, sect. 127.
56 Dumont, *Vergnügen und Schmerz*, 57.
57 See KGW VII/1, 322.
58 KGW VIII/3, 150 (*The Will to Power*, sect. 699).
59 Nietzsche, *Twilight of the Idols*, 'Maxims and Arrows', sect. 12. It is only fair to point out that this is not how Englishmen see themselves. As A.P. Herbert puts it, 'The Englishman never enjoys himself except for a noble purpose': *Uncommon Law* (London: Eyre Methuen, 1977), 198.
60 KGW VIII/3, 70 (*The Will to Power*, sect. 695).
61 KGW VIII/2, 33 (*The Will to Power*, sect. 516).
62 KGW VIII/1, 200 (*The Will to Power*, sect. 1045).

Chapter 10

Ressentiment, Revenge and Punishment

Of all the philosophers who have looked beyond punishment to the motives and forces which lie behind it, both as a moral concept and as a social institution, Friedrich Nietzsche is the most prominent. However, as with the other themes we have explored in previous chapters, it is easy to overlook or misunderstand some of his most important ideas when the setting within which they were developed is disregarded. In this final chapter, Nietzsche's thinking on justice and punishment will be seen in the context of his dialogue with several contemporary writers. One of these has already been mentioned – Eugen Dühring, an influential thinker at one time in ethics and politics, as well as metaphysics. The other is Paul Rée, whose personal relationship to Nietzsche has often been discussed, but whose importance here lies in his 'historical' approach to morality, which opened the way towards what Nietzsche later called a 'genealogy of morals'.

For later readers, Nietzsche's use of the category of *ressentiment* in his analysis of morality has been particularly influential. Often he is credited with inventing this as a philosophical concept. The most notable promoter of that view is Max Scheler, whose book *Ressentiment* opens with the statement: 'Among the scanty discoveries which have been made in recent times about the origin of moral judgments, Friedrich Nietzsche's discovery that *ressentiment* can be the source of such value judgments is the most profound.'[1] Yet Scheler is wrong in attributing this 'discovery' to Nietzsche: the term *ressentiment* was already well-established in the writings of another philosopher, Eugen Dühring. Nietzsche's use of the term differs from Dühring's primarily in his very different valuation of *ressentiment* – a 'revaluation' (*Umwertung*) or 'reversal of perspective' which is characteristic of Nietzsche's thinking, and is a more subtle process than the simple replacement of one concept by a different one.

A striking feature of Nietzsche's philosophy is his frequent insistence that all human concepts are historical phenomena, a claim applicable to the principles of morality and religion as well as those of knowledge. Even those concepts which seem most permanent, he argues, have undergone many changes, evolving according to either external influences or their own inner tendencies. As a consequence, any interpretation of an idea which refers to its given form must be misleading, especially when it tries to explain the idea by proposing a 'higher' origin. This, too, was an unusual idea for its time, but one must note here the influence of another contemporary writer, Nietzsche's close friend for some years, Paul Rée. His attempt to construct a 'history of moral sensations', based on naturalistic assumptions, was a catalyst for Nietzsche's own conception of a history (or more properly, a prehistory) of moral values such as 'good' and 'evil'.

It is these two writers who will feature most prominently in our discussion of Nietzsche's treatment of revenge and punishment. From Rée, Nietzsche derived his important idea of the approach which he later called 'genealogical'; and it was Dühring who inspired, or rather provoked, his critique of the notion of revenge. More than any other work of Nietzsche, it is *On the Genealogy of Morals* that brings together these elements to constitute his most powerful attack on these problems. Yet there is no question of reducing Nietzsche's thinking to either of these earlier approaches, or even to a combination of the two – and such a combination would be impossible in any case. We could put Dühring's and Rée's accounts of punishment in a familiar setting by designating them as 'retributive' and 'utilitarian' respectively. But if such a labelling, abstracting from the individual features of their views, is an oversimplification, it at least points to the scope of their general concepts, and it helps account for their usefulness for Nietzsche's own thinking on justice and punishment. While they may have been negative, rather than positive, influences, they did define the moral and philosophical issues he addressed.

Dühring's Theory of Revenge

The proposition that justice and revenge are inseparably linked is asserted with force and conviction by a philosopher we have encountered in earlier chapters, Eugen Dühring. In books such as *Der Werth des Lebens*, first published in 1865, Dühring argues that the origin of the concept of justice lies in the impulse to retaliate against those who have done us some injury. Dühring uses the French word *ressentiment* for this 'reactive feeling', adding that its outward expression has a more familiar title – revenge.[2] The desire for revenge, he suggests, occurs naturally and involuntarily, like any other feeling.[3] It is not prompted by a moral judgement, arising in turn out of some purely rational conception of justice. On the contrary, our determination of injustice is the expression of our feelings of *ressentiment* against those who do harm. For practical reasons, society has found it desirable to establish its own monopoly of revenge, rather than leaving it in the hands of individuals. The form of the judgement alters accordingly: abstract thinking about justice and injustice is expressed in impersonal and universal ideas.[4] Yet the underlying impulse remains the same.

Dühring considers two other accounts of punishment, but only to reject them as inadequate. One is the 'formalist' view which identifies justice with an equivalence or symmetry between an offence and its punishment. While Dühring does not say whom he has in mind, Kant would be a prominent representative of this approach. For Kant insists that punishment 'can never be inflicted merely as a means to promote some other good for the criminal himself or for civil society. It must always be inflicted upon him only *because he has committed a crime*'.[5] Since this direct relation alone is admitted as determining what is appropriate, it also decides the nature and extent of the punishment. For instance, the principle of 'like for like' clearly requires the death penalty for those convicted of murder. Is this retribution to be identified with revenge? Kant says not, because 'no punishment, no matter from whom it comes, may be inflicted out of hatred'.[6] The civil power which imposes punishment represents a higher authority than any individual person, and its actions spring not from passions, but from the original contract on which the state's constitution is based. Kant argues further that only a law of retribution 'can specify definitely the quality and the quantity of punishment'.[7] Any other criterion will introduce considerations which vary according to particular circumstances. In any case, they will be external to justice; and since, for Kant, justice exists either in its pure form or not at all, any mixture of principles amounts to its elimination.

For a basic rebuttal of any 'formalist' theory of morality, Dühring urges that abstract concepts alone can never supply what is needed for justifying actions. Theoretical reason cannot make the transition from an 'is' to an 'ought' and, for this reason, moral ideas must find their grounding in the feelings or drives which occur in human beings and motivate their actions.[8] Only these can supply the material content required for any exercise of practical reasoning. It is just as well that *ressentiment* is not the only feeling of this kind; Dühring recognizes natural impulses of love and sympathy which can be broadened to encompass humanity as a whole. In addition, we have a desire for the good opinion of others, and that is an important factor in moral development.[9] Yet where an understanding of justice is concerned, Dühring's emphasis is always on the feeling of *ressentiment* and its corollary, the drive for revenge, since it is from these alone that our conception of injustice is derived.

The formalist approach is represented by the *lex talionis*, which prescribes a punishment similar to the crime – an eye for an eye, and a tooth for a tooth. Dühring objects that this does not go far enough. He writes: 'The infliction of the same harm, or one corresponding in magnitude, is not at all sufficient to restore equality.'[10] When that arbitrary restriction is imposed on the scope of punishment, just and unjust suffering are treated as the same thing. Fortunately, Dühring observes, the natural drive for revenge does not limit itself to the magnitude of the offence; it normally goes further, and rightly so, in his opinion. For 'only with an surplus of visible reaction is injustice as such actually dealt with'. What the *lex talionis* considers is only the outward, visible aspect of the crime. The real problem is the wrongful intrusion of one will into the domain of another, a fact which cannot be simply identified with observable events. Accordingly, the solution is to negate the offending will, but this cannot be achieved simply by a reaction of equal magnitude.

> The amount of harm which an adequate atonement, i.e. satisfaction of revenge, requires must be greater than the harm committed, and in particular, the force directed against the will of the wrongdoer must more than outweigh the lack of regard for others shown by that will in the crime.[11]

This rejection of the *lex talionis* as too inhibiting does not imply that Dühring is prepared to give the impulse towards vengeance a completely free rein. He allows that it can easily go too far, and so bring about a new injustice, this time imputable to the person seeking revenge. Feelings are hard to measure, and their assessment varies from person to person. Also, the *ressentiment* aroused by a particular injury may combine with some distinct prejudice, or with a hostility arising from other experiences. These uncertainties are good reasons for not leaving revenge to the judgement of individual persons; society as a whole is more consistent and reliable in fixing upon the punishment that fits the crime.

Another theory of justice considered by Dühring does at least adopt a material basis for its practical recommendations: it takes punishment to be justified by its consequences, and in particular by its success in reducing the likelihood of future offences. As Dühring points out, it is the threat of punishment that has this effect, and punishment itself is required only to give that threat the credibility it requires to act as a deterrent.[12] Dühring's criticism of the utilitarian approach is similar to that of Kant – that it fails to satisfy the demand for justice. States do impose some penalties which can be understood only as deterring measures, but that is because the rules they enforce have nothing to do with acts of injustice. An entire system of law enforcement based on this principle would be no more than a form of 'terrorism'. For while any act of justice may serve as a deterrent, not every deterrent involves an act of justice. Our concept of injustice is grounded in a natural drive which is quite separate from instruments of social control over behaviour. Dühring concludes that criminal justice, even in its ideal form, is just 'the public organisation of revenge'.[13] And while a fear of revenge may well deter potential aggressors, that is not the point of revenge.

Nietzsche's Response to Dühring

Much of Nietzsche's thinking about morality is a dialogue with Dühring. In 1875 he made a detailed summary of *Der Werth des Lebens*, adding his own critical comments, many of which point forward to his later writings. For instance, he sketches an analysis of Christian morality, accusing it of directing revenge against oneself.[14] In *On the Genealogy of Morals*, written twelve years later, Nietzsche develops these themes in much greater detail and explains his opposition to Dühring's standpoint. He says that it is an attempt 'to sanctify *revenge* under the name of *justice* – as if justice were basically merely a further development of the feeling of being aggrieved – and then to glorify not only revenge but all reactive impulses in general'.[15] Nietzsche is not defending the formalism that Dühring wanted to contest. His objection is that Dühring has overlooked another, and even more important, class of affects and impulses – the *active* ones. Looking at systems of law, he argues, we see that they are set up not by the weak, in order to satisfy their reactive feelings, but rather by individuals or groups who are 'active, strong, spontaneous, aggressive'.

In some ways, then, Dühring's thinking coincides with Nietzsche's. Both find a measure of self-deception, even of hypocrisy, in the conventional attitude towards revenge. On the other hand, Nietzsche's conclusion is that, in so far as punishment is legalized revenge, it must be eliminated: 'Let us do away with the concept *sin* – and let us quickly send after it the concept *punishment!*'[16] Here, Nietzsche is choosing the other horn of the moral dilemma posed by an identification of punishment with revenge. But why take this option, rather than change our view of revenge? To answer this question, and to reach an understanding of Nietzsche's position, we must look more closely at the nature of revenge.

Just what is wrong with revenge? Once again, a certain answer seems evident: revenge is morally wrong. For once, Nietzsche seems to be in full agreement with the Judaeo-Christian tradition. And he is far from alone in this. In her book *Wild Justice*, Susan Jacoby remarks on the 'taboo' attached to revenge in modern Western culture.[17] Witnesses in criminal trials, she observes, are supposed to disavow any desire for revenge when giving evidence against the accused, even – or rather, especially – when they are themselves the victims of criminal violence. They must present themselves as motivated by a disinterested concern for truth and justice; otherwise, the credibility of their testimony will be reduced in the public eye. She cites court proceedings in which witnesses against an alleged war criminal were, in effect, forced to make a public declaration of forgiveness in order to have their factual testimony accepted as evidence.[18]

The underlying assumption is that justice and revenge are mutually exclusive, and that punishment can properly be justified only in terms of general and impersonal considerations, such as the deterrence of future offences. Whether it is possible for us to achieve this objective standpoint is another matter. Jacoby draws attention to the persistent, although unacknowledged, presence of revenge in our thinking about crime and punishment. She argues that our failure to recognize and accept this has harmful consequences: as with other cases of repression, the denied impulse is liable to express itself in ways that are more damaging, both to oneself and to others. However, if punishment is recognised as retribution – 'legalized revenge' without the pejorative connotation – it is, for just this reason, kept in proportion to the offence, without becoming an outbreak of unbounded destruction.

What, then, is Nietzsche's critique of revenge? It is common enough to see revenge condemned, but not so common to see it *criticized*. That implies something quite different: it means understanding revenge not as a crime, but rather as a *mistake*. To make such a judgement we would have to identify revenge as having a rationale, as aiming at something above and beyond the pain of the other person. That in turn would make it possible to assess the success or failure of revenge in its own terms, apart from moral considerations. One common way of doing this is to regard revenge as an attempt to regain one's honour or social prestige. Adequate or not, this is at any rate a genuine explanation since it, in effect, reduces revenge to something that is easier to understand, or at least more familiar. What is more important is that this account turns revenge from a backward-looking motive into a forward-looking one. Like most other human actions, what it achieves, or tries to achieve, is simply some later state of affairs. Its success or failure is therefore defined by the course of events which it is designed to influence. This account is quite successful in dispelling the puzzle that attaches to revenge as an act concerned with the past rather than future. If anything, it may be too successful, eliminating something that we still feel is the most striking feature of this concept.

Perhaps revenge has *no* such rationale; perhaps it is just a sort of instinct which, as a matter of fact, occurs in human beings and, like other instincts, seeks its own satisfaction.[19] This is not as arbitrary as it appears. Such an impulse could have considerable value in the struggle for existence, since it seems plausible to suppose that individuals and groups known to be highly vengeful are less likely to be injured by others.[20] Nietzsche has a certain sympathy with this approach – up to a point. In *On the Genealogy of Morals* he endorses the attempt to understand an affect such as revenge in terms of its biological function, and even to defend it as valuable on that score; but he insists that, by itself, this is a one-sided approach. We must also consider 'another group of affects which, it seems to me, are of even greater biological value than these reactive affects and consequently deserve even more to be scientifically evaluated and esteemed'.[21] Here, Nietzsche has in mind the active and creative expressions of the will to power, which he thinks are overlooked in evolutionary theories. He is prepared to confront the biological approach on its own ground, by attacking the notion of the drive for self-preservation as too narrow for explaining the behaviour of living things.[22]

Yet Nietzsche also has a more radical criticism to make. He says that an appeal to revenge as an instinct does *not* explain the deliberate infliction of suffering: 'for revenge merely leads us back to the same problem: "how can making suffer constitute a compensation?"'[23] The problem is that of making sense of this pattern of action. Elsewhere Nietzsche is very sceptical about some common interpretations of human activities. He insists, for example, that the sexual instinct is aimed not at continuing the species – although that is no doubt its biological function – but only at its own satisfaction. Similarly, the pleasure of eating has nothing to do with self-preservation.[24] What lies behind these misleading interpretations is a refusal to look at everyday activities in their own terms. Revenge is a different case, but there is a similar tendency to explain it away, either by taking it as a basic instinct, not requiring further interpretation, or by turning it into a social phenomenon, expressing the need to maintain one's public prestige. Either alternative overlooks the important problem about revenge: how can making suffer constitute a compensation?

If revenge is supposed to achieve some further outcome, the important question is whether it succeeds in its aim or not. Schopenhauer is one philosopher who gives a negative answer and offers a genuine critique of revenge. At first, he simply condemns revenge, saying that 'Such a thing is wickedness and cruelty, and cannot be ethically justified'.[25] But he goes on to argue that revenge is misguided in accepting the principle of individuation at face value, and failing to appreciate that it does not apply beyond the phenomenal realm: 'It does not see to what extent the offender and the offended are in themselves one, and that it is the same inner nature which, not recognising itself in its own phenomenon, bears both the pain and the guilt.'[26] A utilitarian approach to punishment – one which restricts its attention to observable consequences – makes good sense in its own terms, and so is quite acceptable to Schopenhauer (and to Nietzsche, for that matter). But if we are thinking in moral rather than legal concepts, we need to go further and reach a conception of 'eternal' rather than 'temporal' justice. This, Schopenhauer observes, is expressed in the Christian prohibition on revenge. Eternal justice requires no such assistance from human efforts; it belongs to the timeless inner nature of the world, within which crime and punishment belong to one and the same being, and so must forever maintain a perfect balance.[27]

Nietzsche's account is quite different, but he too wants to criticize revenge, and not just condemn it. It is difficult to say whether he succeeds, given the fragmentary nature of his approaches to this theme but, since that is a problem we face with many of his important ideas, it provides no excuse for not trying to achieve a coherent picture. What makes his approach of special interest is its suggestion of a rationale which is not reducible to a forward-looking motive. It is clear, however, that Nietzsche considers revenge to be unsuccessful. His Zarathustra insists that revenge must be overcome in all its forms: 'For *that man be delivered from revenge*, that is for me the bridge to the highest hope, and a rainbow after long storms.'[28] Revenge fails simply because 'no deed can be annihilated'. What does this failure consist in? Revenge may be aimed against the deeds of the past, but in practice it takes as its target a more accessible object – namely, 'all who can suffer'.[29] Yet why should making others suffer reduce or eliminate one's own suffering? If their pain elicits sympathy or pity, it has the opposite effect, since such a response '*increases* the amount of suffering in the world'.[30] We must find further conditions here and, among these, reference to the past must clearly be the crucial factor. Drawing on a moral vocabulary, we can begin to construct an appropriate account in the following way.

Revenge attempts to redirect its own suffering on to another. For this to come to anything, several conditions must apply. First, the suffering must be identified as the *effect* of some past event. Second, that event must be grasped as an action for which some other person was *responsible*. Third, that other must be identifiable as the *same* person on whom revenge is now taken. These mediating links are supposed to make it possible for the suffering one inflicts on the other to eliminate the power of the past event to cause one's own suffering. They enable revenge to remove the blockage which is the source of the frustration of the will, and to complete a circuit which, as long as it remains partial, can only provoke anger and melancholy.

There is no question here of eliminating the past act, or even of trying to do so. In fact, revenge seems to stand in a certain complicity with what it purports to condemn. This is a familiar enough phenomenon in everyday life, where we see people taking a pride of ownership in their grievances and maintaining them in good condition. But if revenge is successful on its own terms, it should free us from the past. The past can never come to an end, but it can, on this model, be turned into something self-contained, and thus separable from the ongoing course of becoming. Such a past would be completed, over and done with, a genuine 'bygone' – and therefore a perfect rather than imperfect tense.

The task of redemption is announced by Zarathustra as one of transformation:

> To redeem what is past in man and to re-create all 'It was' until the will says, 'Thus I willed it! Thus shall I will it' – this I called redemption and this alone I taught them to call redemption.[31]

Revenge attempts to do something which is similar to this, yet different. If the past event is an 'It was', the past act of the other is a 'Thus you willed it', and the other's present responsibility a 'Thus you will it'. In retracing this path, revenge is, in effect, purporting to turn 'It was' into 'Thus you willed it' and then into 'Thus you will it'. The infliction of pain, a negation of the will, is intended to eliminate this last element and, on passing back round the circle, to negate the others, until one's own present suffering is also eliminated.

Yet Nietzsche holds that all this is futile, because the links on which the closing of the circuit depends, such as causality, responsibility and personal identity, are illusory ones. He attacks these three concepts again and again: 'But thought is one thing, the deed is another, and the image of the deed still another: the wheel of causality does not roll between them.'[32] 'No one is accountable for his deeds, no one for his nature; to judge is the same thing as to be unjust.'[33] 'He who is punished is never he who performed the deed. He is always the scapegoat.'[34] These pronouncements are straightforward and categorical. They condemn the moral vocabulary (taken here to include terms such as 'cause' and effect') for failing to express anything in reality. Statements made in these terms are, Nietzsche thinks, *false*. The inescapable conclusion is that the structure of revenge is an illusion from beginning to end, in that each of its key concepts has been identified as a fiction. The general features of Nietzsche's critique can be summed up rather briefly along the following lines.

Causality is, he thinks, a false concept. There are no causes and effects, only continuing processes; successive states of affairs are abstracted by us from the flow of becoming, and later reunited, after a fashion, by causal relations. We noted in Chapter 5 his rejection of action at a distance in time as providing an explanation of the course of events. In any case, the necessity of the connection between two successive states would present an insoluble puzzle. The usual appeal to 'laws of nature' is an anthropomorphic interpretation of the world, Nietzsche argues in *Beyond Good and Evil*.[35] It suggests that things are somehow constrained, prevented from going their own way, by the intervention of a dominating total power. In contrast, he presents becoming as consisting in extended processes, which are somehow 'entangled' with one another. There is certainly a necessity in what happens (expressed, for instance, in the law of conservation of energy) but it is just the necessity whereby everything – that is, every process – is what it is.

Guilt is another concept that Nietzsche often attacks. The relation between subject and object is something that we introduce into events, thereby turning processes into actions: 'The interpretation of an event as either an act or the suffering of an act (– thus every act a suffering) says: every change, every becoming-other, presupposes an author and someone upon whom "change" is effected.'[36] Such a schema allows the causal relation to be elaborated in accordance with the moral agenda. Once the subject is separated from its activity, it can be regarded as free to express itself in either of several activities.

> For just as the popular mind separates the lightning from its flash and takes the latter for an *action*, for the operation of a subject called lightning, so popular morality also separates strength from expressions of strength, as if there were a neutral substratum behind the strong man, which was *free* to express strength or not to do so.[37]

The concept of free will isolates the source of guilt: 'It is because man *regards* himself as free, not because he is free, that he feels remorse and pangs of conscience.'[38] But that feeling is an illusion, Nietzsche insists. Not only can we point to the incoherence of the concept of an impulse coming from nowhere, but we can also give an account of the origins of this 'moral sensation', in an extension of moral judgement from outcomes, first to actions, and then to agents themselves. Contrasting with all this is an understanding of becoming as a process which cannot be divided into subject and object, or taken as either acting and being acted upon. Nietzsche wants to affirm what he calls the 'innocence of becoming', abandoning those interpretations that serve the aims of revenge.

Nietzsche is also firmly opposed to the related notion of repentance. In a notebook entry headed 'Against Repentance', he comments: 'I do not like this kind of cowardice towards one's own deeds.' Not only does repentance represent an undesirable trait of character, he continues, it is in any case ineffective, for 'No action can be undone by being regretted'.[39] As long as we choose to think in moral terms, therefore, guilt must be acknowledged as something permanent. The only alternatives are a belief in some supernatural power which annuls guilt, presumably changing the past in the process or, on the other hand, a rejection of the whole notion of guilt. As an affirmer of the innocence of becoming, Nietzsche supports the second alternative. His critique of repentance is really part of a broader critique of revenge, in its several forms, since repentance is just 'revenge upon oneself'.[40]

Responsibility for actions carried out at other times is bound up with personal identity, which in turn presupposes the unitary self that is the 'subject' of action. The concept of the self as transcending the passage of time is crucial to the justification of revenge: by suspending the difference between present and past, it allows revenge to be understood as a willing that extends to what has been. Philosophers have assumed that our inner experience reveals the existence of this self, and with an immediate certainty. Yet, Nietzsche argues, a more careful approach – that of an expert philologist – shows that what seems to be text here is really interpretation. Instead of saying 'I think', we might instead say 'it thinks'. But 'even the "it" contains an *interpretation* of the process, and does not belong to the process itself'.[41] The assumption that every process involves an agent is a 'grammatical habit', imposed upon us as an 'invisible spell' by our language, which requires a subject and predicate in propositions.[42] While we cannot very well get away from this, we can think of the self in a different way – not as a single permanent subject, but as 'a multiplicity of subjects, whose interaction and struggle is the basis of our thought and our consciousness in general'.[43] On this view, the notions of personal identity and responsibility are an irrelevance.

As well as criticizing these concepts as either false or incoherent, Nietzsche suggests that they cannot be separated from their roles in the rationalization of revenge. The moral element may be apparent in the concept of agency, but it applies in the other cases as well. Why else would we be so concerned about personal identity, if not to allot responsibility for past events? Even causality has an ulterior motive: 'Belief in cause and effect has its place in the strongest of instincts, in that of revenge.'[44] As a 'psychologist', Nietzsche tries to uncover the motives behind modes of thinking which profess their neutrality and objectivity. Both philosophical systems and particular concepts, he thinks, express hidden intentions and personality traits. Revenge is not the only such drive, but it has a particular importance for its prevalence in our familiar ways of thinking, especially in the ideas centring upon the moral point of view, and for its aptitude for disguising itself in seemingly innocuous forms.

Paul Rée's Account of Punishment

If Nietzsche's dialogue with Dühring extends well beyond the realm of moral value, his corresponding relation to Paul Rée is far more narrowly focused. Let us begin by looking at the ideas of Rée's book, *The Origin of the Moral Sensations*. Succinct and well-written, this is the most impressive of his philosophical productions. Its standpoint, he announces in the Foreword, is that of a scientific theory which first observes empirical phenomena and then looks into their origins. We feel some acts as good, others as evil. From the latter comes the guilty conscience and the feeling of justice which calls for punishment. How are these phenomena to be explained? Kant and Schopenhauer thought that their origin must be transcendent, but Rée rejects this claim, writing: 'The moral man stands no closer to the intelligible world than the physical man.'[45] In contrast, Lamarck and Darwin have traced moral phenomena back to natural causes, and Rée takes their discussions as his model.

The starting-point for his argument is the presence of both egoistic and unegoistic drives in every person. Thinkers such as Helvétius have tried to explain altruism away – as aiming merely at eliminating our own sympathetic suffering – but that assumes an imaginative element which is not always present in altruism. Darwin suggests one explanation of this phenomenon by identifying a social instinct in lower animals, apparently a widening of the parental instinct, intensified through natural selection. Whatever its origin may be, altruism is the determining element for morality.[46] We judge unegoistic acts to be morally good, rare though they are in pure form. Why do we make this judgement? After all, egoistic acts may benefit others: a doctor who cures for money is as useful to a patient as any altruistic colleague. But there are so many harmful forms of egotism that, from its beginnings, human society has found it necessary to hold them in check. Because egoistic motives are stronger and more numerous than unegoistic ones, habits which favour altruistic action need to be systematically encouraged and reinforced. Like Lamarck (and to some extent Darwin himself) Rée assumes that acquired habits can be passed on to later generations as innate characteristics.

Rée argues that our moral sentiments are the result of changes occurring over many generations. What occurs is a transfer of meaning from the outer to the inner – that is, from consequences to motives. Since the connection between the two is forgotten or disregarded, relative judgements in which 'good' means useful *for* something are replaced by absolute ones. We have become habituated to regard altruistic action as good in itself, apart from its outcomes. This is a useful habit, since it provides us with rules of conduct which are beneficial. Nevertheless it is, strictly speaking, an error.

In a chapter on the feeling of justice, Rée gives an explanation of the concept of retribution which parallels his earlier account of moral ideas. It is, he observes, sometimes said that the purpose of punishment is to satisfy our demand that wrongdoers must be made to suffer for what they have done. However, Rée replies, this sentiment can be explained in a way that does not carry any implication that retribution is an actual occurrence. He presents the feeling of justice as the product of two factors. One is an illusion arising from the routine character of punishment. From an early age, children are told, 'You are being punished because you have done this', not ' … so that you will not do it again'.[47] Similarly, the original purpose of the law is never evident in its practice: judges simply condemn whoever has broken the law, without referring to the underlying purpose of the penalty. Hence, in each case it *seems* that only the immediate case is in question.

The other factor in Rée's analysis of the impulse toward retribution is a belief in free will. He assumes that this is an error, and that our actions are always determined by our mental and physical state at the time. If there is an inner conflict, the strongest motive will prevail. Any subsequent impression that it need not have done so is just a failure to recall the earlier situation. A bad conscience is usually associated with this illusion, although Rée notes that it also has a more general form: we may reflect that a blameworthy act has arisen from our character, and be unhappy at having such a character: in that case, our regret is directed not at the single act but at the whole personality. But the same point is valid here: we are not responsible for our personalities, since they are the necessary result of upbringing and circumstances. Hence, Rée concludes, a person of insight will experience little or no regret of this broader kind.

Once the origin of the feeling of justice is understood, Rée concludes, it can be seen that punishment does not constitute atonement, but can serve only for the prevention of future harm. If we recognize the necessity of all actions, we will no longer hold anyone as responsible.[48] But that is not a licence for the unrestrained expression of egoism, for it leaves open the question of influence and control over behaviour. Where the unegoistic drives are too weak to withstand the egoistic ones, society provides another motive for its own protection, the fear of punishment. The original makers of laws had only deterrence in mind, according to Rée.[49] The feeling of justice was not a factor in their invention of punishment, and seems only to confuse the issue when invoked at later times as either explanation or justification.

It is perhaps surprising that Rée does not account for retribution as the expression of a drive for revenge. He treats the latter separately and interprets it, following Schopenhauer closely, as an attempt to remedy the loss of self-esteem caused by any deliberate injury. One can at least see from this version that revenge may serve as a strong motive for action, whereas retribution, on Rée's account, seems to have no such driving force. Being only an impression gained from already existing practices of punishment, it seems to be a social construction of relatively recent origin. This separation of punishment from either revenge or retribution seems a weakness for Rée's theory. In correspondence with Nietzsche shortly after the publication of *Der Ursprung der moralischen Empfindungen*, he acknowledged the need to establish some connection between these phenomena.

> The most mistaken thing about my latest work (as you said already, but I did not want to admit – probably because in that case I would have had to revise a lot) is the historical development of punishment (although I still hold that the philosophical view of punishment as merely a means to an end is correct). Now since the most essential mark of a bad act is that it deserves punishment (according to general opinion) a work on the origin of moral consciousness and its history has nothing more important to investigate than precisely the origin of punishment, i.e. it has to investigate the way the belief has developed in human history that certain actions must be followed by suffering and punishment. What we encounter everywhere as a preliminary stage is blood revenge, and to find out about this in various countries, I am studying all the systems of criminal law I can and primitive cultures. In addition, classical antiquity, half in the original language, half in translation.[50]

Rée carried out this programme in considerable detail in his next book, *Die Entstehung des Gewissens*. Here, an abundance of historical scholarship is exhibited, although the theory it supports is no different from the earlier one. In 1879 Rée wrote to Nietzsche that most of his new work would be a history of punishment – 'and it arose not from revenge, but from opposition to revenge'.[51] About half of the book is a discussion of punishment, which

Rée indeed treats as a substitute for revenge, rather than as a modified version of the same impulse. He proposes a development which involves an intermediate stage – one which shares features of both revenge and true punishment.

As before, it is assumed that what motivates revenge is the feeling of inferiority. The satisfaction gained by revenge is thus negative in kind, since it is just the removal of this painful feeling. In primitive cultures revenge is widely practised. However, this is not to be confused with punishment, understood as an expression of the feeling of justice: historians who run the two together are mistaken.[52] Revenge, as Rée analyses the concept, has no necessary connection with injustice. One may seek revenge for an injury without feeling that one has been unfairly treated.[53] A more advanced society uses payment (*Abkauf*) as a substitute for revenge. This is Rée's second stage, and he provides many examples drawn from his studies in ethnology. In these cultures, revenge is restrained by a recognition of places of asylum, and a standard price is fixed for expiating each type of offence; even murder can be paid for at the going rate. The distinction between intentional and unintentional injury is not yet made. The state mediates disputes and guarantees the validity of the settlement. Before long, however, the state becomes the main party in this process of resolution. The offender now owes a debt to society, and payment is therefore made not to the injured person but to the state.

Only later still do we arrive at true punishment. According to Rée, this arises when the state's concern shifts to preventing unlawful actions, rather than exacting repayment for what has already committed. Punishment is used as a practical measure, designed with deterrence in mind. And since it is deliberate action that is influenced by the threat of punishment, the distinction between the intentional and unintentional becomes important for the first time. Revenge was already partially eliminated by the substitution of payment for retaliation; now it is wholly replaced.[54] Rée takes pains to deny that the state has simply taken over the task of revenge on behalf of the individual. As he puts it, the state is not the 'bravo' of its aggrieved members. Nor, for that matter, is the state taking revenge on its own behalf when it punishes: its aim is simply to restore peace, and not to satisfy any vengeful feeling. For Rée, the feeling of justice is a recent development, a 'parvenu'.[55] Historians who interpret old revenge customs as punishment are just projecting our modern attitude back to earlier times.

Nietzsche's Response to Rée

While it is always clear that Nietzsche is wholeheartedly in disagreement with Dühring's defence of punishment as revenge, his relation to Rée's account of the concealed origins of punishment is far more ambiguous. One might not guess this from the preface to *On the Genealogy of Morals*, written in 1887, where Nietzsche writes:

> The first impulse to publish something of my hypotheses concerning the origin of morality was given me by a clear, tidy, and shrewd – also precocious – little book in which I encountered distinctly for the first time an upside-down and perverse species of genealogical hypothesis, the genuinely *English* type, that attracted me – with the power of attraction which everything contrary, everything antipodal possesses. The title of the little book was *The Origin of the Moral Sensations*; its author Dr Paul Rée; the year in which it appeared 1877. Perhaps I have never read anything to which I would have said to myself No, proposition by proposition, conclusion by conclusion, than I did to this book: yet quite without ill-humour or impatience.

Rée and Nietzsche had been friends during what proved a crucial period of intellectual development for each. They had been in daily contact and shared a constant interchange of ideas while living and working in Sorrento: Nietzsche on a collection of aphorisms in the style of Rée's *Psychologische Beobachtungen*, and Rée on a long essay in moral philosophy, in the style of Nietzsche's *The Birth of Tragedy*. The close connection between the respective outcomes was emphasized by their common publisher, Ernst Schmeitzner, in announcing the appearance of Nietzsche's book *Human, All-Too-Human*:

> As a moralist Nietzsche arrives by way of the historical approach at very fruitful conclusions; e.g. the grounding of morality in metaphysics, as proposed by Schopenhauer, is found to be untenable, since historical philosophy has already achieved a natural history of the development of morality: in the work of Paul Rée listed below, *Der Ursprung der moralischen Empfindungen*, which is broadened and developed by Nietzsche.[56]

Nietzsche might not have seen himself as a follower of Rée – and Schmeitzner was not the person to observe their differences – but one cannot deny that the link is there. It has been observed that *Human, All-Too-Human* is the work of Nietzsche which, more than any other, is dominated by another mind. How, then, do we account for the extraordinary display of manoeuvring to minimize and deny the influence of Rée which marks the preface to *On the Genealogy of Morals*? There Nietzsche offers a reading of *Human, All-Too-Human* which is wholly distorted by his eagerness to explain away his debt to Rée. The language of the work was, he explains, not really his own; he offered alternatives to Rée's theses, but did not explicitly rebut them, because refutation is not his style; and anyway, he admits some vacillation and backsliding. Finally, despite his disavowal of refutation, Nietzsche cites evidence for the difference between his standpoint and Rée's. He does this by listing those sections of *Human, All-Too-Human* and its two sequels in which the differences can be seen, and in which the themes of *On the Genealogy of Morals* are prefigured. The real problem for Nietzsche, he says, is not the origin of morality, but the *value* of morality. Having read this, we note that *On the Genealogy of Morals* opens with a critique of the 'English psychologists', but the view attributed to Spencer is Rée's thesis that we have *forgotten* that 'good' originally meant 'useful'.

In *On the Genealogy of Morals*, Nietzsche describes the history of punishment, arguing that the procedure itself is older and more enduring than the meaning or purpose which has been projected into it in recent times. This contrast is a common pattern, since 'whatever exists, having somehow come into being, is again and again reinterpreted to new ends'.[57] Punishment, as we know it, has a long history in the course of which it has served many different purposes. In consequence, it now has a mixture of quite different meanings, not a single meaning. It may provide a recompense to those who have been injured, if only at the level of their feelings – the object that Dühring singles out for a privileged status when he identifies *ressentiment* as the original motive behind all punishment. But punishment may simply negate the offender's ability to do further harm, or effect the expulsion of an undesirable element from the community. Another immediate and practical use of punishment lies in the confining of the disturbing effect which any crime has on social stability to a limited region.

Some of the functions of punishment listed by Nietzsche here are broader in scope and aimed at the long term. He notes that punishment may serve to enhance respect for the authority that determines and imposes the penalty. Or it may impress itself on the memory, ensuring that the law is never forgotten. Sometimes punishment is addressed to the advantages formerly enjoyed by the offender, and is designed as a repayment for them. It may be the payment of a fee by the wrongdoer for protection from further revenge from the offended party. It may be a practical compromise with demands for revenge coming from groups whose power has to be reckoned with by the state. It may be a war against rebellion against the order of society, or a celebration of victory over the enemy. This list, Nietzsche remarks, is 'certainly not complete'. However, he adds that one function often cited in justification of punishment should *not* be included. The idea that punishment produces a feeling of guilt in the offender is, he argues, not confirmed by experience. Its effect is more often than not just the opposite: the offender becomes hardened in resistance to the demands of the community. Alternatively, it may have a wholly destructive effect and bring about a general demoralization.

This refusal to adopt a narrow formulation of the issues concerning punishment finds a close parallel in Nietzsche's observations on revenge in *The Wanderer and His Shadow*. He specifically denies that revenge is a single phenomenon for which some such definition could be supplied.[58] It may, he says, represent an immediate response which expresses only the instinct of self-preservation, or a more deliberate attempt at restoring the self-esteem lost by injury. Which motive is at work in revenge is often hard to tell, even for the individual who is taking revenge. These comments also apply to Nietzsche's view of punishment understood as a social institution, for he believes that there is an overlap between punishment and revenge, even if they are not simply the same thing. Another passage in *The Wanderer and His Shadow* is closely linked to this one, stating a principle which covers not only revenge and punishment, but many other features of human life:

Which is more temporary, the soul or the body? In matters of law, morality and religion, what is most external and visible, such as custom, behaviour and ceremony, has the most *endurance*; it is the *body* to which a *new soul* is always being added. The cult is, like a fixed word-text, always being newly interpreted; concepts and sensations are the fluid element, practices the solid.[59]

Here Nietzsche arranges a number of oppositions – custom and feeling, body and soul, text and interpretation, solid and fluid – in parallel fashion, to make a point about social life: that the same practice may have very different meanings at different times. For Nietzsche, the distinction between punishment as a material practice and the further functions which it has or is believed to have implies that there is no single explanation of justification of punishment. So any attempt to assign a single meaning to the concept is misguided: 'Today it is impossible to say for certain *why* people are really punished: all concepts in which an entire process is semiotically concentrated elude definition; only that which has no history is definable.'[60] Here Nietzsche's historical approach is taken to its ultimate conclusion: a radical rejection of the tradition of philosophical inquiry which investigates the meanings of concepts like that of punishment, and thus a rejection of the presuppositions common to the retributivists and utilitarians of his time.

Notes

1. Max Scheler, *Ressentiment*, trans. William W. Holdheim (New York: Schocken Books, 1972), 43.
2. Eugen Dühring, *Der Werth des Lebens. Eine philosophische Betrachtung* (Breslau: Verlag von Eduard Trewendt, 1865), VIII; and *Cursus der Philosophie als streng wissenschaftlicher Weltanschauung und Lebensgestaltung* (Leipzig: Erich Koschny, 1875), 224.
3. Similarly, the British jurist James Fitzjames Stephen asserted that hatred of wrongdoers is 'a healthy natural sentiment' which is, and ought to be, satisfied by legal punishment. See J.F. Stephen, *A History of the Criminal Law of England* (London: Macmillan, 1883), Vol. 2, 82. This social institution is, Stephen suggests, to hatred and revenge what marriage is to sexual passion – an analogy repeated by Susan Jacoby in *Wild Justice: The Evolution of Revenge* (New York: Harper and Row, 1983), 12–13.
4. Dühring, *Der Werth des Lebens*, 21. Cf. KGW IV/1, 217.
5. Immanuel Kant, *The Metaphysics of Morals*, trans. Mary McGregor (Cambridge: Cambridge University Press, 1991), 140.
6. Ibid., 253.
7. Ibid., 141.
8. Dühring, *Der Werth des Lebens*, 20.
9. Ibid., 81.
10. Dühring, *Cursus der Philosophie*, 227–28.
11. Ibid., 234.
12. Ibid., 226.
13. Ibid.; see also Dühring, *Der Werth des Lebens*, 78; and KGW IV/1, 227.
14. KGW IV/1, 256.
15. Friedrich Nietzsche, *On the Genealogy of Morals*, Second Essay, sect. 11.
16. Friedrich Nietzsche, *Daybreak*, sect. 202.
17. Jacoby, *Wild Justice*, 12.
18. Ibid., 346.

19 Susan Jacoby seems to take this view. She writes: 'On a practical level, the human desire for retribution requires no elaborate philosophical justification': ibid., 9. Of course, on a practical level, nothing requires an elaborate philosophical justification, or even a modest one; but I assume that Jacoby is making a less general claim.
20 Jacoby cites a line from *The Godfather*: 'Accidents don't happen to people who take accidents as a personal insult': ibid., 1.
21 Nietzsche, *On the Genealogy of Morals*, Second Essay, sect. 11.
22 See, for example, Friedrich Nietzsche, *Beyond Good and Evil*, sect. 13.
23 Nietzsche, *On the Genealogy of Morals*, Second Essay, sect. 6.
24 Friedrich Nietzsche, *The Wanderer and His Shadow*, sect. 5; also KGW V/1, 537, 562 and 564.
25 Arthur Schopenhauer, *The World as Will and Representation*, trans. E.F.J. Payne (New York: Dover Publications, 1966), Vol. 1, 348.
26 Ibid., 357.
27 See KGW IV/1, 253–54.
28 Friedrich Nietzsche, *Thus Spake Zarathustra*, 'On the Tarantulas'.
29 Ibid., 'On Redemption'.
30 Nietzsche, *Daybreak*, sect. 134. Nietzsche continues: 'If suffering is here and there indirectly reduced or removed as a consequence of pity, this occasional and on the whole insignificant consequence must not be employed to justify its essential nature, which is, as I have said, harmful.'
31 Nietzsche, *Thus Spake Zarathustra*, 'On Old and New Tablets', sect. 3.
32 Ibid., 'On the Pale Criminal'.
33 Friedrich Nietzsche, *Human, All-Too-Human*, sect. 39.
34 Nietzsche, *Daybreak*, sect. 252.
35 *Beyond Good and Evil*, sect. 22.
36 KGW VIII/1, 136 (*The Will to Power*, sect. 546). For critiques of the 'subject' see KGW VIII/1, 133–34 and 323 (*The Will to Power*, sect. 631 and 481).
37 Nietzsche, *On the Genealogy of Morals*, First Essay, sect. 13.
38 Nietzsche, *Human, All-Too-Human*, sect. 39.
39 KGW VIII/2, 181 (*The Will to Power*, sect. 235).
40 KGW VII/1, 558.
41 Nietzsche, *Beyond Good and Evil*, sect. 17.
42 Ibid., sect. 20.
43 See, for example, KGW VII/3, 382 (*The Will to Power*, sect. 490).
44 KGW VII/1, 412. Cf. ibid.,126.
45 Paul Rée, *Der Ursprung der moralischen Empfindungen* (Chemnitz: Verlag von Ernst Schmeitzner, 1877), VIII. This sentence is quoted by Nietzsche in *Human, All-Too-Human*, sect. 37.
46 Here Rée is following the approach of Arthur Schopenhauer in *On the Basis of Morality*, trans. E.F.J. Payne (Indianapolis and New York: Bobbs-Merrill, 1965).
47 In Rée's later book on conscience, the same point is made again, but this time credited to Paul Johann Anselm Feuerbach. See Paul Rée, *Die Entstehung des Gewissens* (Berlin: Carl Duncker's Verlag, 1885), 192. His reference is to Paul J.A. Feuerbach, *Revision der Grundsätze und Grundbegriffe des positiven peinlichen Rechts* (Erfurt: in der Henningschen Buchhandlung, 1799–1800), Vol. 1, 14.
48 Rée, *Der Ursprung der moralischen Empfindungen*, 42.
49 Ibid., 45.
50 KGB VI/2 (letter of 10 October 1877).
51 Ibid., 1090 (letter of April 1879).
52 Rée, *Die Entstehung des Gewissens*, 39.
53 Ibid., 42–43.
54 Ibid., 108.
55 Ibid., 202.
56 Publisher's announcement at the end of Eugen Dühring, *Robert Mayer der Galilei des neunzehnten Jahrhunderts* (Chemnitz: Ernst Schmeitzner, 1880).

57 Nietzsche, *On the Genealogy of Morals*, Second Essay, sect. 12.
58 Nietzsche, *The Wanderer and His Shadow*, sect. 33.
59 Ibid., sect. 77.
60 Nietzsche, *On the Genealogy of Morals*, Second Essay, sect. 13.

Bibliography

Writings of Friedrich Nietzsche

Kritische Gesamtausgabe: Briefwechsel, ed. Giorgio Colli and Mazzino Montinari, Berlin: de Gruyter, 1975 – .
Kritische Gesamtausgabe: Werke, ed. Giorgio Colli and Mazzino Montinari, Berlin: de Gruyter, 1973 – .
Historische-Kritische Gesamtausgabe: Werke, ed. H.J. Mette and Karl Schlechta, München: C.H. Beck'sche Verlagsbuchhandlung, 1937 – .
Nietzsches Briefe an Peter Gast, ed. Peter Gast, Leipzig: Insel-Verlag, 1924.

Secondary Works

Abel, Günter, *Nietzsche: Die Dynamik der Willen zur Macht und die ewige Wiederkehr*, Berlin: de Gruyter, 1984.
Andler, Charles, *Nietzsche, sa vie et sa pensée*, 3rd edn, Paris: Librairie Gallimard, 1958.
Anonymous, 'Sensation and Science', *Nature*, 14 July 1872, 177–78.
Anonymous, 'Spiritualism in Germany', *The Nation*, 12 February 1880, 113–14.
Ansell-Pearson, Keith (ed.), *Nietzsche and Modern German Thought*, London and New York: Routledge, 1991.
Aquinas, Thomas, *Summa theologiae*, 61 vols, London: Blackfriars, 1965–81.
Aristotle, *The Basic Works of Aristotle*, ed. Richard McKeon, New York: Random House, 1941.
Avenarius, Richard, *Philosophie als Denken der Welt gemäss dem Princip des kleinsten Kraftmasses. Prolegomena zu einer Kritik der reinen Erfahrung*, Leipzig: Fues's Verlag, 1876.
Babich, Babette E., *Nietzsche's Philosophy of Science: Reflecting Science on the Ground of Art and Life*, Albany, NY: State University of New York Press, 1994.
Babich, Babette E. and Robert S. Cohen (eds), *Nietzsche, Epistemology, and Philosophy of Science: Nietzsche and the Sciences II*, Dordrecht: Kluwer Academic Publishers, 1999.
Babich, Babette E. and Robert S. Cohen (eds), *Nietzsche, Theories of Knowledge, and Critical Theory: Nietzsche and the Sciences I*, Dordrecht: Kluwer Academic Publishers, 1999.
Baudelaire, Charles, *Les Paradis artificiels*, ed. Jacques Crépet, Paris: Louis Conard, 1928.
Bauer, Martin, 'Zur Genealogie von Nietzsches Kraftbegriff. Nietzsches

Auseinandersetzung mit J.G. Vogt', *Nietzsche-Studien*, 13 (1984), 211–27.

Becker, Oskar, *Dasein und Dawesen: Gesammelte philosophische Aufsätze*, Pfullingen: Verlag Günther Neske, 1963.

Bois, Henri, 'Le finitisme de Dühring', *L'Année philosophique*, 20 (1909), 93–124.

Bois, Henri, 'Le "Retour éternel" de Nietzsche', *L'Année philosophique*, 24 (1913), 145–84.

Bork, Alfred M., 'The Fourth Dimension in Nineteenth-Century Physics', *Isis*, 55 (1964), 326–38.

Boscovich, Roger Joseph, *A Theory of Natural Philosophy*, trans. J.M. Child, Cambridge, MA: MIT Press, 1966.

Brobjer, Thomas H., 'Nietzsche's Reading and Private Library, 1885–1889', *Journal of the History of Ideas*, 58 (1997), 663–93.

Brush, Stephen G. (ed.), *Kinetic Theory*, 2 vols, Oxford: Pergamon Press, 1966.

Brush, Stephen G., *The Temperature of History*, New York: Burt Franklin, 1978.

Brush, Stephen G., 'Nietzsche's Recurrence Revisited: The French Connection', *Journal of the History of Philosophy*, 19 (1981), 235–38.

Buechner, Alexander, *Un philosophe amateur. Essai biographique sur Léon Dumont 1837–1877 avec des extraits de sa correspondance*, Paris: Librairie Félix Alcan, 1884.

Calder, William M. III, 'The Wilamowitz–Nietzsche Struggle: New Documents and a Reappraisal', *Nietzsche-Studien*, 12 (1983), 214–54.

Cantor, Georg, *Gesammelte Abhandlungen*, ed. Ernst Zermelo, Berlin: Verlag von Julius Springer, 1932. Reprint, Hildesheim: Georg Olms, 1962.

Capek, Milic, 'The Theory of Eternal Recurrence in Modern Philosophy of Science, with Special Reference to C.S. Peirce', *Journal of Philosophy*, 57 (1960), 289–96.

Capek, Milic, *The Philosophical Impact of Contemporary Physics*, New York: Van Nostrand Reinhold Company, 1961.

Capek, Milic, 'Eternal Return' in Paul Edwards (ed.), *The Encyclopedia of Philosophy*, New York: The Macmillan Company and The Free Press, 1967, Vol. 3, 61–63.

Capek, Milic, 'Eternal Recurrence – Once More', *Transactions of the Charles S. Peirce Society*, 19 (1983), 141–53.

Carroll, Lewis, 'What Achilles said to the Tortoise', *Mind*, 4 (1895), 278–80.

Caspari, Otto, *Die Thomson'sche Hypothese von der endlichen Temperaturausgleichung im Weltall beleuchtet vom philosophischen Gesichtspunkte*, Stuttgart: Verlagsbuchhandlung von August Horster, 1874.

Caspari, Otto, *Der Zusammenhang der Dinge: Gesammelte philosophische Aufsätze*, Breslau: Verlag von Eduard Trewendt, 1881.

Claparède-Spir, Hélène, 'Friedrich Nietzsche und Afrikan Spir', *Philosophie und Leben*, 6 (1930), 242–50.

Couprie, Dirk L., '"Hätte die Welt ein Ziel, […] so wäre es […] mit allem

Werden längst zu Ende." Ein Beitrag zur Geschichte einer Argumentation', *Nietzsche-Studien*, 27 (1998), 107–18.
Danto, Arthur, 'Nietzsche', in D.J. O'Connor (ed.), *A Critical History of Western Philosophy*, New York: The Free Press, 1964.
Danto, Arthur, *Nietzsche as Philosopher*, New York: The Macmillan Company, 1965.
Davidson, Donald, 'Events as Particulars', *Nous*, 4 (1970), 25–32.
Deleuze, Gilles, *Nietzsche and Philosophy*, trans. Hugh Tomlinson, London: The Athlone Press, 1983.
De Morgan, Augustus, *A Budget of Paradoxes*, ed. David Eugene Smith, 2nd edn, Chicago: Open Court, 1915. Reprint, Freeport, NY: Books for Libraries Press, 1969.
d'Espérance, Elizabeth, *Shadow Land or Light From the Other Side*, London: George Redway, 1897.
D'Iorio, Paolo, 'Cosmologie de l'éternel retour', *Nietzsche-Studien*, 24 (1995), 62–123.
D'Iorio, Paolo, 'La superstition des philosophes critiques', *Nietzsche-Studien*, 22 (1993), 257–94.
Duhem, Pierre, *Le Système du monde*, 10 vols, Paris: Hermann, 1914–59.
Dühring, Eugen, *Der Werth des Lebens. Eine philosophische Betrachtung*, Breslau: Verlag von Eduard Trewendt, 1865.
Dühring, Eugen, *Cursus der Philosophie als streng wissenschaftlicher Weltanschauung und Lebensgestaltung*, Leipzig: Erich Koschny, 1875.
Dühring, Eugen, *Robert Mayer der Galilei des neunzehnten Jahrhunderts*, Chemnitz: Ernst Schmeitzner, 1880.
Dumont, Léon, *Théorie scientifique de la sensibilité. Le plaisir et la peine*, Paris: Librairie Germer Baillière, 1875.
Dumont, Léon, *Vergnügen und Schmerz. Zur Lehre den Gefühlen*, Leipzig: F.A. Brockhaus, 1876.
Einstein, Albert., H.A. Lorentz, H. Weyl and H. Minkowski, *The Principle of Relativity*, New York: Dover Publications, 1952.
Faraday, Michael, *Experimental Researches in Electricity*, New York: Dover Publications, 1965.
Feuerbach, Paul Johann Anselm, *Revision der Grundsätze und Grundbegriffe des positiven peinlichen Rechts*, 2 vols, Erfurt: in der Henningschen Buchhandlung, 1799–1800.
Fick, Adolf, *Gesammelte Schriften von Adolf Fick, in vier Bänden*, Würzburg: Stahel'sche Verlags-Anstalt, 1903.
Fodor, Nandor, *Encyclopaedia of Psychic Science*, New York: University Books, 1966.
Freeman, Kathleen, *Ancilla to the Pre-Socratic Philosophers*, Oxford: Basil Blackwell, 1948.
Freud, Sigmund, *The Standard Edition of the Complete Psychological Works of Sigmund Freud*, ed. James Strachey and Anna Freud, London: Hogarth Press, 1953–1975.
Fritz, Kurt von, 'The Discovery of Incommensurability by Hippasus of Metapontum', *Annals of Mathematics*, 46 (1945), 242–64.

Galileo, *Dialogues Concerning the Two Chief World Systems*, trans. Stillman Drake, 2nd edn, Berkeley, CA: University of California Press, 1967.

Goethe, Johann Wolfgang von, *Briefwechsel mit Friedrich Schiller. Gedenkenausgabe der Werke, Briefe und Gespräche*, ed. Ernest Beutler, Zürich: Artemis-Verlag, 1949.

Goodman, Nelson, *The Structure of Appearance*, Cambridge, MA: Harvard University Press, 1951.

Grant, Edward, 'Nicole Oresme and his *De proportionibus proportionum*', *Isis*, 51 (1960), 293–314.

Grant, Edward, 'Nicole Oresme and the Commensurability or Incommensurability of the Celestial Motions', *Archive for History of Exact Sciences*, 1 (1960–62), 420–58.

Grant, Edward, *Oresme and the Kinematics of Circular Motion*, Madison, WI: University of Wisconsin Press, 1971.

Gründer, Karlfried, *Der Streit um Nietzsches 'Geburt der Tragödie'*, Hildesheim: Georg Olms Verlagsbuchhandlung, 1969.

Hartmann, Eduard von, *Philosophie des Unbewussten*, 3rd edn, Berlin: Carl Dunckers Verlag, 1871.

Heath, T.L., *The Works of Archimedes*, Cambridge: Cambridge University Press, 1897. Reprint, New York: Dover Publications, 1953.

Heath, T.L., *Aristarchus of Samos*, Oxford: Clarendon Press, 1913.

Heidegger, Martin, *Nietzsche*, trans. David F. Krell, 4 vols, San Francisco: Harper and Row, 1980.

Helmholtz, Hermann von, 'Helmholtz on the Use and Abuse of the Deductive Method in Physical Science', *Nature*, 24 December 1874, 149–51 and 14 January 1875, 211–12.

Helmholtz, Hermann von, *Popular Scientific Lectures*, New York: Dover Publications, 1962.

Helmholtz, Hermann von, *Helmholtz's Treatise on Physiological Optics*, ed. J.P.C. Southall, New York: Dover Publications, 1962.

Henderson, Linda D., *The Fourth Dimension and Non-Euclidean Geometry in Modern Art*, Princeton, NJ: Princeton University Press, 1983.

Herbart, Johann Friedrich, *Sämtliche Werke*, ed. Karl Kehrbach and Otto Flügel, 19 vols, Aalen: Scientia Verlag, 1964.

Herbert, A.P., *Uncommon Law*, London: Eyre Methuen, 1977.

Hollingdale, R.J., *Nietzsche*, London: Routledge and Kegan Paul, 1973.

Hume, David, *A Treatise of Human Nature*, ed. L.A. Selby-Bigge, Oxford: Clarendon Press, 1888.

Jacoby, Susan, *Wild Justice: The Evolution of Revenge*, New York: Harper and Row, 1983.

Jaki, Stanley L., *The Paradox of Olbers' Paradox*, New York: Herder and Herder, 1969.

Janz, Curt Paul, *Friedrich Nietzsche Biographie*, 3 vols, München: Deutsche Taschenbuch Verlag, 1981.

Jaspers, Karl, *Nietzsche: An Introduction to the Understanding of his Philosophical Activity*, trans. Charles F. Wallraff and Frederick J. Schmitz, Chicago: Henry Regnery Company, 1965.

Kant, Immanuel, *Critique of Pure Reason*, trans. Norman Kemp Smith, London: Macmillan, 1929.
Kant, Immanuel, *Prolegomena to any Future Metaphysics that will be able to present itself as a Science*, trans. Peter G. Lucas, Manchester: Manchester University Press, 1953.
Kant, Immanuel, *The Metaphysics of Morals*, trans. Mary McGregor, Cambridge: Cambridge University Press, 1991.
Klossowski, Pierre, *Nietzsche and the Vicious Circle*, trans. Daniel W. Smith, London: The Athlone Press, 1997.
Köselitz, Heinrich, 'Musikalische Philister', in Curt Paul Janz, *Friedrich Nietzsche Biographie*, München: Deutscher Taschenbuch Verlag, 1981, Band 3, 246–55.
Krueger, Jerry, 'Nietzschean Recurrence as a Cosmological Hypothesis', *Journal of the History of Philosophy*, 16 (1978), 435–44.
Lampert, Laurence, *Nietzsche's Teaching*, New Haven and London: Yale University Press, 1986.
Lange, Friedrich Albert, *Geschichte des Materialismus und Kritik seiner Bedeutung in der Gegenwart*, Iserlohn: Verlag von J. Baedecker, 1866.
Lange, Friedrich Albert, *The History of Materialism and Criticism of its Present Importance*, trans. E.C. Thomas, 3rd edn, London: Routledge and Kegan Paul, 1925.
Laplace, Pierre-Simon, *A Philosophical Essay on Probabilities*, trans. F.W. Truscott and F.L. Emory, New York: Dover Publications, 1952.
Lewis, C.S., *The Problem of Pain*, London: Geoffrey Bles, 1940.
Liebmann, Otto, *Kant und die Epigonen. Eine kritische Abhandlung*, Stuttgart: Carl Schober, 1865.
Lindsay, Robert Bruce, *Julius Robert Mayer: Prophet of Energy*, Oxford: Pergamon Press, 1973.
Lingis, Alphonso, *Deathbound Subjectivity*, Bloomington and Indianapolis: Indiana University Press, 1989.
Lombard, Lawrence B., *Events: A Metaphysical Study*, London: Routledge and Kegan Paul, 1986.
Lotze, Hermann, *Metaphysic*, ed. Bernard Bosanquet, 2nd edn, Oxford: Clarendon Press, 1887.
Love, Frederick R., *Nietzsche's Saint Peter: Genesis and Cultivation of an Illusion*, Berlin and New York: de Gruyter, 1981.
Löwith, Karl, *Nietzsche's Philosophy of the Eternal Recurrence of the Same*, trans. J. Harvey Lomax, Berkeley, CA: University of California Press, 1999.
Lucian, 8 vols, Loeb Classical Library, Cambridge, MA: Harvard University Press, 1913–67.
Mach, Ernst, *Popular Scientific Lectures*, trans. T.J. McCormack, La Salle, IL: Open Court, 1894.
Magnus, Bernd, *Nietzsche's Existential Imperative*, Bloomington and London: Indiana University Press, 1978.
Maimonides, Moses, *The Guide of the Perplexed*, trans. Schlomo Pines, 2 vols, Chicago: Chicago University Press, 1963.

Mainländer, Philipp, *Die Philosophie der Erlösung*, Berlin: Verlag von Theobald Grieben, 1876.

Manning, H.P. (ed.), *The Fourth Dimension Simply Explained*, New York: Mum and Co., 1910.

Mansfeld, Jaap, 'The Wilamowitz–Nietzsche Struggle: Another New Document and Some Further Comments', *Nietzsche-Studien*, 15 (1986).

Marx, Karl and Friedrich Engels, *Collected Works*, London: Lawrence and Wishart, 1975–.

Mayer, Julius Robert, 'The Motions of Organisms and their Relation to Metabolism', in R.B. Lindsay (ed.), *Julius Robert Mayer: Prophet of Energy*, Oxford: Pergamon Press, 1973.

Meyer, Kenneth R., 'An Application of Poincaré's Recurrence Theorem to Academic Administration', *The American Mathematical Monthly*, 88 (1981), 32–33.

Mill, John Stuart, *A System of Logic*, 7th edn, London: Longmans, Green, Reader, and Dyer, 1868.

Mittasch, Alwin, *Friedrich Nietzsche als Naturphilosoph*, Stuttgart: Alfred Kröner Verlag, 1952.

Moles, Alistair, 'Nietzsche's Eternal Recurrence as Riemannian Cosmology', *International Studies in Philosophy*, 21 (1989), 21–35.

Moles, Alistair, *Nietzsche's Philosophy of Nature and Cosmology*, New York: Peter Lang, 1990.

Morgan, George A. Jr, *What Nietzsche Means*, Cambridge, MA: Harvard University Press, 1941.

Moser, Fanny, *Der Okkultismus: Täuschungen und Tatsachen*, München: Verlag von Ernst Reinhardt, 1935.

Müller-Lauter, Wolfgang, *Nietzsche: Seine Philosophie der Gegensätze und die Gegensätze seiner Philosophie*, Berlin and New York: de Gruyter, 1971.

Neumann, Carl, *Die Principien der Elektrodynamik. Eine mathematische Untersuchung*, Tübingen: Heinrich Laupp, 1868.

Nohl, Hermann, 'Eine historische Quelle zu Nietzsches Perspektivismus: G. Teichmüller, die wirkliche und die scheinbare Welt', *Zeitschrift für Philosophie und philosophische Kritik*, 149 (1913), 106–15.

Oppenheimer, Jane M., 'Science and Nationality: The Case of Karl Ernst von Baer 1792–1876', *Proceedings of the American Philosophical Society*, 134 (1990), 75–82.

Oresme, Nicole, *De proportionibus proportionum and Ad pauca respicientes*, ed. and trans. Edward Grant, Madison, WI: University of Wisconsin Press, 1966.

Paracelsus, *The Hermetic and Alchemical Writings of Paracelsus*, ed. A.E. Waite, London: James Elliot, 1894.

Pearsall, Ronald, *The Table-Rappers*, London: Michael Joseph, 1972.

Pfeiffer, Ernst (ed.), *Friedrich Nietzsche Paul Rée Lou von Salomé: Die Dokumente ihrer Begegnung*, Frankfurt-am-Main: Insel Verlag, 1970.

Poincaré, Henri, *Oeuvres de Henri Poincaré*, 11 vols, Paris: Gauthier-Villars, 1916–56.

Poincaré, Henri, *Les méthodes nouvelles de la mécanique céleste*, 3 vols, Paris: Gauthier-Villars et fils, 1892–99. Reprint, New York: Dover Publications, 1957.

Poincaré, Henri, 'On the Three-Body Problem and the Equations of Dynamics', in Stephen G. Brush (ed.), *Kinetic Theory*, Vol. 2, Oxford: Pergamon Press, 1966.

Proclus, *The Elements of Theology*, trans. E. R. Dodds, 2nd edn, Oxford: Clarendon Press, 1963.

Quine, Willard Van Orman, 'Events and Reification', in Ernest LePore and Brian P. McLaughlin (eds), *Actions and Events: Perspectives on the Philosophy of Donald Davidson*, Oxford: Basil Blackwell, 1985.

Rée, Paul, *Der Ursprung der moralischen Empfindungen*, Chemnitz: Verlag von Ernst Schmeitzner, 1877.

Rée, Paul, *Die Entstehung des Gewissens*, Berlin: Carl Duncker's Verlag, 1885.

Reid, Thomas, *Philosophical Works*, 8th edn, Edinburgh: James Thin, 1895. Reprint, Hildesheim: Georg Olms, 1967.

Ribenboim, Paulo, *The Book of Prime Number Records*, New York: Springer-Verlag, 1988.

Richardson, John, *Nietzsche's System*, New York and Oxford: Oxford University Press, 1966.

Rucker, Rudy v.B., *Infinity and the Mind*, Brighton: Harvester Press, 1982.

Rucker, Rudy v.B., *The Fourth Dimension and How to Get There*, Harmondsworth: Penguin Books, 1985.

Russell, Bertrand, *An Essay on the Foundations of Geometry*, New York: Dover Books, 1956.

Salaquarda, Jörg, 'Nietzsche und Lange', *Nietzsche-Studien*, 7 (1978), 236–53.

Schacht, Richard, *Nietzsche*, London: Routledge and Kegan Paul, 1983.

Scheler, Max, *Ressentiment*, trans. W.W. Holdheim, New York: Schocken Books, 1972.

Schlechta, Karl and Anni Anders, *Friedrich Nietzsche: Von den verborgenen Anfängen seines Philosophierens*, Stuttgart and Bad Cannstatt: Friedrich Frommann Verlag, 1962.

Schopenhauer, Arthur, *On the Basis of Morality*, trans. E.F.J. Payne, Indianapolis and New York: Bobbs-Merrill, 1965.

Schopenhauer, Arthur, *The World as Will and Representation*, trans. E.F.J. Payne, 2 vols, New York: Peter Smith, 1969.

Schopenhauer, Arthur, *Parerga and Paralipomena*, trans. E.F.J. Payne, 2 vols, Oxford, Clarendon Press, 1974.

Schopenhauer, Arthur, *On the Fourfold Root of the Principle of Sufficient Reason*, trans. E.F.J. Payne, La Salle, IL: Open Court, 1974.

Seigfried, Hans, 'Law, Regularity and Sameness: A Nietzschean Account', *Man and World*, 3 (1973), 386.

Sextus Empiricus, 4 vols, trans. R.G. Bury, Loeb Classical Library, London: Heinemann, 1933–45.

Simmel, Georg, *Schopenhauer and Nietzsche*, trans. Helmut Loiskandl, Deena

Weinstein and Michael Weinstein, Amherst, MA: The University of Massachusetts Press, 1986.
Small, Robin, 'Nietzsche's God', *Philosophy Today*, 26 (1982), 41-53.
Small, Robin, 'Absolute Becoming and Absolute Necessity', *International Studies in Philosophy*, 21 (1989), 125-34.
Small, Robin, 'Incommensurability and Recurrence: From Oresme to Simmel', *Journal of the History of Ideas*, 52 (1991), 121-37.
Small, Robin, 'Eugen Karl Dühring', in *The Routledge Encyclopedia of Philosophy*, ed. Edward Craig, London: Routledge, 1998, Vol. 3, 147-49.
Small, Robin, 'Zarathustra's Gateway', *History of Philosophy Quarterly*, 15 (1998), 79-98.
Soll, Ivan, 'Reflections on Recurrence: A Re-examination of Nietzsche's Doctrine, die Ewige Wiederkehr des Gleichen', in Robert Solomon (ed.), *Nietzsche: A Collection of Critical Essays*, New York: Doubleday Anchor, 1973, 322-42.
Spiekermann, Klaus, 'Nietzsches Beweise für die ewige Wiederkehr', *Nietzsche-Studien*, 17 (1988), 497-504.
Spiekermann, Klaus, *Naturwissenschaft als subjektlose Macht? Nietzsches Kritik physikalisher Grundkonzepte*, Berlin and New York: de Gruyter, 1992.
Spir, African, *Forschung nach der Gewissheit in der Erkenntnis der Wirklichkeit*, Leipzig: Förster und Findel, 1869.
Spir, African, *Denken und Wirklichkeit. Versuch einer Erneuerung der kritischen Philosophie*, 2 vols, Leipzig: J.G. Findel, 1873.
Spir, African, *Gesammelte Schriften*, 4 vols, Leipzig: Verlag von J.G. Findel, 1883-84.
Spir, African, *Nouvelles esquisses de philosophie critique*, Paris: Félix Alcan, 1899.
Spir, African, *Right and Wrong*, trans. A.F. Falconer, Edinburgh: Oliver and Boyd, 1954.
Stack, George J., 'Nietzsche and Lange', *The Modern Schoolman*, 57 (1980), 137-49.
Stack, George J., 'Nietzsche and Boscovich's Natural Philosophy', *Pacific Philosophical Quarterly*, 62 (1981), 69-87.
Stack, George J., *Lange and Nietzsche*, Berlin and New York: de Gruyter, 1983.
Stack, George J., 'Eternal Recurrence Again', *Philosophy Today*, 28 (1984), 242-63.
Stack, George J., 'Riemann's Geometry and Eternal Recurrence as Cosmological Hypothesis: A Reply', *International Studies in Philosophy*, 21 (1989), 37-40.
Stambaugh, Joan, *Nietzsche's Thought of Eternal Return*, Baltimore and London: The Johns Hopkins University Press, 1972.
Stambaugh, Joan, *The Problem of Time in Nietzsche*, trans. John F. Humphrey, Lewisburg: Bucknell University Press, 1987.
Stephen, James Fitzjames, *A History of the Criminal Law of England*, 3 vols, London: Macmillan, 1883.

Sterling, M.C., 'Recent Discussions of Eternal Recurrence: Some Critical Comments', *Nietzsche-Studien*, 6 (1977), 261–91.
Strauss, David Friedrich, *Der alte und der neue Glaube*, Leipzig: Verlag von S. Hirzel, 1872.
Strong, Tracy B., *Friedrich Nietzsche and the Politics of Transfiguration*, Berkeley, CA: University of California Press, 1975.
Tait, P.G., 'Zöllner's Scientific Papers', *Nature*, 28 March 1878, 420–22.
Taylor, Richard, 'Causation', *The Monist*, 47 (1962–63), 287–313.
Teichmüller, Gustav, *Aristotelische Forschungen*, 3 vols, Halle: G.E. Barthel, 1867–73.
Teichmüller, Gustav, *Darwinismus und Philosophie*, Dorpat: Verlag von C. Mattiesen, 1877.
Teichmüller, Gustav, *Neue Studien zur Geschichte der Begriffe*, Cotha: F.A. Perthes, 1879.
Teichmüller, Gustav, *Die wirkliche und die scheinbare Welt. Neue Grundlegung der Metaphysik*, Breslau: Verlag von Wilhelm Koebner, 1882.
Thomson, William, *Mathematical and Physical Papers*, Cambridge: Cambridge University Press, 1882.
Thomson, William and P.G. Tait, *Handbuch der theoretischen Physik*, trans. Hermann von Helmholtz and Georg Wertheim, 2nd edn, Braunschweig: Druck und Verlag von Friedrich Vieweg und Sohn, 1874.
Tipler, Frank J. (ed.), *Essays in General Relativity*, New York: Academic Press, 1980.
Treiber, Hubert, '"Der Ausland" – Die "reichste und gediegenste Registratur" naturwissenschaftlich-philosophischer Titel in Nietzsches "idealer Bibliothek"', *Nietzsche-Studien*, 25 (1996), 394–412.
Ulrici, Hermann, 'Der sogennante Spiritismus. Eine philosophische Frage', *Zeitschrift für Philosophie und philosophische Kritik* (1878), 239–71.
Ulrici, Hermann, *Der sogenannte Spiritismus. Eine wissenschaftliche Frage*, Halle: Pfeffer, 1879.
Van Fraassen, Bas C., 'Capek on Eternal Recurrence', *Journal of Philosophy*, 59 (1962), 371–75.
Van Steenberghen, Fernand, *Thomas Aquinas and Radical Aristotelianism*, Washington, DC: The Catholic University of America Press, 1980.
Vogt, Johannes Gustav, *Die Kraft. Eine real-monistische Weltanschauung*, Leipzig: Verlag von Haupt und Tischler, 1878.
Von Wright, G.H., *Norm and Action: A Logical Enquiry*, London: Routledge and Kegan Paul, 1963.
Weitzenböck, Roland W., *Der vierdimensionale Raum*, Basel-Stuttgart: Birkhäuser Verlag, 1956.
Whitlock, Greg, 'Roger Boscovich, Benedict de Spinoza and Friedrich Nietzsche: The Untold Story', *Nietzsche-Studien*, 25 (1996), 200–220.
Whitlock, Greg, 'Examining Nietzsche's "Time Atom Theory" Fragment from 1873', *Nietzsche-Studien*, 26 (1997), 350–60.
Whorf, Benjamin Lee, *Language Thought and Reality*, ed. John B. Carroll. Cambridge, MA: MIT Press, 1956.

Wilcox, John T., *Truth and Value in Nietzsche*, Ann Arbor, MI: University of Michigan Press, 1974.
Wundt, Wilhelm, *Der Spiritismus. Eine sogennante wissenschaftliche Frage*, Leipzig: Wilhelm Engelmann, 1879.
Zeldin, Mary-Barbara, 'Spir, Afrikan Alexandrovich', in *The Encyclopedia of Philosophy*, ed. Paul Edwards, New York: The Macmillan Company and The Free Press, 1967, Vol. 7, 544.
Zermelo, Ernst, 'On the Mechanical Explanation of Irreversible Processes', in S.G. Brush (ed.), *Kinetic Theory*, Vol. 2., Oxford: Pergamon Press, 1966.
Zöllner, Johann Carl Friedrich, *Über die Natur der Cometen. Beiträge zur Geschichte und Theorie der Erkenntnis*, 2nd edn, Leipzig: Verlag von Wilhelm Engelmann, 1872.
Zöllner, Johann Carl Friedrich, *Principien einer elektrodynamischen Theorie der Materie. Erster Band*, Leipzig: Verlag von Wilhelm Engelmann, 1876.
Zöllner, Johann Carl Friedrich, *Wissenschaftliche Abhandlungen*, 4 vols, Leipzig: Commissionsverlag von L. Staackmann, 1878–81.
Zöllner, Johann Carl Friedrich, *Das Deutsche Volk und seine Professoren. Eine Sammlung von Citaten ohne Commentar. Zur Aufklärung und Belehrung des deutschen Volkes zusammengestellt von Friedrich Zöllner*, Leipzig: Commissionsverlag von L. Staackmann, 1880.
Zöllner, Johann Carl Friedrich, *Zur Aufklärung des deutschen Volkes über Inhalt und Aufgabe der wissenschaftlichen Abhandlungen von Friedrich Zöllner*, Leipzig: Commissionsverlag von L. Staackmann, 1880.
Zöllner, Johann Carl Friedrich, *Transcendental Physics*, trans. Charles Carlton Massey, 4th edn, Boston: Colby and Rich, 1888. Reprint, New York: Arno Press, 1976.
Zöllner, Johann Carl Friedrich, *Beiträge zur Deutschen Judenfrage mit academischen Arabesken als Unterlagen zu einer Reform der Deutschen Universitäten*, Leipzig: Verlag von Oswald Mutze, 1894.
Zuboff, Arnold, 'Nietzsche and Eternal Recurrence', in Robert Solomon (ed.), *Nietzsche: A Collection of Critical Essays*, New York: Doubleday Anchor, 1973, 343–57.

Index

absolute becoming, doctrine of xvii, 1, 6–11
action at a distance 14–15, 88, 178
altruism 180–81
Anaxagoras xvi, 87, 156
Anders, Anni 63
anticipations of perception, principle of 163
anti-Semitism 71
approximation 124–8, 131
Aquinas, St Thomas 21, 34
Aristotle 4–5, 14, 27, 34–5, 42, 53
astrology 119, 124–7
atomism 81, 86, 92, 141, 155–7, 163
Avenarius, Richard 83, 86
Averroes 21

Becker, Oskar 32–4
becoming, concept of 12, 54–5, 86, 90, 100, 179; *see also* absolute becoming
beginning of the world 25–6, 93
Bentley, Richard 15
Bismarck, Otto von 71
Bois-Reymond, Emil du xiii, 62
Bonaventure, St 21, 26, 34
Boscovich, Roger Joseph xviii, 13, 90–92, 108, 112, 117–18, 135, 141, 155
Boyle, Robert 81, 155
Brentano, Franz 44
Büchner, Ludwig xii

Cardan, Jerome 167
Carnot's theorem 94, 143
Caspari, Otto xii, 42–3, 87, 94, 135, 138, 143–6
causality, concept of 86–90, 109, 178–80
cause and effect, simultaneity of 14–15
chance 117
Christianity xiv, 46, 174–7
commensurability and incommensurability 119–25, 130
Condillac, Etienne de 153

conservation of energy 28, 60–61, 89, 135, 139, 147–8, 166, 179
conservation of matter 28
convergence, 'astronomical' and 'geometrical' approaches to 131–2
Copernicus, Nicolaus 90–91, 155

Darwin, Charles xii, 45, 53, 60, 164, 167, 180–81
de Fundis, John 124
definite number, law of xviii, 23–4, 37, 112
Democritus xvi, 81, 86–7, 156–7, 161
Descartes, René 44, 48, 146
determinism 108–13
dialectical materialism xii
'dice game' analogy 108–13
Diogenes Laertius 156
Dove, Alfred 63–4
Drossbach, Maximilian xii
Duhem, Pierre 124–6, 132
Dühring, Eugen xii, xviii–xix, 21–33, 62, 112, 140–41, 171–5, 180, 183
Dumont, Léon xiii, 164–7

eating, pleasure of 176
'economy' principle in science 82–3, 92–3, 149
Eglinton, William 71
egoism 180–82
Einstein, Albert 66
Emerson, Ralph Waldo xi
Empedocles 87, 156
empiricism 2
energy, 'positive' and 'negative' 137
Engels, Friedrich xii
entropy 143, 146
Epicurean view of pleasure and pain 167
Epicurus 81
epistemology 31, 48, 71
equilibrium state *see* 'final state' problem
d'Espérance, Elizabeth 71–3
eternal recurrence

doctrine of xvii–xix, 6, 11–12, 21, 31–7 *passim*, 53–4, 85, 95–6, 99–106, 110–13, 159–60
  mathematics of 117–32
  physics of 135–50
Eucken, Rudolf 41
'evaporation' of forces 148
everyday experience 44
evolution, theory of xiii, 45, 164

Faraday, Michael 92, 155
Fick, Adolf 87–9
'final state' problem 66, 93, 95, 99–107, 137, 143–6
finitude and finitism 23–4
force
  centres of 95, 137–8, 148, 155, 160
  concept of xvii–xix, 95, 135–6
  connection with concept of power 147–50
  'directing' as distinct from 'driving' 149
  'essence' of 106–7
  forms of 139, 144
  law of 91, 135
Förster, Bernhard 71
fourth dimension 67–70
free will 179, 181
Fritzsch, Ernst Wilhelm 64

Gassendi, Pierre 81
Gauss, Karl Friedrich 65
'genealogical' approach to revenge and punishment 172
al-Ghazali, Abu Mohammed 21, 26
God 26, 43, 52, 103, 118, 142, 149
Goethe, Johann Wolfgang von 41, 168
'Great Year' doctrine 119–21, 125, 127
guilt 179

Haeckel, Ernst xii, 45
Hansen, Carl 71
Hartmann, Eduard von xii–xiii, xviii, 23–6, 64, 167
hedonism 153–4, 166–8
Hegel, Georg Wilhelm Friedrich xi
Heidegger, Martin 159
Helmholtz, Hermann von xii–xiii, 47, 60–62, 66, 94, 143, 146, 157
Helvétius, Claude 180–81

Heraclitus xvi–xvii, 1, 7, 9, 16, 44, 86, 90, 106, 150, 159, 167
Herbart, J.F. xvii, 2–4, 8–9, 15–16
Hippocrates 156
Homer 51
Hope, Elizabeth *see* d'Espérance, Elizabeth
Hume, David 15

idealism xv, 44, 46, 49, 154, 157–8
Im neuen Reich 63–4
impossibility, concepts of 105–7
instinct 167; *see also* sexual instinct
intentionality 102–4
interference, concept of 144–5
intuition 30–31, 45–6, 55
irrational numbers 123–4

Jacoby, Susan 175
Joule, James 139
justice, concept of xix, 172–7, 181–3

Kant, Immanuel xi, xiv–xv, 2–3, 8, 30–33, 42, 45–6, 51, 60–61, 68, 88–9, 136, 157, 162–3, 168, 172–4, 180
Kepler, Johannes 60, 129
kinetic energy 136–7, 141, 148
Kirchhoff, Robert 61, 87
Köselitz, Heinrich xii, 73–4, 95, 139–42, 147, 150

Lamarck, Jean Baptiste de 180–81
Lange, Friedrich Albert xiii, xv, xix, 23, 47–8, 71, 156–9
Lankester, Ray 67
Laplace, Pierre Simon 110
Leibniz, Gottfried xi–xii, 94, 135, 138, 142, 146
Lewis, C.S. 162
lex talonis 173–4
Liebmann, Otto 2
Locke, John 153, 159
logic 3
Lotze, Hermann 43
Lucretius 81, 141

Mach, Ernst 82–3
magnitudes, intensive and extensive 161–3
Maimonides, Moses 5–6

Mainländer, Philipp xii, xviii, 23, 26
material substance, concept of 90–92
materialism xii, xv–xix, 45–6, 85–7
  philosophical 157
  and sensualism 154–9
  see also dialectical materialism
Mayer, (Julius) Robert xiii, xix, 135–6, 139–42, 147–50
mechanism xviii, 81–5, 90, 93–6, 137, 143, 146, 156–7
metaphysical thinking 3
Mill, John Stuart 112–13
Möbius, A.F. 68–9
Mohr, Friedrich 148
Moleschott, Jacob xii
monadism 146
morality xix–xx, 164, 171–4, 181–2
Musikalisches Wochenblatt 64

naive realism 136
national characters, German and English xii, 60
natural selection xiii, 45, 164, 181
Nature 61
nature, laws of 92, 178
necessity, concept of 99–101
Neumann, Carl 15
Newton, Isaac xii, 14–15, 66, 89–90, 94, 129
Nietzsche, Elisabeth 71–4
Nietzsche, Friedrich
  Beyond Good and Evil xv, 3–4, 42, 47–9, 82–3, 85, 149, 156–8, 178
  The Birth of Tragedy 42, 62, 64
  Daybreak 140–41, 156
  The Gay Science 1, 3, 6, 42, 85, 138–9, 146, 149, 153–6, 167
  On the Genealogy of Morals 172, 174, 176, 183–5
  Human, All-too-Human 2–3, 49, 84, 140, 150, 164, 184
  Philosophy in the Tragic Age of the Greeks xvi, 2, 11
  Thus Spake Zarathustra 34, 42–3, 50–55, 59, 63, 74–5, 127, 149–50, 153, 168, 178
  'On Truth and Lies in an Extra-Moral Sense' 63
  Twilight of the Idols xiv, 158
  Untimely Meditations 63–4

The Wanderer and His Shadow 185–6
nihilism 48, 95–6
Nohl, Hermann 41

Ockham's razor 82
Olbers' paradox 66
Oresme, Nicole 118–27, 130–31, 160
Overbeck, Franz 42–3, 87

pain and pleasure *see* pleasure and pain
Paneth, Joseph 74
Parmenides xvi, 2–3, 11
Pericles 156
personal identity 180
perspective, concept of 45–7
perspectivism 41, 47–8, 54–5
  temporal 52–3
'phenomenal' and 'sub-phenomenal' differences 126–7
philology 86, 180
π, irrationality of 123–4
Plato and Platonism xiv, 41, 43, 53, 68, 81, 154
pleasure and pain, theory of 164–8
Poincaré, Henri 128–32
positivism xii, 23, 49
possibility
  concepts of 99–100, 105–6
  logical and empirical 100, 107
potential energy 147–8
power, concept of 147–50
probability theory 108–13
properties of things 105–6, 160
Protagoras 44
punishment, theories of 172–8, 181–6
Puschmann, Theodor 64
Pythagorean thought 160

qualities of things 160–64
quantities, differences between 161–2

realism 23, 26, 31, 44
recurrence theorem 128–32
reductionism, scientific 84
Rée, Paul xix, 42, 72–4, 150, 164, 171–2, 180–84
repentance 179
responsibility for actions 179
ressentiment xix–xx, 171–4, 185
retribution 173, 181–2

revenge 172–85
Rohde, Erwin 41, 62–4

Salomé, Lou 72–4
'sameness' as distinct from similarity 127–8
Scheler, Max 171
Schmeitzner, Ernst xii, 140, 184
Schopenhauer, Arthur xi–xii, xvi, 14, 26, 32–3, 61, 88, 167, 176–84 *passim*
science as interpretation rather than explanation 85, 87
scientific method 81–3
semiotic knowledge 44–7
sensations 163–6
senses, semiotic status of 46
sensualism xix, 49, 153–4, 168
and materialism 154–9
Sextus Empiricus 5
sexual instinct 176
Simmel, Georg 118–19, 122–8 *passim*, 131, 160
Slade, Henry 67–9
solar system, stability of 129–30
Sophocles 156
space
concepts of 8, 13, 45
Euclidian and Riemannian 65–6, 70
Spir, African xiii–xvii, 1–6, 9, 11, 15–16, 48–9
spiritualism 67–8, 71–5
Steffensen, Karl 41
Stendhal 153
Stokes, George Gabriel 61
Strauss, David Friedrich 64
sublimation, concept of 84
symmetry 69

Tait, P.G. 60–61
Teichmüller, Gustav xvi, 41–55 *passim*, 86
thermodynamics
first law of 147
second law of xiii, 66, 128–9, 132, 145

Thomson, William xiii, 60–61, 66, 93–5, 143, 146
three-body problem 129
Thucydides 156
time
circularity of 34–6, 53, 55
divisibility of xvii, 1, 4–8, 12–14, 51
empirical reality of 3–4
infinitude of xviii, 21–2, 27–37, 51–4
perspectival conception of 45, 49–54
relational theory of 34–6
sense of 7–8, 13
time-atom theory 12–15, 89
Tipler, Frank J. 132
Trendelenburg, Adolf 41, 43
'true world' xiv, 3, 49, 55, 158

unconscious inference 63
University of Basel 41
'untimeliness' xi, 84, 95–6
utilitarianism 166, 168, 186

Vogt, Johannes Gustav xi–xiii, xviii, 135–9, 142–3, 146–7
Vogt, Karl xii, 136
von Baer, Karl Ernst xiii, xvi, 7, 51
vulgarization, philosophical xii

Wagner, Richard 23, 62, 64, 72, 75
Wallace, Alfred Russel 60–61
wave theory of heat 145
Weber, Wilhelm 60–61
Wilamowitz-Möllendorff, Ulrich von 62–3
'will to power' theory 16, 29, 83–4, 106–7, 145, 149, 167, 176
Wirth, Moritz 59, 71
Wundt, Wilhelm 67–8

Zeno 11
Zermelo, Ernst 128–9
Zöllner, Friedrich xiii, xviii, 13–14, 59–71, 74–5, 95, 148
Zuboff, Arnold 104, 125–6